1987.

JUSTINIAN AND THEODORA

JUSTINIAN AND THEODORA

ROBERT BROWNING

With 29 illustrations and 7 maps

THAMES AND HUDSON

First published in the United States in 1987 by
Thames and Hudson Inc., 500 Fifth Avenue,
New York, New York 10110

Library of Congress Catalog Card Number 86-50886

Printed and bound in Great Britain

JUSTINIAN AND THEODORA

ROBERT BROWNING

With 29 illustrations and 7 maps

THAMES AND HUDSON

© 1971 Robert Browning
This revised edition © 1987 Thames and Hudson Ltd, London

First published in the United States in 1987 by
Thames and Hudson Inc., 500 Fifth Avenue,
New York, New York 10110

Library of Congress Catalog Card Number 86-50886

Printed and bound in Great Britain

Contents

Preface

Many books have been written on the age of Justinian. The present work may be justified in that it tries to depict the events as they may have appeared to the emperor himself and to his astonishing consort. Roman emperors were not arbitrary dictators. They depended on their personal advisers and on a cumbersome bureaucracy both for their knowledge of what was going on and for the execution of their decisions. Often their sphere of decision was narrowly limited. But if decisions were made at all, only the emperor could make them. Justinian and Theodora were autocrats who knew what they wanted, who persevered through endless checks and failures, who impressed their personalities upon an age more firmly than any of their predecessors since Augustus, five and a half centuries earlier.

Many have helped in the production of this book. Thanks are due especially to Patricia Vanags, who first suggested that I write it, to Susan Phillpott, whose experience and judgement were so readily available, to Colleen Chesterman, who helped to collect and choose the illustrations, and to Susan Archer, who typed the manuscript, much of it twice.

ROBERT BROWNING

Preface to Revised Edition

The opportunity offered by the reedition of this book has enabled me to correct many slips and infelicities in the first edition, to change the text here and there to take account of recent research, and to bring the bibliography up to date. In the sixteen years which have passed it has become more and more clear that the sixth century was a major turning point in the transition from antiquity to the Middle Ages. Whether we believe that great men make history or that history makes great men, the importance of Justinian and his unlikely consort remains as great as ever.

Genealogical Tables

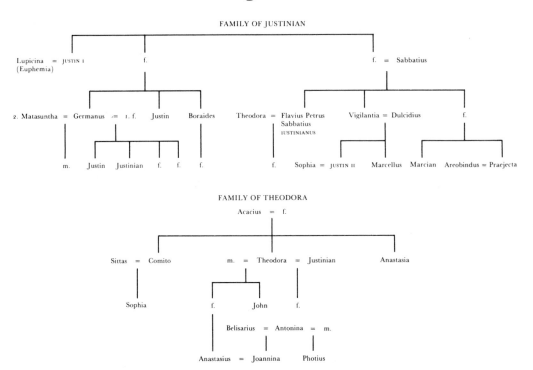

FAMILY OF JUSTINIAN

Lupicina = JUSTIN I   f.   f. = Sabbatius
(Euphemia)

2. Matasuntha = Germanus = 1. f.   Justin   Boraides   Theodora = Flavius Petrus   Vigilantia = Dulcidius   f.
                                       Sabbatius
                                       IUSTINIANUS

m.   Justin   Justinian   f.   f.   f.   f.   Sophia = JUSTIN II   Marcellus   Marcian   Areobindus = Praejecta

FAMILY OF THEODORA

Acacius = f.

Sittas = Comito   m. = Theodora = Justinian   Anastasia

Sophia   f.   John   f.

Belisarius = Antonina = m.

Anastasius = Joannina   Photius

8

Introduction

The Roman empire of the sixth century AD was in many respects different from that of the generally more familiar first and second centuries. It would be out of place to attempt even to outline its history in the intervening centuries. The subject of this book is after all Justinian. But a brief summary of the more important changes that took place between the reign of Constantine (307-37) and that of Anastasius (491-518), with whose death the narrative opens, may save a great deal of explanation later and avoid certain confusions and misconceptions.

When Constantine proclaimed himself Augustus in 307, he ruled only in Britain and Gaul. The rest of the empire was in the hands of other emperors, sometimes as many as six. This was a continuation of the chaos of the third century, when the armies raised their commanders to the purple and more or less permanent civil war prevailed in the empire. Over the years Constantine eliminated his rivals one by one, until in 324 he ruled alone from the Clyde to the Euphrates. The Roman empire, always a single, unitary state in theory, had once more become one in practice.

But it was not enough to win power by force of arms. What is won by the sword may be lost by the sword; and men feel no especial loyalty towards their conquerors. Constantine needed to be not only a sovereign, but a legitimate sovereign. The old constitutional theory – it was never entirely realized – whereby imperial power was conferred by the consensus of army, senate and people – had been utterly devalued during the civil wars of the third century. Emperors like Aurelian (270-5) and Diocletian (284-305) had tried to win the acceptance of their power by claiming for it some kind of divine sanction: Aurelian called himself a god, a kind of earthly representative of the universal sun god, whose cult he encouraged; and Diocletian set up an elaborate system of personal relationships between himself and his colleagues on the one hand and Jupiter and Hercules on the other. In fact for most people Jupiter and Hercules were a kind of shorthand for different manifestations of a supreme deity. Few now took the Olympians at face value.

Constantine turned for legitimation to the god of the Christians. Like all his contemporaries he was a religious, indeed a superstitious, man. And he had a sense of mission. So he was always alert for signs of divine interest in his own success; needless to say, he received them from time to time. Christians were not particularly numerous in the empire, and least of all in its western provinces, which Constantine knew best. And Christianity had made little progress as yet among the upper classes of Roman society. There were Christians, however, in Constantine's family, including his mother Helen; and from his earliest days he must have had some familiarity with Christian doctrine and practice. On the eve of his decisive battle against Maxentius at the gates of Rome on 28 October 312 he and his army saw some unusual celestial phenomenon – perhaps a solar halo – which he interpreted as a cross, the sign of the Christians. And that night, so he told his biographer Eusebius twenty years later, he had a dream which convinced him that the god of the Christians was indeed the true ruler of the universe. Fortified by this revelation he went out to battle and won an overwhelming victory, which set him on the path to power throughout the empire. From then on the Christians were first put on an equal footing with other, less exclusive, religions, and then favoured by grants of money, building of churches, and so on. From being the religion of a somewhat inward-looking and sectarian minority drawn largely from merchants and artisans of oriental origin or connection, Christianity spread during the reigns of Constantine and his sons throughout all classes of the empire. Originally an illegal, semi-clandestine and occasionally persecuted organization, the Christian church now became rich, influential and public. Christianity was not yet the only tolerated religion; but it was the religion favoured by the state. Men in high positions were convinced that upon the correctness of its doctrines and observances the continuance of divine favour, and thus the security of the state, depended. Hence arose the need for the imperial power to intervene in ecclesiastical disputes, and an increasingly close cohabitation of state and church.

Much has been written on the nature of Constantine's conversion to Christianity. The question, in so far as it concerns the psychology of an individual, is irrelevant to the subject of this book. What is important is that, from Constantine on, the power of an emperor is not merely a function of the armed forces at his call, but a token of his having been chosen by God to rule. Moreover the Roman empire was no longer merely a state, and a very powerful and extensive one. It was part of a divine plan for the salvation of mankind – the one Christian empire, which belonged to a different order of being from other political communities, and which in the fullness of time would become coextensive with the human race. This did not imply that emperors could not be overthrown. Their defeat would itself be proof that they had by their sins forfeited divine favour. But it did put the legitimacy of a ruling emperor and of all his acts of state upon a new footing. And it implied a tight relationship between state and church, which were opposite sides of the same coin.

The re-establishment of the unity of the empire as a Christian empire is the major accomplishment of Constantine. But other changes instituted by him were important. During the anarchy of the third century, emperors had often resided with their armies rather than at Rome. Milan, and the legionary headquarters of Trier and Sirmium (Sremska Mitrovica) had become seats of power in the west. In the east Nicomedia, Antioch and Alexandria were on occasion imperial residences. Rome became increasingly a city enjoying prestige but no power. It was awkwardly situated off the main military roads, and as the seat of the senate – a still influential caste of rich landowners – it was ill fitted to be the capital of an absolute monarch. So Constantine, his rivals all overthrown, was merely following the pattern established by his predecessors when he set up his capital elsewhere than at

Rome. His choice fell upon Byzantium, an ancient Greek city on the European shore of the Bosphorus with a magnificent natural harbour. Renamed the City of Constantine – Constantinopolis – and the New Rome, it was formally inaugurated on 11 May 330. It was to be a copy of the old Rome, with its senate, its city prefect, its fourteen city wards, its hippodrome, and so on. But it was to be a Christian city from the first, with no pagan cult sites or traditions. The establishment of the new capital implied no division of the empire, but rather symbolized its new unity.

East and west diverge

The reigns of Constantine and his sons (307-61) were in the main years of external peace, as well as internal unity. Slowly the empire recovered from the chaos of the third century. A new coinage, supported by the immense quantities of treasure confiscated by Constantine, replaced the debased and inflationary issues of his predecessors. A new, simplified system of taxation of the primary producers, partly in money and partly in kind, guaranteed the state revenues. To ensure the payment of taxes and the performance of certain essential functions, such as the maintenance of the food supply to the great cities or the provision of recruits for the army, more and more citizens were tied to their jobs, which became hereditary, even in the female line: he who married a baker's daughter had to become a baker. It was an uncomfortable, harsh world for many. But men knew where they stood. And prolonged peace brought some attendant increase in prosperity.

In the later fourth century there was sometimes more than one emperor, and responsibility for rule might be divided on a geographical basis, as between the brothers Valentinian (364-75) and Valens (364-78). But this was merely a matter of administrative convenience. The Roman empire still formed a single state. And in view of its theological legitimation, it could scarcely be otherwise: two independent emperors were as inconceivable as two omnipotent deities. In practice, however, there was a growing differentiation between the eastern and western halves of the empire. The next century was to bring this into sharp focus. In the meantime it is clear that the strength of the empire lay more in the lands of ancient civilization and largely Greek speech around the eastern Mediterranean rather than in the lands of recent Romanization and mainly Latin speech of the west. The east held the bulk of natural resources, of industry, of population. Its cities were more numerous, its trade better developed, and its Christian communities older and more widespread.

It also offered a greater prize to invaders. In 376 a large body of Goths, living outside the frontiers north of the lower Danube, were pressed by a westward sweep of the Huns through the steppe lands from central Asia. They demanded to be settled as federate allies on imperial territory, south of the Danube. The matter was mishandled, promises were not always kept, imperial officials were unsympathetic and grasping. In the outcome the Goths decided to take by force what they could not get by negotiation. Their army – a cavalry force – advanced on Constantinople. The emperor Valens went out to meet them. The Roman army was shattered, and the emperor himself killed, in the battle of Adrianople on 9 August 378. The Gothic problem was henceforth one of the main preoccupations of any Roman government.

The man who cleared up the mess after Adrianople was Theodosius (378-95), a Roman general of Spanish origin who was proclaimed emperor by the army. He had to deal with a number of rival claimants as well as with pressure of foreign peoples all round the northern frontiers of the empire; but he succeeded for the time being in settling the problem of the Goths established on imperial territory, and in coming to an agreement with Sapor III, the new Persian king, which ensured peace on the eastern frontier for a century. A devout, indeed fanatical, Christian, he persecuted with equal zeal the remaining pagan groups among the upper classes and the dissident factions within the Christian Church. Theodosius moved tirelessly to and fro throughout the empire, which in his view, as in that of his age, was a single whole, though its problems varied in detail between east and west. When he died in 395 he left two young sons, aged eighteen and eleven respectively. The elder, Arcadius, was to rule in Constantinople; the younger, Honorius, in the west. Neither was old enough to exercise real power.

In fact the division between the two halves of the empire became deep and permanent. They became two separate states, though ideally remaining constituent parts of a transcendent whole: the Christian Roman empire. The reasons for the permanence of the division are complex. At the lowest level there was jealousy and conflict of interest between the ministers in east and west with whom lay the real power after Theodosius' death. There were differences in the military situation. For demographic and economic reasons the recruitment of an effective army from the peasantry was difficult in both east and west. But the more populous east, where there were certainly more free peasants than in the west, could at least provide some troops from its internal resources. The west could provide scarcely any. Hence its greater dependence on foreign contingents – either recruited as individuals into units of the Roman army or, more recently, fighting under their own chiefs, with their own organization and weapons. Hence, too, the predominance in the west during the fifth century of the commander-in-chief, who can make and unmake emperors. He was usually, though not always, a foreigner, most often a German. In the defence of the east a greater role was played by mountaineers from Thrace, from the Armenian massif, and from the Taurus mountains, where the half-Hellenized Isaurians provided both unskilled labour for the cities and recruits for the army.

The east, then, was richer, more stable, more able to protect itself than the west. And although lip-service was regularly paid to the unity of the empire, in practice no eastern ruler could for long risk weakening his own position to save the west, even supposing it were possible to do so. So the rift continued. The legislation of each emperor was valid only in his own half of the empire. His coinage in general circulated only in his own realm. While the movement of individuals was never actively hindered, there was much less personal and intellectual contact between the two halves than in the preceding century: knowledge of Greek became rarer in the west; officials no longer passed in the course of their career from one half to the other. At the same time a series of external blows fell on the west – mainly because it offered an easier target. A group of Goths, under their king Alaric, who had wandered menacingly about the Balkans were turned westwards by the diplomacy of Constantinople. Refused a military command and land for his followers to settle on, Alaric captured Rome on 24 August 410 and held the Eternal City to ransom. Men ought not to have been surprised. But they were, for it was eight hundred years since the city had last been taken by a foreign foe. The shock was stunning inasmuch as it challenged preconceived ideas of the eternity of Roman power. The surviving pagans – and they were numerous and influential in the west – argued that it was all the fault of the Christians and proved the falsity of Christian doctrine. Augustine, bishop of Hippo in Numidia, began to compose his *City of God* in answer to such arguments. The Roman empire, he explained, was an historical phenomenon like any other state, which came into being and would pass away. The only permanent community was that of the church visible and invisible, the City of God.

Alaric's sack of Rome was only the most striking of a series of blows struck by external enemies in the early years of the fifth century, in Gaul, in north Italy, in Spain. What the new invaders sought was land to settle on. And they were given it in accordance with a pattern already set by Theodosius. In certain areas of the empire one-third of each estate was granted to one or more barbarian heads of families, in return for military service. This was the theory, based on the system of billeting troops on landowners which had been in force for centuries and was known as *hospitalitas*. In practice it might mean anything from the payment of a tax by landlords to maintain a mercenary force, to the effective surrender of whole provinces to foreign control. For these foreigners came in whole tribes and nations, under their own rulers and governed by their own laws.

Under this system, Salian Franks were settled in northern Gaul, Burgundians in Savoy, Visigoths in south-western Gaul, Suevi and Vandals in Spain, Alans, Ostrogoths and Huns in Pannonia (Hungary). The Vandals under their king Gaiseric crossed from Spain to Africa in 435, their invasion disguised by the fiction of *hospitalitas*. A few years later they had taken Carthage, and set up a wholly independent kingdom in Africa, the granary of Rome. Their rule was soon extended to Sicily, Sardinia, Corsica and the Balearics – they were the only barbarian kingdom to take seriously the question of sea power – and in 455 they captured and sacked Rome for the second time in half a century.

The results of this widespread settlement of barbarian peoples were disastrous for the western empire. First of all the devastation which they wrought in their path reduced still further the slender surplus over day-to-day needs which sustained the central state structure. Secondly, large areas within provinces, and sometimes whole provinces, became barbarian enclaves, paying no tax to the central government and effectively outside its control. Thirdly, it became impossible for certain provinces to be defended militarily. Britain was the first to be abandoned, early in the fifth century. The seizure of Africa (Tunisia) by the Vandals meant that other Roman provinces of north Africa had to be given up because of difficulty of communications, while the growing power of the Vandal fleet led to the abandonment of Corsica, Sardinia and the Balearics. By the middle of the fifth century, Roman authority had become shadowy in most of Gaul and Spain; though there were pockets of territory in Gaul administered and taxed by Roman officials right up to the last decades of the century.

In the territories taken over by the barbarians the situation varied. Vandal Africa at first practised a kind of apartheid, with a ruling aristocracy of Vandal warriors; in Spain and even more so in Gaul the great Roman landowners, anxious to save what they could of their wealth and influence, found a community of interest with the barbarian princes, who in their turn came more and more to resemble Roman territorial magnates. The cities dwindled in size, and life centred increasingly on the great estates. To the mass of the peasants it may have mattered little whether they depended on a Roman emperor or on a German king.

The Goths in Italy

Meanwhile the great Roman military commanders – whether Roman by origin, like Aetius and Boniface, or barbarian, like Ricimer the Suevian – strove above all to maintain their own power, rather like Chinese warlords of the 1920s. They made and unmade puppet emperors in Rome – some of them children – as part of their manoeuvring between the pressure of the barbarians, the prestige of the senate, and the diplomacy of Constantinople. When the last of these Masters of Soldiers, Odovacar the Herule, decided to dispense altogether with the child-emperor Romulus Augustulus in 476 and to rule Italy directly – as the Franks ruled Gaul and the Visigoths Spain – it struck few men at the time that the Roman empire in the west had come to an end. In theory it still existed. In practice it had long ceased to count.

Odovacar's kingdom was short-lived. The eastern emperor Zeno in Constantinople wanted a more tractable neighbour, and one more ready to recognize the theoretical unity of the empire. His government in 488 urged the Ostrogoths of Pannonia, under their king Theodoric of the royal house of the Amals, to eject Odovocar. This the Ostrogoths did in a series of bloody campaigns which lasted until 493. In the meantime Zeno had died and been succeeded by Anastasius. It was between Anastasius and Theodoric that a *modus vivendi* was established which lasted until Theodoric's death in 526. Theoretically, Theodoric ruled over his Roman subjects – the vast majority of the population of Italy – as

Master of Soldiers and representative of the emperor in Constantinople, and over his Gothic subjects as their hereditary king. His coins bore the portrait of Anastasius; he named one of the two consuls – by now the consulate had become an empty but prestigious dignity – of each year; and he addressed himself with deference to the Roman senate. But in fact he ruled Italy independently. He had of course to take account of the wishes of the Roman magnates who composed the senate, no less than of those of the Gothic warriors who made up his army. But in spite of all convenient legal fictions, Ostrogothic Italy was as much severed from the empire as Frankish Gaul, Visigothic Spain or Vandal Africa.

There had been divisions in the Christian church before Constantine, some over points of doctrine, others over church organization. As Christianity became first a tolerated religion, then a favoured religion and finally the official religion of the empire, the divisions continued, and their importance increased. For the government it was a matter of life and death to support the true church, for only so could divine favour be secured and maintained. For churchmen it was vital to secure imperial patronage and support – and control of the great wealth which the church now possessed – for the group to which they themselves belonged. Thus state involvement in ecclesiastical disputes became inevitable. The first fundamental division that the state had to deal with was concerned with the nature of the Trinity and the relations of Father, Son and Holy Spirit. An influential group, called Arians after their founder, Arius, an Alexandrian priest, took the view that the Son was subordinate to the Father, and condemned as heretics the majority who regarded them as of the same nature. Every Christian community in the empire was split, as bishops excommunicated one another. Constantine cared little for the refinements of theology, and had many Arians among his closest collaborators. But he did care for the unity of the church, which alone could guarantee the legitimacy of his own rule. So he convened a council of bishops from throughout the empire at Nicaea in 325 to settle the problem of Arianism. The council, not without pressure from the civil authorities, declared the doctrines of Arius and his followers to be heretical; and the emperor duly exiled some of the Arian leaders to remote parts of the empire. For two generations Arianism continued to have many adherents, and attempts were made to set up a parallel church organization to that of the Orthodox. Indeed Arianism enjoyed imperial patronage under Valens, himself an Arian. But thereafter the Arian communities within the empire rapidly dwindled away.

Outside the frontiers it was a different matter. Christianity had been brought to the Visigoths when they were still living north of the Danube by a group of Arian Gothic clergy settled in Moesia (northern Bulgaria). The leader of this group was Wulfila, whose Gothic translation of the Bible, the oldest text in any Germanic language, still survives in part. From the Visigoths, Arian Christianity spread swiftly through the various Germanic peoples on the move in central and eastern Europe. The outcome was that the majority of the Germanic peoples who settled in the western provinces of the empire in the fifth century were Arians, and so heretics in the eyes of their Orthodox Roman subjects. This was the situation of the Visigoths, the Ostrogoths, the Vandals, the Suevi and the Burgundians. Only the leaders of the Franks, who entered Gaul directly from their homeland in the Low Countries, and hence had no contact with the mainly eastern Arianism, embraced the Nicaean faith.

In the fifth century disputes on the nature of the Trinity died down, and the Nicaean creed was generally accepted – except among the Arian Germans. But a new and complex quarrel about the nature of Christ began to divide the church in the east. The western church, like western society, had different problems to deal with, reeling as it was under the impact of the barbarian invasions. The complexities of the discussion need not detain us.

Divisions in the Church

The influence of late Greek philosophy, personal ambitions, the national feeling of the non-Greek peoples of the southern and eastern provinces all played a part. And since the hope of salvation of individual Christians appeared to depend on the relation of the divine and the human in Christ, passions were aroused among the mass of believers. A series of church councils convoked by the emperors in the fifth century condemned both Nestorianism – that is, the view that Jesus was in the full sense a man, upon whom divinity was superimposed – and Monophysitism – that is, the doctrine that Christ was essentially divine, and that there was in him no conflict between a human and a divine nature. The Nestorians soon ceased to have any influence within the empire, though the numerous Christian communities in Persia were largely Nestorian, and Nestorian missionaries travelled right across central Asia to China. Nestorians therefore tended to be suspected, not always unjustly, of pro-Persian sentiments. The Monophysites, who were anathematized by the Council of Chalcedon in 451, were another matter. The great centres of Monophysite Christianity were Egypt and Syria, but there were many Monophysite sympathizers throughout the empire, and particularly in Constantinople. The emperor Anastasius himself adhered to the Monophysite cause. The Pope and the western church had no sympathy for Monophysite doctrines. Any inclination to make concessions to the Monophysites in Constantinople at once provoked hostility, amounting sometimes to schism, on the part of the Pope and the western church. Any doctrinal *rapprochement* with the west drove the masses of Syria and Egypt, and a substantial section of the population of the rest of the eastern empire, into sullen opposition to the ruling power. Yet by definition there could only be one church, as there could only be one empire.

1   The path to power

On the night of 9 July 518, in the Great Palace overlooking the Sea of Marmara, the old emperor Anastasius died. It was a night of violent storms, and some said he had been struck by lightning as a punishment for his heretical views. For he was a devout Monophysite, as were most of his Egyptian and many of his Syrian subjects, believing that in the incarnation Christ remained wholly divine, and had no distinct human nature.

If the thunderbolt which struck the Great Palace was really aimed at Anastasius, the Almighty had long stayed his hand, for the emperor was eighty-seven years old. Twenty-seven years earlier the empress Ariadne, widow of his predecessor Zeno, had chosen him to succeed to the throne and had reinforced her choice by marrying him. At that time Anastasius was a commander of the silentiaries, gentlemen-ushers of the court, and nothing in his previous life had marked him out for greatness. Perhaps the senate, in inviting Ariadne to choose the new emperor, had hoped for a *fainéant* ruler, who would leave the real power in the hands of the court aristocracy. If so, they were disappointed. Anastasius, in spite of his age and lack of experience, showed himself a subtle and talented diplomat, an administrator unafraid of radical change, and a brilliant financier. He left the treasury full, the prestige of the empire high and its frontiers stable, the apparatus of government efficient and just.

Like many cultured men of his age, he was an amateur theologian; he had even been considered as a possible candidate for the vacant see of Antioch. Before his unexpected accession he had acquired the habit of preaching sermons in the churches of Constantinople. This was contrary to canon law, since he was a layman. But it was above all the Monophysite tone of his homilies which gave offence. And before long the Patriarch Euphemius, with the approval of the emperor Zeno, forbade him to preach and smashed the quasi-episcopal throne on which it was his habit to sit in church.

Once in power his support of the Monophysites had become open and highly effective, in spite of the declaration of orthodoxy which the Patriarch had exacted from him. Monophysite candidates were appointed to Patriarchal and Metropolitan sees, Orthodox leaders were arrested and exiled, relations with the Pope and with the Catholic Roman aristocracy of Italy became strained. A Monophysite addition to the liturgy in the Church of the Holy Wisdom on Sunday, 4 November 512 provoked a riot, which the government brutally suppressed. Within a few days Constantinople was in an uproar. Crowds roamed the streets setting fire to houses of the emperor's relatives and calling for the elevation to the throne of Areobindus, a general who had distinguished himself in the Persian war a few years before. Areobindus wisely found urgent business outside Constantinople; Anastasius, realizing that things were getting out of hand, recalled his police and soldiers, and faced twenty thousand of his infuriated subjects from the Kathisma, the imperial box, in the Hippodrome. He appeared without his crown, offered to abdicate and begged the people to choose a new emperor. He was a tall, handsome man, and the white hair of age had only increased the dignity of his appearance, while long years at court had made him a good actor. The crowd, which had at first greeted him with insults, began to waver. Soon a dialogue began between a court functionary with a stentorian voice and the spokesman of the crowd. Concessions were promised, appeals made to loyalty; and before long the citizens dispersed in good humour. No sooner had Anastasius gained this tactical advantage than he proceeded to exploit it. His police launched a savage campaign of arrests and executions in the city. Subdued, intimidated and leaderless, the citizenry could no longer offer effective opposition to their emperor's heretical faith.

But outside the city, others were ready to take up the struggle. Vitalian, a general in command of Gothic and Bulgarian troops in the province of Scythia (Dobrudja) and himself probably a Romanized Thracian, was a fervent Chalcedonian and an ambitious man. The elderly emperor had designated no successor. Orthodox faith and self-interest pointed in the same direction, and Vitalian was not slow to follow their call. He had the open support of the leading prelates in exile, and probably the covert support of the Holy See, while he was on good terms with the Ostrogothic king Theodoric in Italy. In 513 he headed a revolt: disaffected peasants flocked to his standard, and within a few months he was at the gates of Constantinople with fifty thousand men. The city walls, built by Theodosius II eighty years before, were impregnable if defended, and the imperial fleet by its control of the sea guaranteed the maintenance of supplies to the city. Anastasius made haste to grant tax concessions to the Asiatic provinces, lest they too should join Vitalian, and to corrupt with gifts Vitalian's principal officers. It seems likely that Vitalian counted on an uprising within the city. But the emperor's skilful combination of concessions and threats, and the efficiency of his police, forestalled treachery. Vitalian withdrew northward along the Black Sea coast, fought a few indecisive engagements with the pursuing imperial army, and then – near Varna – fell on their camp by surprise, massacred three-quarters of them and took prisoner their commander-in-chief Hypatius, the emperor's nephew.

Inside the walls of Constantinople things began to stir; there were riots in the Hippodrome, and the chief of police, the Prefect of the Watch, was assassinated. Anastasius managed to re-establish control. But as Vitalian once again marched down the coast towards Constantinople, this time supported by a fleet from the Black Sea ports, the emperor's position became grave. Anastasius, however, was not the man to lose his head in an emergency. He could not offer serious military resistance, and against an enemy with sea power he might not hold the city indefinitely. Vitalian, on the other hand, could not risk either a lost battle or an extended siege. The situation was ripe for negotiation. Anastasius offered 3900 pounds of gold and the command of the armies of Thrace, and promised to call the next summer a general council of the church under the presidency of the Pope to re-establish religious unity. Vitalian withdrew well content to the Danube frontier. But the church council never took place: neither Anastasius nor Pope Hormisdas would yield an inch of principle, and soon there was deadlock. Resentful and disappointed, Vitalian took the field again in autumn 515 and marched on Constantinople. But this time the emperor was ready for him. Vitalian's fleet was set on fire and destroyed as it lay at anchor, and his army was outmanoeuvred and suffered a crushing defeat. Three of his generals were captured and put to death; but the rebel himself, with a sizeable force, succeeded in escaping to Anchialos, near Burgas, where he enjoyed the support of the population. There he nursed his resentment and bided his time. After all Anastasius was now eighty-four.

When he died he left the succession to the throne entirely open. A Roman emperor ruled neither by right of succession nor by right of conquest. His power was delegated to him by the people, and in the first place by the senate and the army. Such was the theory, and it reflected political reality. Nevertheless Anastasius' recent predecessors had always taken care to nominate a co-emperor or to designate a successor before their death; or, like Zeno, had left an empress with the prestige and influence to manage the transfer of power. Anastasius' wife was already dead, and his only child was an illegitimate son of his youth who had vanished without trace. He had, however, three nephews who had been prominent in public affairs, of whom the senior was Hypatius, the general upon whom Vitalian had inflicted so humiliating a defeat a few years before. Hypatius did not share his uncle's religious views, and on that count would have been acceptable to senate, army and people. But his defeat had reduced his stature, and in any case, as Master of Soldiers in the east, he was doubtless at his headquarters in Antioch; it would take several weeks for the news of the emperor's death to reach him. Still he was a force to be reckoned with. Vitalian, with his Gothic and Bulgarian army, was ten days' march away to the north. A quick settlement of the succession was imperative or there was a risk of civil war.

The prize was a high one. The first officers of state to learn of the death of the emperor were Celer, the Master of Offices (head of the civil service, with special responsibility for foreign relations), and Justin, Count of the Excubitors (commander of one of the palace regiments). Both of these men had troops under their command, but those of Celer, the *candidati* and the regiments of the Scholae, were ornamental detachments of palace guards. Justin's Excubitors could fight if need be. Both alerted their troops during the night. In the morning the high officials, the Patriarch, and the senate were summoned by Celer to the palace to deliberate on the choice of a successor, while the people thronged into the Hippodrome, acclaiming the senate and calling for a quick settlement. Groups of palace guards appeared from time to time in the Hippodrome, putting forward the names of candidates, which were rejected by the crowd – no doubt they were meant to be rejected. There were scuffles between the Scholae and the Excubitors, and some were killed. Justin made an appearance in the Hippodrome to establish order, and his soldiers began to call his name as emperor. He declined the honour. A free fight broke out in the Hippodrome, as names were bandied about. Soon a menacing crowd was beating on the ivory doors of the chamber where the senate was in session. The frightened dignitaries offered the throne to Justin, who seemed to have more command of the situation than anyone else, but still he refused. The disorder grew greater, and finally Justin yielded to the entreaties of the senate. Before the vast throng he was elevated upon a shield – a German custom long adopted by the Roman army – and an officer placed a golden chain on his head in lieu of a diadem. The standards of the soldiers, which had been lowered in mourning, were raised, and a shout of acclamation re-echoed throughout the Hippodrome. The Excubitors formed themselves in a protective screen around their commander, and when they stepped aside he was revealed clad in imperial robes. The Patriarch John placed the diadem on his head. Through the voice of his herald the new emperor spoke:

The Emperor Caesar Justin, victorious, ever Augustus. Assuming empire by universal choice and with the blessing of almighty God, we beseech divine Providence to enable us in Its mercy to do all in the interests of you and of the state. It is our care to keep you, with the help of God, in all prosperity and to preserve each one of you with all good will, love and freedom from care. To mark the happy occasion of my accession I bestow on each of you five gold pieces and one pound of silver. (Constantine Porphyrogenitus, *On the Ceremonies of the Court* I.93.)

It is not possible, here, to discern the network of intrigue and plotting which brought Justin to the throne. His office was not one of the highest, and his career had been undistinguished. Such a man could reach the heights of power only by playing skilfully on the ambitions and fears of his powerful rivals. What is known of the events of 10 July is only a fraction of the whole story.

What kind of man was the new emperor, and who were his closest associates? Justin, like the other candidates whose names were put forward, followed the creed of Chalcedon, formulated by the ecumenical council of 451, according to which Christ combined in His person divine and human nature in indissoluble unity. He was a self-made man, a soldier risen from the ranks – one of the regular channels of social mobility in the late Roman empire. Procopius the historian, in the rancorous and scurrilous memoir which he wrote for private circulation, had this to say of him many years later:

When Leo occupied the imperial throne of Byzantium, three young farmers of Illyrian origin, Zimarchus, Dityvistus, and Justin, who came from Bederiana, had been waging an endless war at home with poverty. So they determined to get away from it all and went off to join the army. They covered the whole distance to Byzantium on foot, carrying on their own shoulders their cloaks, in which they had nothing on arrival but some dry biscuits put in before they left home. Their names were entered in the army lists, and the Emperor picked them out to serve in the palace guard, as they were all men of exceptional physique.

Some time later, when Anastasius had succeeded to the imperial power, he was involved in war with the Isaurians [the half-hellenized inhabitants of the Taurus mountains, over whom the government's control was nominal], who had taken up arms against him. He sent an army of considerable size to deal with them, the commander being John the Hunchback. This John had locked up Justin in prison because of some misdemeanour, intending to dispatch him on the following day. This he would have done but for a dream which came to him in time to prevent it. The general said that in his dream he was confronted by a being of colossal size, too mighty in every way to be taken for human. This being commanded him to release the man whom he had that day imprisoned: he himself on waking from sleep dismissed the vision from his mind. But when the next night came, he dreamt that he again heard the same words as before, but remained just as unwilling to carry out the order. Then for the third time the vision stood over him, threatening total ruin unless he did as he was told, and adding that one day he would be in grave danger, and then he would need this man and his family.

This occurrence enabled Justin to survive his immediate danger; and as time went on he acquired great power. The emperor Anastasius gave him command of the palace guards; and when he himself passed from the scene, Justin on the strength of this command succeeded to the throne, though he was by now a doddering old man and totally illiterate – in common parlance he did not know his ABC – an unheard of thing in a Roman. (Procopius, *Secret History* 6. 2-11.)

The exact location of Bederiana is uncertain but it is most probably in the neighbourhood of Nish in Yugoslavia. This was a region of Latin speech in late antiquity, though its economic links were with the Greek east. The population was of Thracian stock, though by now long Romanized. Justin's two companions on his journey to Constantinople had Thracian names – Zimarchus was in fact a common name in regions of Thracian speech – and there is no doubt that the Thracian language – an Indo-European tongue more closely related to Armenian than to any other surviving language – continued to be spoken in parts of the northern Balkans until the early Middle Ages, particularly in the countryside. Justin may well have learnt Thracian at his mother's knee, though from his earliest childhood he would also have known Latin. Greek he must have learnt when he came to Constantinople.

A Romanized Thracian peasant, then, who comes to Constantinople to seek his fortune. Probably a younger son, whose elder brother inherited the family farm. And probably about 470 – Leo's reign was from 457 to 474. If he was aged twenty then, he would be sixty-eight when Anastasius died. A man of little culture – though we need not take too seriously Procopius' tale that he was illiterate and used a wooden stencil to sign his name. The same story is told of the Gothic king Theodoric, who had received a thorough classical education at Constantinople in his youth. Byzantine army-officers might not have a literary education, but they had to be able to read and write. Justin's advancement was slow – through the long years of palace duty, campaigns, and tours in the provinces – but he did rise out of the ranks. By the early 490s he was already commanding a regiment of the guards in the field. He must have been a man of intelligence and ability, probably of ambition too. Unlike the legionaries of classical Rome, soldiers of the late empire could marry; but their unions often had a temporary and informal character. Justin was married to a woman called Lupicina, who was said by his enemies to be a foreigner, an ex-slave, whom he had bought from another man to be his concubine. When her husband became emperor she assumed the more prestigious name of Euphemia. There were no children.

Justin perhaps never returned to Bederiana. But he had a strong sense of family, and once he began to rise in the world he sent for several of his young nephews, gave them the careful education that he himself lacked, and launched them on a career in the capital. One of these, Germanus, became a brilliant and successful general, something of a *grand seigneur*, and married as his second wife Matasuntha, grand-daughter of Theodoric the Gothic king of Italy and widow of his successor King Vitiges. He died in 550 while in command of an army, leaving two sons, Justin and Justinian, of whom the elder was, like his father, a distinguished soldier. Germanus' brothers Boraides (once again a Thracian name) and Justus were also brought to the capital and rose high in the military hierarchy.

Another of the nephews whom Justin launched in the world was called Petrus Sabbatius. He was a son of Justin's sister, and came from the village of Tauresium, near Bederiana. His mother had left Bederiana to marry a farmer – his name was probably Sabbatius – in a nearby village. Their only son was born there about 482. It is not known when his successful uncle sent from Constantinople for him, for the life of this man is cloaked in darkness until he reached his later thirties. Procopius, who disliked him, said that he spoke barbarous Greek in later life, which would suggest that he was at least twelve, and probably older, when he left his Latin-speaking village. Many years later, however, when Petrus Sabbatius had become the emperor Justinian, he too sent for a young relative from Bederiana and gave him a good education in Latin and Greek. The boy was aged eight, the usual age for beginning grammar school, and this may well have been the age at which Petrus Sabbatius joined his uncle in Constantinople, no doubt swiftly transported there by the imperial post and treated with deference and respect. Not for him the long journey on foot, with hard biscuits rolled up in his cloak. We know no details of his early life in the capital, but it is clear that he had the best education, in both Greek and Latin, that the empire could provide. In later life he showed himself a man of wide culture, who never ceased to study. But his interests led him to the Greek Church Fathers, whose works he knew intimately, rather than to the literature and thought of classical Greece.

All of Justin's nephews and great-nephews of whom anything certain is known, with the exception of the future Justin II, followed a military career. This was the world Justin knew and understood. Only they did not begin in the ranks, as their uncle had. It is thus probable that Petrus Sabbatius, his formal education completed, was enrolled in one of the élite corps of palace guards. At any rate, when his uncle succeeded Anastasius, he was a *candidatus*, an officer of the Scholae regiment. He was the least military of men, however, and once his uncle became Count of the Excubitors his attendance at parades must have become infrequent. His eyes were on greater things.

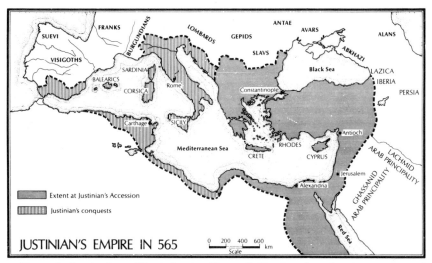

FRANKS
SUEVI
VISIGOTHS
BURGUNDIANS
LOMBARDS
GEPIDS
SLAVS
ANTAE
AVARS
ALANS
ABKHAZI
Black Sea
LAZICA
IBERIA
PERSIA
SARDINIA
BALEARICS
CORSICA
Rome
Constantinople
Carthage
SICILY
Mediterranean Sea
RHODES
CRETE
CYPRUS
Antioch
ARAB PRINCIPALITY
LACHMID PRINCIPALITY
GHASSANID ARAB PRINCIPALITY
Jerusalem
Alexandria
Red Sea

Extent at Justinian's Accession

Justinian's conquests

JUSTINIAN'S EMPIRE IN 565

0 200 400 600 km
Scale

From the beginning of Justin's reign Petrus Sabbatius played an important and decisive role. The old emperor was doubtless a gallant soldier, and nearly half a century of imperial service had given him considerable worldly wisdom. But he was not at his ease in the sophisticated world of the metropolitan aristocracy, nor could he cope with the complexities of foreign policy or the subtle interrelation of church and state. And in any case he seems to have drifted rapidly into senility. At the beginning of his uncle's reign Petrus Sabbatius was promoted to the post of Count of the Domestics. Originally this officer had been in charge of the officer-cadets attached to the palace, but had long ago become an important member of the consistory, the inner cabinet which advised the emperor from day to day. It is more than likely that the whole complex intrigue which brought so unlikely a figure as Justin to the summit of power was conceived and directed by his able and ambitious nephew, now a man in his later thirties, with twenty years' experience of life in the ruling circles of the empire. Some time before his uncle's accession, he had begun to call himself Flavius Petrus Sabbatius Justinianus. This probably means that he had been adopted by Justin as his heir, a distinction never conferred on his cousin Germanus. Justin was an old man, and the loyalty he had always shown towards his Thracian peasant family led him to look for a successor among the members of that family. The complexities of governing an empire which, though reduced in area over the preceding century, still extended from the Adriatic to the Euphrates and from the Danube to the Cataracts of the Nile, were beyond his grasp. It was to Justinian that he turned for aid and advice. In the eyes of contemporary writers Justinian was the power behind the throne during the nine years of Justin's rule. But they wrote in Justinian's reign, and with hindsight. It must not be forgotten that Germanus, by all accounts an able man, with a following among the aristocracy, was always a potential emperor. Most of Justin's ministers seem to have been run-of-the-mill functionaries of no distinction. But his chief minister Proclus, Quaestor of the Sacred Palace (chief law officer of the empire), was a powerful figure, of antique integrity. The poem inscribed on his statue in Constantinople runs:

I am Proclus, son of Paul of Byzantium. The Imperial Palace took me from a flourishing practice in the halls of Justice, that I might be the trusty mouthpiece of the mighty emperor. This bronze effigy declares how great were the rewards of my exploits. Son and father won like prizes, but in winning the consular fasces the son outdid the father. (*Greek Anthology* 16. 48.)

Proclus may have been of imperial calibre, though a lawyer-emperor would have been unprecedented; so Justinian's path to power was by no means smooth. The course it followed will be seen, but first a glance at the state of the empire in 518.

Relations with the Goths

In March 455 the western emperor Valentinian III was murdered. His death marked the beginning of the collapse of Roman power in the west. The remote and unimportant province of Britain had already been lost at the beginning of the fifth century. Gaul had been invaded again and again by Visigoths, Burgundians and Huns, and now the Franks were establishing themselves in the north and east of the province. But Roman authority was still maintained by Roman arms over large areas. Spain had been overrun by the Visigoths, who set up a kingdom there. And since 439 the rich and hitherto peaceful north African provinces were in the hands of the Vandals. A few months after Valentinian's death, Rome itself was sacked by a Vandal force from Africa.

In the next twenty years a succession of shadowy emperors – protégés of the eastern empire, of the Gaulish magnates, of the Roman senate or of the Visigoths – reigned in Ravenna, while what real power there was belonged to the Romanized Suevian Ricimer, commander-in-chief of the army. When this tough warlord died in 472, the end was not far off. A Roman from Illyria, Orestes, who as a young man had lived as a hostage at the barbaric court of Attila, proclaimed as emperor his son Romulus Augustulus. The young man was hated and despised by the army in north Italy, consisting by this time almost entirely of German mercenary contingents. The commander of these, Odovacar the Herule, unable to obtain grants of land for his soldiers, decided to simplify the situation by dispensing with an emperor for the west. Romulus Augustulus was sent packing, and Odovacar governed Italy and the neighbouring territories under the nominal authority of the eastern emperor in Constantinople. In the meantime Gaul had fallen to Franks and Burgundians.

In appearance Odovacar's measure re-established the unity of the empire, divided since 395 into two parts. Theoretically the two emperors had acted in consort – *unanimitas* was the watchword. In practice each half went its own way.

In the east there was no loss of territory and no gradual collapse of Roman authority. It is true that at the death of the emperor Marcian in 457 the Alan general Aspar was the real master of the empire in the east as the Suevian Ricimer was in the west, and that he succeeded in putting on the throne his own nominee, Leo I. However, the eastern half of the empire, which contained the bulk of its population and wealth, remained territorially intact. Its economy was hardly affected, and its complex administrative machinery continued to function untrammeled. Furthermore, it was not ultimately dependent on German mercenaries for its defence. Leo raised an army from the tough and only superficially hellenized Isaurians of the Taurus mountains, whose leader Zeno became his son-in-law and ultimate successor. With the aid of Zeno and his followers, Aspar was murdered in 471. Zeno succeeded Leo on his death in 474. The main military threat which faced him came from the Ostrogoths, who ranged up and down the Balkan peninsula in search of land to settle on. Odovacar in Italy caused continual frontier troubles. By a brilliant stroke of diplomacy Zeno succeeded in sending Theodoric and his Ostrogothic army of twenty thousand men to evict Odovacar from Italy in the name of the empire. It took five years of bloody warfare before the task was accomplished. Theodoric was both king of the Ostrogoths and Patrician and Master of Soldiers of the eastern empire. This at any rate was the constitutional fiction. In reality he ruled Italy as an absolute monarch. But he was as anxious as Zeno and his successor Anastasius to maintain the fiction. It made control of his Roman subjects, who far outnumbered the Goths, easier. The Romans in Italy continued to be governed by Roman law and to preserve unchanged their way of life, including the great estates of the magnates. They were debarred from military service, as the Goths were debarred from holding civil office. Theodoric's coins bore the effigy of the emperor on the obverse, and his own monogram on the reverse, as if he were some kind of Roman magistrate. But real power lay with his court in Ravenna, not with the senate in Rome or with the emperor in Constantinople.

Thus the whole of the Mediterranean world west of a line from Ljubljana to the deserts of Libya was severed from the empire. The division corresponded only roughly with that between the Latin-speaking and the Greek-speaking world. Sicily was still largely Greek, and Latin was spoken over a vast area of the Balkans. And Latin was the language of state administration and law in the east, though Greek was the language of civic administration and of culture. Life in the lost provinces had changed little for the mass of the people. The shepherds were different, but the sheep continued to be fleeced as before.

Religious schism followed the line of political severance. The Council of Chalcedon in 451 had not united the Church. Monophysite doctrines were widely held in parts of the east, particularly in Egypt and Syria. Zeno had tried to win over the support of the Monophysites by promulgating a decree, the so-called *Henoticon*, which made some concessions to their point of view. It did not satisfy the Monophysites. And in the west, where Monophysite views were virtually unknown, it provoked a horrified reaction. In 484 Pope Felix III excommunicated

Acacius, the Patriarch of Constantinople who had inspired the Henoticon, and all his followers. The breach between the bishop of Rome and the emperor in Constantinople was welcome to Odovacar, as it no doubt was to the rulers of the other Germanic kingdoms of the west. It meant that their Roman subjects were less likely to look for help and support to a ruler whom they regarded as a heretic. It thus reinforced, at the level of theology, the political division of the Mediterranean world.

The first problem with which the new government had to deal was that of religious unity. Justin, the empress Euphemia and Justinian were themselves firm supporters of the doctrines of the Council of Chalcedon. But there was more to it than that. The church had a network of communications which penetrated into every town and village of the empire. Internal security demanded that this network function in the interests of the state and not against it. In a world in which all from the emperor to the humblest peasant were convinced that the prosperity of the realm and their own salvation depended upon correct religious belief, heresy and schism were a threat to the unity of the empire and the loyalty of its subjects. If Justinian already dreamed of re-establishing the authority of the empire in the west, as he must have, then he had to seek to win the support of the Italians, and above all of the Roman senatorial aristocracy. At the same time there were regions of the empire that were so firmly committed to the Monophysite faith that to seek to impose on them the doctrines of Chalcedon would inevitably alienate them and drive them to disaffection. The chief of these was Egypt, from which Constantinople drew the bulk of its grain supply. A government which could not maintain the system of free distribution of bread to many of the citizens of the capital and stable bread prices for the rest would have serious trouble on its own doorstep.

Hence the new government in its first month of office forced the Patriarch of Constantinople – a nominee of Anastasius – to repudiate his pro-Monophysite views, calling synods at Constantinople, Jerusalem, Tyre and Apamea which proclaimed their adherence to the faith of Chalcedon, expelling from their sees those Monophysite bishops who had not anticipated events and fled on the news of Anastasius' death, and recalling the many dignitaries, civil and ecclesiastical, who had been exiled in the previous reign. Egypt was left alone, and it was there that many of the exiled Monophysite clergy found refuge. Among these was Severus, Metropolitan (archbishop to whom the diocesan bishops of a province are subordinate) of Antioch, the leading theologian and propagandist among the Monophysites. Others slipped over the frontier into Persian territory, where the Nestorian church (followers of Nestorius, who taught that Christ was a man upon whom divinity had been superimposed; persecuted in the empire, they were the main Christian community in Persia) received them with coolness. Diplomatic measures were taken to discourage the Persians from granting them asylum. The first aim of the government was to re-establish Orthodox influence in Syria, where there was still a strong Orthodox party, and so to isolate Egypt from the rest of the empire. In this aim it was entirely successful, at any rate for a while.

At the same time an envoy was sent to Pope Hormisdas, bearing letters from the emperor, from the Patriarch, and from Justinian, to prepare a reconciliation. King Theodoric may well have been sorry to see the trump card thus snatched from his hand, but there was little he could do about it once the Pope had accepted the emperor's overtures. His only course was to negotiate a settlement whereby he recognized in theory the sovereignty of the emperor and at the same time had the *de facto* rule of himself and his successors guaranteed by Constantinople. This he did. His son-in-law Eutharic was formally recognized by Justin as the heir-apparent to the Ostrogothic kingdom, adopted by him in accordance with Germanic custom in a ceremony which would have no validity in Roman law, and designated consul for 519 along with the emperor himself. When on 1 January 519 Flavius Eutharicus Cillica entered Rome to inaugurate his consulship with unexampled splendour and munificence, many of the western exiles who formed a pressure-group at Constantinople felt that their cause was lost. And those western Roman senators who had dreamed of a restored western empire under their own nominee at last admitted that the western empire was ended, and had to make their peace with Ravenna and Constantinople alike. Their reappraisal of the situation was symbolized when their leader Boethius became in 519 Master of Offices under Theodoric and had two sons designated consuls for 522.

The Pope, who had little understanding of the situation in the eastern provinces, pressed the imperial government to depose Timothy IV, the Monophysite Patriarch of Alexandria, and to begin a campaign of religious repression in Egypt. But the government stood firm, and ultimately Hormisdas had to accept the typically Byzantine compromise that what was criminal heresy elsewhere was orthodox and legitimate in Egypt.

Tension between Constantinople and Ravenna

In Italy the Gothic government was nervous of Byzantine intentions, in spite of the recognition of Eutharic. In 522 Eutharic died, leaving a widow, Amalasuntha the daughter of King Theodoric, and two young children, Athalaric and Matasuntha. Theodoric was over seventy, and the problem of the succession was grave. The Franks and the Burgundians were stirring on the northern and western frontiers of the kingdom of Italy. There were rumours of plots and counter-plots. The atmosphere in Ravenna was buzzing with suspicion. In 523 Pope Hormisdas, a loyal friend of Theodoric, died. The king's intelligence service intercepted letters from leading Roman senators to the emperor in Constantinople, which put the writers under suspicion of disaffection. Boethius, the Master of Offices, tried to suppress the evidence; but he had enemies among the Roman aristocracy who were glad to denounce him. An investigation was held in the presence of Theodoric. After evidence had been given against one leading senator, Albinus, Boethius was unwise enough to observe that if Albinus was guilty, so was Boethius himself and the whole Roman senate. This was too much for the king. For the first time since his accession he used terror against the senate, the organ of the ruling class of Italy. Boethius and some others were arrested. His successor in office, Cassiodorus, tried to mollify the king. But Theodoric was determined to make an example of Boethius. He was held in prison in Pavia and there put to death, with every refinement of cruelty, on 23 October 524. During his imprisonment he wrote his *Consolation of Philosophy*, a book read and translated throughout the Middle Ages. The earliest English translation was made by King Alfred in the ninth century. Medieval readers – and some of their modern followers – supposed that the *Consolation* was a work of Christian piety. In fact there is no mention of Christianity in it and nothing specifically Christian in its ideas. The erudite leader of the Roman senate, devout Christian though he doubtless was, turned in his hour of need to the pagan, neo-Platonist tradition.

When the news reached Justinian, his indignation must have been tempered with pleasure. The Roman upper classes of Italy were now detached from all loyalty to the Gothic monarchy, and committed to the cause of the emperor. And not a single Byzantine soldier had moved from his barracks. Thousands would have to move however, and many never to return, before the hopes kindled in Justinian's heart in 524 could be realized.

In summer 526 the old King Theodoric died. In the words of a scholar who had no cause to admire the Germans, 'he was certainly one of the greatest statesmen the German race has ever produced, and perhaps the one who has deserved best of the human race'. His daughter Amalasuntha became regent until the majority of her son Athalaric; conciliatory gestures were made towards the Roman senate, and pro-Roman ministers appointed. The boy king wrote a humble letter to Justin, assuring the emperor of his everlasting respect and begging his august protection. The Gothic nobility, chafing at the unnatural rule of a woman, began to mutter that their queen and her son were forgetting Gothic dignity in their anxiety to win the favour of the distant emperor.

The other frontiers

In the other German kingdom, which straddled the Mediterranean – that of the Vandals in Africa, Sicily and Sardinia – changes were taking place too. In 523, after an inglorious reign of twenty-seven years, King Thrasamund died. The bizarre law of succession established by Gaiseric, the founder of the kingdom, brought to the throne Hilderic, a mild, cultivated, spineless man of sixty-six, grandson of the western Roman emperor Valentinian III. The new king at once stopped the persecution of Catholics which had marked the Vandal kingdom since its foundation. Exiled clerics were recalled, elections held to vacant sees. The Vandal system of 'apartheid' was abandoned, and with it vanished the claim of the tiny

Vandal minority to rule. King Hilderic, feeling himself more Roman than Vandal, entered into friendly correspondence with Justinian – but not with the emperor Justin who was his contemporary – and the astute prince neglected nothing which might bind the king's affection. Hilderic went so far as to have coins struck bearing the effigy of Justin, a tacit admission of Byzantine suzerainty. In the meantime the Moorish tribesmen pressed on the frontiers of the Vandal kingdom, and its Roman subjects, no longer terrorized, began to look towards Constantinople. Encouraged, no doubt, by Justinian, Hilderic put to death the Ostrogoths in the entourage of the dowager queen Amalafrida, who opposed his pro-Roman policy, and later arrested Amalafrida herself. When she died in captivity, Hilderic's enemies drew the obvious conclusion. All possibility of a common front between the Gothic and Vandal kingdoms was now excluded.

On the eastern frontier the new Byzantine government was no longer bound by a religious policy which ensured the sullen hostility of most of its subjects, and was able to pass to the offensive. The main theatres of war were in Mesopotamia and the Caucasus. But things were happening to the south, by the straits of Bab-el-Mandeb at the mouth of the Red Sea. Of no strategic value to either the Roman empire or Sassanid Persia, this region was of some commercial importance to both. It was from there that both Byzantium and Persia imported frankincense and other perfumes. But more significant was the long-distance trade in spices with India and the East Indies, and in silk, raw and worked, with China. Indian products could reach the Mediterranean world via the Persian Gulf, whose ports were in Persian hands, or through the Red Sea to Egyptian ports. Control of the straits by Byzantium enabled it to circumvent a possible Persian blockade; control by Persia enabled it to cut off these essential supplies – which were used in the preservation of autumn-killed meat over the winter – from Roman markets. Silk might come from China by several overland or sea routes which passed through Persian territory, and hence could be blocked. Only two routes circumvented Persia, that across the steppe north of the Caspian Sea to Black Sea ports, and that through the Red Sea to Egypt. Silk was not an article of general consumption like spice. But as a prestige possession, as a badge of rank, as a reward for merit, its role in the Mediterranean society of late antiquity was a striking one. An increase in price or a decrease in supply would pose many problems to the government in Constantinople. Throughout the sixth century much care was devoted to preventing Persian monopoly control of the Silk Road.

Here is the account of an early sixth-century Greek sea-captain:

Now this country of silk is situated in the remotest of all the Indies, and lies to the left of those who enter the Indian sea, far beyond the Persian Gulf and the island called by the Indians Selediba and by the Greeks Taprobane (Sri Lanka). It is called Tzinitza, and is surrounded on the left by the ocean, just as Barbaria (the Horn of Africa) is surrounded by it on the right. The Indian philosophers called the Brahmins say that if you stretch a cord from Tzinitza to pass through Persia and onward to the Roman dominions, the middle of the earth would be quite correctly traced, and they are perhaps right. For the country in question deflects considerably to the left, so that the loads of silk passing by land through one nation after another reach Persia in a comparatively short time, while the route by sea to Persia is vastly greater . . . He then who comes by land from Tzinitza to Persia shortens very considerably the length of the journey. This is why there is always to be found a great quantity of silk in Persia. Beyond Tzinitza there is neither navigation nor any land to inhabit. (Cosmas Indicopleustes, *Christian Topography* 2. 137-138.)

The peoples of the high mountain land of Ethiopia and Eritrea were by the sixth century largely Christian – but Monophysite Christians, since they had been converted from Egypt and their obedience was to the Patriarch of Alexandria. The state of Axum had established its hegemony over its neighbours, and extended its power across the straits to the Yemen. Monophysites might be heretics within the empire, but outside its frontiers they were Christians, entitled to the protection and support of the Christian emperor – when it suited his purposes. Ethiopian control of the Yemen meant in fact Roman control of the straits. The interior of the Arabian peninsula was largely a zone of Persian influence. Its prosperous Jewish communities, engaged in long-distance caravan trade, enjoyed special Persian protection, because they were unlikely to support a Christian regime in which Jews were the object of discrimination. Hence Judaism made many proselytes among the Semitic peoples of south Arabia. At the beginning of Justin's reign a Jewish prince of the Himyarites, Dhu-Nuwas, succeeded in expelling the Ethiopian garrison from the Yemen, and began to persecute the Christians in his country. The news of the persecution spread to the Monophysite communities of the empire. Timothy, the Patriarch of Alexandria, called on his spiritual son Ella Atsbeha, King of Axum, to intervene with Ethiopian forces. Jewish leaders in Palestine, fearful of reprisals, called on Dhu-Nuwas to end his persecution. Finally the Roman emperor, or his far-seeing nephew, seems to have addressed himself to Ella Atsbeha. A great Ethiopian expedition was launched, Dhu-Nuwas was defeated and killed, and Christianity was restored in the Yemen. What had been a trivial squabble between two neighbouring south Semitic peoples had become part of a world conflict.

At the northern end of the long frontier between the Roman and Persian empires lay the kingdom of Lazica – the ancient Colchis, today the western part of the Georgian Soviet Socialist Republic. Until the middle of the fifth century it had belonged to the Roman sphere of influence. The emperor Leo I had allowed it to fall under Persian control. Its kings went to Ctesiphon for their investiture, and the Zoroastrian religion had a quasi-official status among the upper classes. In 522 when King Damnazes died, his son Tzath decided to come to Constantinople for investiture, no doubt as a result of secret discussions with Justin's government. He was baptized, and from then on his kingdom was a Roman protectorate. This change of allegiance blocked off the only Persian access to the Black Sea, which became a Roman lake apart from a few ports on its north coast still held by Gothic rulers; and these were speedily dealt with. It also meant that a corridor through which the Huns of the steppes could be allowed to raid Roman territory was now sealed off. And it added Lazica to a chain of more or less Christian states stretching across Transcaucasia from the Black Sea to the Caspian – Lazica, Iberia (eastern Georgia), and Albania (Azerbaijan), from which Christian missionaries crossed the Caucasian mountains and evangelized the nomadic Hun tribes in their own tongue during the reign of Justin.

Persian response to this diplomatic victory, which so much weakened Persia's strategic position, was at first surprisingly mild. The Great King protested: he could do little else. He was still struggling to suppress a widespread movement of social protest in his own country – that of the Mazdakites, who preached a utopian and primitivist communism. And he was anxious to secure the succession for his favourite third son, Chosroes, against the claims of his elder brothers. Indeed he tried to get Justin to adopt Chosroes, as a hundred years earlier the Roman emperor Arcadius had had his infant son Theodosius formally adopted by the Great King Yezdgerd I. Justinian, who was hypnotized by his designs for the restoration of Roman power in the west, nearly fell into the trap. It was Proclus who pointed out to him that this might enable Chosroes to claim the heritage of his adoptive father – the Roman empire. So the reply was sent that the Roman emperor could not adopt a barbarian under Roman law. Chosroes could only be adopted by the German custom of adoption by arms, like the emperor's other barbarian vassals. The Great King Kavadh was provoked to action by this studied insult, and in 526 sent an army into Iberia, whose king Gurgen was taking a clearly pro-Roman attitude. The Romans replied by a deep raid into Persian Armenia, led by two young Thracian officers, friends of Justinian, Belisarius and Sittas. A second raid was repulsed by a Persian force. Further south, on the desert frontier, the formidable Arab leader Al-Mundhir, ruler of the pro-Persian kingdom of the Lakhmids, on the eastern border of the empire, recommenced his incursions into Roman territory. The local Roman commander mounted a counter-attack, which ended in chaos and failure. He was replaced by Belisarius, and an experienced general, Hypatius, nephew of the former emperor Anastasius, was re-appointed commander-in-chief in the east. These frontier skirmishes, following on twenty years of peace between the two empires, looked like the prelude to a new major war. But on 1 August 527 Justin died, leaving Justinian as sole emperor; and for Justinian a war with Persia had very low priority. So a cease-fire was arranged and negotiations begun.

The city of Constantine

The city in which the rest of Justinian's life was to be spent had been founded in 658 BC by colonists from Megara in Greece, who called it Byzantium. It was already nearly a thousand years old when Constantine established his capital there in 330 AD. Situated on a hilly peninsula between the Sea of Marmara and a long deep-water inlet, the Golden Horn, it was admirably placed for trade between the Mediterranean and the Black Sea, and had long been prosperous. Constantine greatly extended its area, adorned it with churches and public buildings of every kind, and protected it by a wall across the peninsula from sea to sea. The new capital prospered and soon outgrew Constantine's walls; a new line of walls was built by Theodosius II in the early part of the fifth century, further up the peninsula. They still stand, majestic and grim.

By the sixth century the population of the city was something between five hundred thousand and one million. It was of motley origin. Greeks from all over the empire, hellenized Thracians, westerners from Italy and Africa, Latin-speaking Illyrians from the western Balkans, Greek-speakers from Asia Minor, as well as others who still spoke one of the ancient tongues of that land, descendants of Hittites and Lydians and Lycians, Aramaic-speaking Syrians, Copts from Egypt, Armenians from their high plateau in the east, Jews, Goths and Herules and Gepids

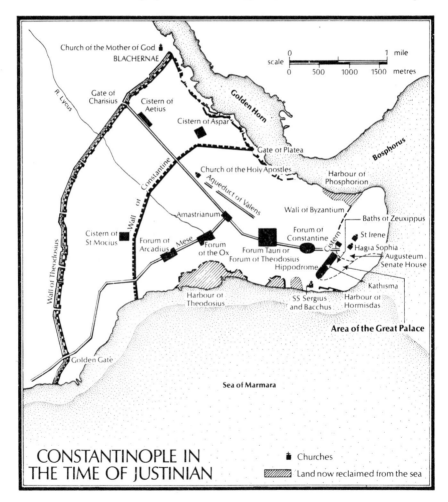

CONSTANTINOPLE IN
THE TIME OF JUSTINIAN

- Churches
- Land now reclaimed from the sea

from the Germanic lands to the north, jostled one another in its streets and squares. The common language of everyday speech was Greek. The imperial government, the army and the law-courts used Latin.

The centre of the city, the site of the market place of the old Megarian colony, was the Augusteum, an open square on high ground about half a mile from the tip of the peninsula. Grouped round the square were the great church of the Holy Wisdom – Hagia Sophia – built by Constantine and his son Constantius, the Senate House, the public baths of Zeuxippus, adorned with statues from all over the Greek world, the entrance to the Hippodrome, and the huge bronze gateway to the Great Palace. The palace itself, built on a series of terraces sloping down from the Hippodrome to the Sea of Marmara, was by Justinian's time a vast, untidy complex of halls, churches, pavilions, courtyards, barracks and gardens. No Versailles, it was rather a Kremlin, with monuments of every emperor from Constantine onwards.

From the Augusteum a broad street led westwards, lined by colonnaded porticoes and broken by a series of open squares, usually with a column or obelisk in the centre, to the Golden Gate, the southernmost of the gates in the Theodosian walls, about five miles distant. This street, called the Mese or main street, was the principal artery of the life of the city. From one of the squares into which it opened out, the Amastrianum, a branch led north-westwards to the Gate of Charisius. These broad main streets were linked and surrounded by a tangle of narrow lanes, following the irregular contours of the terrain and opening out from time to time into small squares. Of churches there were hundreds, mostly quite small. The numerous monasteries varied from modest establishments of a few monks in a private dwelling to rich institutions with hundreds of monks and more than as many servitors.

The houses of the rich presented a blank brick wall to the street on the ground floor and were built round interior courtyards, often containing gardens and fountains. The upper floors had bow windows, from which the ladies of the household might watch the animated life of the street below. There were many more modest patio-style houses. But the majority of the citizens lived in much more humble dwellings, off narrow passageways leading from the street. And many of them had no dwelling at all. Chronic unemployment was a feature of life in the capital of the empire. Homeless beggars slept under piles of rags between the columns of the porticoes. Many monasteries and churches had hostels for the homeless, or kitchens in which free meals were prepared for the destitute.

Since much timber was used in building, and many of the poorer houses were constructed entirely of wood, the danger of fire was ever present. And once started, it spread rapidly through the narrow lanes, fanned by the wind which blew up or down the valleys between the city's hills. There was a fire brigade, but it could do little to quell a major outbreak. The problem of getting water to the conflagration in sufficient quantity was one which ancient technology never solved. The water was available in the great cisterns, but buckets and wooden hand-pumps were all that the firemen had to transport it. In addition to the danger of spontaneous fires, there was that of arson. An angry crowd might set fire to the house of an unpopular magistrate or to some public building which symbolized for them the authority against which their hatred was directed. The great riot of January 532 saw whole quarters of the city devastated by incendiarism.

A large part of the population was engaged, directly or indirectly, in the service of the imperial government or the court. Not only were there countless porters, ushers, and minor functionaries, and an ever-growing army of clerks, shorthand-writers and accountants in the various departments of state, patiently awaiting promotion by seniority. Constantinople was also the centre of a number of luxury trades whose principal customers were to be found in the court and among the higher officers of state. Goldsmiths, silversmiths, jewellers, ivory-carvers, workers in inlay and enamel, weavers of brocade, sculptors and mosaicists found a ready market in the capital. And the maintenance and repair of the Great Palace and the various other public buildings engaged innumerable builders, architects, engineers, masons, bricklayers and plumbers.

Bread was distributed free or at low fixed price to all registered householders in the city; and measures were taken to prevent inflationary prices for other basic foodstuffs, such as pork and wine. Fish alone, which supplied the bulk of the people's protein requirements, was not controlled: one cannot hoard fish. The desire to stabilize food prices is a feature of all ancient city life. When transport is difficult and expensive, large agglomerations of people are particularly vulnerable to natural shortages, abetted by private hoarding and speculation by the rich. And the bigger the city, the bigger the problem. An imperial residence in particular needed contented citizens. Hunger and discontent could build up to riot pressure, and riot might take on a political tone: emperors had been murdered by angry city crowds.

The machinery through which this control of prices was operated was that of the guilds. Established in the first place perhaps for the protection of the producers, these had over the centuries been adapted by the state to the protection of the consumers and through them the security of the government. There was a guild for every trade, operating under the city prefect.

The distinction between manufacturer and retailer hardly existed. Most articles were made in small booths open to the street and sold by the manufacturer. There was scarcely any large-scale industry, apart from the imperial armament workshops. Each trade had its own quarter, the perfumers in the Augusteum, the bronze workers at the east end of the Mese, the horse-dealers in the Amastrianum square, and so on. This pattern of trade is still familiar in oriental cities today.

Much of the domestic work in all but the poorest households was still done by slaves; and where a craftsman's family helped him at his work, the slave or slaves were involved too. But slavery no longer played a major role in industrial production or in agriculture, apart from special cases such as mining and the production of purple dye, both extremely unpleasant occupations. The unskilled workmen who built and repaired Hagia Sophia – and they must have numbered thousands – were not slaves but Isaurians, free workmen from the wild Taurus mountains in the south of Asia Minor. So too were the porters who carried crushing loads on their backs through the narrow streets, many of them impassable to wheeled vehicles.

Dignitaries moved about the city on horseback, accompanied by an entourage; lesser men had mules or donkeys; and ladies of rank were conveyed in closed coaches drawn by mules, or in sedan-chairs. The mass of the citizens went about their business on foot, and the streets were filled with noisy, bustling crowds from sunrise to sunset. By the wharves which lined the Golden Horn foods from all over the empire and far beyond its boundaries – from Britain and Scandinavia to China – were loaded and unloaded by half-starved day-labourers. Cattle, sheep and pigs were driven through the streets from the city gates to the butchers' slaughtering yards. Often enough some of them were quietly diverted to the enclosed patio of some rich house. Stalls lined all the streets wide enough to contain them, and itinerant vendors of cooked foods wove their way through the crowds, crying their wares.

Far more of life was lived in the open air than in most European cities of today, even during the cold, damp winters. The extremes of wealth and poverty were displayed before the eyes of all. The situation could rapidly become explosive. The reign of Justinian was punctuated by riots and demonstrations, which sometimes became menacing and on one occasion, in January 532, nearly toppled him from his throne.

Ancient governments gave to the populace of their great cities not only bread, but circuses. In Constantinople the chariot-races in the Hippodrome, a copy on a slightly smaller scale of the Circus Maximus at Rome, offered excitement and spectacle in plenty. The races, with their combination of vicarious danger and partisan passion, could serve as a safety-valve for popular discontent. But the anonymity and the sense of solidarity which the tens of thousands of spectators cramming the benches enjoyed provided an unparalleled opportunity for the expression of popular feeling. The cheer-leaders of the circus factions could become the spokesmen of the people. In moments of tension they voiced the demands of their supporters and engaged in dialogues with the emperor or the presiding magistrate which could turn into real political confrontations – in one of which Anastasius had nearly lost his throne. The balance of force was on the side of the authorities, of course. The crowd in the Hippodrome was unarmed, and the emperor had his soldiers. But when popular feeling ran high there was no guarantee that the soldiers would carry out their orders, or that they had not already transferred their loyalty to a new candidate for the throne. And in any case a massacre of the citizens was unlikely to win support: forethought and flexibility were better instruments of power than brute force. The citizens of Constantinople had no political rights in the modern sense; but an emperor had always to reckon with them.

This consideration, as well as the natural desire for aggrandizement, explains the care which every emperor since Constantine had taken to adorn the city with public works. Water was collected from the hills of Thrace and led in aqueducts to great underground cisterns, which ensured a plentiful supply of water both to the numerous public baths and to the fountains and stand-pipes at almost every street corner. Hospitals, with doctors paid from state funds, provided the rudiments of a public medical service. A system of underground drains with brick pipes carried the waste products of the city to outlets on the Sea of Marmara or the Golden Horn. Porticoes and halls and covered markets gave shelter from the sun in summer and from the rain in winter. Since the fifth century shopkeepers were obliged to keep lights burning outside their premises at night, thus providing a rudimentary system of street lighting.

The only permanent military garrison was that provided by the regiments of the Palace Guard, some of whom were more ornamental than formidable. But the Prefect of the City, and later a new officer, the Praetor of the Plebs, had at his disposal a considerable police force, of which little is known in detail. And there were often formations of the regular army stationed in the vicinity of the capital, who could be called upon to maintain order. However, a ruler who could not control the people of Constantinople without resorting to force had little hope of staying long in office.

On the accession of his uncle, Justinian had at once been appointed Count of the Domestics and granted the rank of Patrician, the highest that could be conferred upon a subject. In 521 he celebrated his first consulate. The chief task of the holder of this venerable and prestigious office was to hold a series of games in Hippodrome and amphitheatre, and to distribute largesse to the populace. A man seeking political influence in the capital had much to gain by a well-organized consulate. Justinian made the most of his. Four thousand pounds of gold were spent on largesse and spectacles which included the killing in the amphitheatre of twenty lions and thirty leopards. From 519 he carefully cultivated one of the two great circus parties, the Blues. These organizations, whose primary function was to provide charioteers, acrobats and other performers for the games in the capital and elsewhere, had become something much more. Their professional cheer-leaders could organize the acclamations of the great crowd gathered in the Hippodrome, where numbers gave anonymity to the individual and allowed the expression of hopes and fears, demands and warnings, of which those in power had to take note. Through a network of 'supporters' clubs' in the wards of the city they were able to whip up a crowd or empty the streets at will. The performances of their artistes roused the keenest passions among the spectators; and the two principal parties, the Greens and the Blues, enjoyed from their supporters the fanatical loyalty which some football clubs arouse today. In a city in which there were no political parties and no elections, they served as safety-valves for popular discontent and as means of pressure upon the authorities. A man who aimed at power had much to gain from their support. The two parties were of slightly different social complexion, and enjoyed their support in different quarters of the city. The Blues tended to represent suburban landowners and rentiers, and to be firmly Chalcedonian and a trifle conservative. The Greens drew support from the traders and artisans, many of whom were of Syrian origin, and were inclined to make concessions to Monophysitism and present more radical demands. But these strange organizations are not to be compared with modern political parties. They had no clear-cut programmes, and they were not concerned with elections or office. Yet in the conditions of the time they could become the voice of the people, at any rate of those living within the walls of Constantinople. There were similar Green and Blue circus parties in the major provincial cities, which maintained some kind of loose relation with those in the capital.

Justinian had chosen to attach himself to the Blues. Groups of rowdies belonging to the party became the terror of the city, and no police officer dared lay hands on them because of the patronage they enjoyed. The Greens, on the other hand, were savagely repressed when they ventured in the streets, and driven to even more violent reaction. This gang-fighting in the streets of the city, and to some extent in the provinces too, ensured for Justinian a body of loyal supporters, able in an emergency to control the capital – for Justin was an old and sick man and none knew when his nephew might have to fight for the empire and for his life. It also ensured the success of the games with which he celebrated his consulate. The more old-fashioned professed to be shocked. 'Now that Justinian was fanning the flames and openly spurring on the Blues,' says Procopius sourly, 'the entire Roman empire was shaken to the foundations as if an earthquake or cataclysm had struck it, or as if every city had fallen to the enemy. For everywhere there was utter chaos, and nothing was ever the same again: in the confusion that followed, the laws and the orderly structure of the state were turned upside down.' The activists of the Blues, he goes on, cut their hair short in front and grew it long at the back, with a long moustache and beard, after the fashion of the Huns, and wore tunics with leg-of-mutton sleeves, riding breeches, and Hunnic capes. Their armed bands patrolled the streets at night, robbing wealthy passers-by of their cloaks and their gold or silver buckles and brooches, sometimes finishing off their victims with their daggers. Blackmail, denunciation and protection rackets were added to plain robbery, and no man felt safe. 'It is said,' he goes on, 'that a number of women were forced by their own slaves to yield to suggestions most repugnant to them. . . . Many unwilling boys, with the full knowledge of their fathers, were forced into immoral relations with the partisans; and women who were happily married suffered the same humiliation.' In the meantime Justinian saw to it that miscreants went unpunished, lavished money on the Blues, kept them in his entourage, and had them promoted to magistracies and official positions. This is the account of a hostile witness, a disgruntled conservative, and it doubtless gives a one-sided picture of the way in which the cool-headed and ambitious prince set about ensuring his own future. It was not until 524 or 525, when Justinian was critically ill, that anyone ventured to tell Justin what was going on. For the old emperor lived in senile seclusion in the Great Palace – or preferred to close his eyes to the activities of his trusted nephew. The Prefect of the City, Theodotus Colocynthius (the 'Pumpkin') had many of the Blues hanged or burned alive.

It was doubtless through his connections with the Blues that Justinian learned the superficial affability and accessibility that he later showed as emperor. For he was by nature unsociable, indeed something of a solitary; and it was through the Blues that he met Theodora.

She was some fifteen years younger than he, though like many women she never revealed her age, and she had a chequered and perhaps disreputable past. The circumstantial account given by Procopius, though inspired by bitter hostility and full of damaging imputations, is probably trustworthy in its main facts. Her father Akakios had been a bear-keeper employed by the Green party. Bear-fights, bear hunts, and the performances of acrobats who provoked bears and then saved themselves by their agility were a stock-in-trade of the public performances at the games. Her mother was probably an ex-performer of some kind. Both belonged to the lowest social stratum, one subject to many legal restrictions: a woman who appeared on the stage without her husband's consent was liable to instant divorce; a man who married an actress could not become a bishop; a senator could not marry an actress.

The couple had three daughters, Comito, Theodora and Anastasia. When the eldest girl was not yet seven, Akakios died. His widow at once remarried, hoping that her new husband would succeed to the post of bear-keeper, and thus enable her to bring up her daughters. But another man had already paid the party officials to get the post, and the family found itself destitute. The mother, following what was no doubt a recognized practice, appeared in the circus one day accompanied by the three little girls, decked in flowers, and appealed to the crowd. The Blues, anxious to score a point against the Greens, took them under their protection and gave a job to Theodora's stepfather. No doubt the child was often reminded whom she depended upon for her livelihood. At any rate, throughout her life she remained a fervent supporter of the Blues and an embittered foe of the Greens. Soon her elder sister Comito began appearing on the stage in mimes – rough and usually scurrilous farces, with plenty of knockabout. Theodora accompanied her in minor roles. Her talent for mimicry, her ready wit and her lack of inhibitions soon won her popularity. Actresses in Byzantium were not paragons of chastity. This was a virtue which society did not permit them to practise, and for the lack of which it then reviled them. Procopius dwells upon this period of Theodora's life with the neurotic lasciviousness of a prude. For what it is worth, this is what he says.

For the time being Theodora was still too underdeveloped to be capable of sharing a man's bed or having intercourse like a woman; but she acted as a sort of male prostitute to satisfy customers of the lowest type, and slaves at that, who when accompanying their owners to the theatre seized their opportunity to divert themselves in this revolting fashion; and for some considerable time she remained in a brothel, given up to this unnatural bodily commerce. But as soon as she was old enough and fully developed, she joined the women on the stage and promptly became a courtesan, of the type our ancestors called 'camp follower'. For she was not a flautist or harpist; she was not even qualified to join the corps of dancers; but she merely sold her attractions to anyone who came along, putting her whole body at his disposal. Later she joined the actors in all the business of the theatre, and played a regular part in their stage performances, making herself the butt of their ribald buffoonery. She was extremely clever and had a biting wit, and quickly became popular as a result. There was not an iota of modesty in the wench, and no one ever saw her taken aback; she complied with the most outrageous demands without the slightest hesitation, and she was the sort of girl who if somebody slapped her bottom or boxed her ears would make a jest of it and roar with laughter; and she would throw off her clothes and exhibit naked to all and sundry those parts, both in front and behind, which the rules of decency require to be kept veiled and hidden from masculine eyes.

She used to tease her lovers by keeping them waiting, and by constantly playing about with novel methods of intercourse she could always bring the lascivious to her feet; so far from waiting to be invited by anyone she encountered, she herself by cracking lewd jokes and wiggling her hips suggestively would invite all who came her way, especially if they were still in their teens. Never was anyone so completely given up to unlimited self-indulgence. Often she would go to a party with ten young men or more, all at the peak of their physical powers and with fornication as their chief object in life, and would lie with all her fellow-diners in turn the whole night long: when she had reduced them all to a state of exhaustion she would go to their menials, as many as thirty on occasions, and copulate with everyone of them; but not even so could she satisfy her lust.

And though she brought three bodily apertures into service, she often found fault with Nature, grumbling that Nature had not made the openings in her nipples wider than is normal, so that she could devise another variety of intercourse in that region. Naturally she was frequently pregnant, but by using all the tricks of the trade she was able to induce immediate abortion.

Often in the theatre too, in full view of all the people, she would throw off her clothes and stand naked in their midst, having only a girdle about her private parts and her groins – not, however, because she was ashamed to expose these also to the public, but because no one is allowed to appear there completely naked: a girdle round the groins is compulsory. With this minimum covering she would spread herself out and lie face upwards on the floor. Servants on whom this task had been imposed would sprinkle barley grains over her private parts, and geese trained for the purpose used to pick them off one by one with their bills and swallow them. Theodora, so far from blushing, when she stood up again actually seemed to be proud of this performance. For she was not only shameless herself, but did more than anyone else to encourage shamelessness. (Procopius, *Secret History* 9. 10-22.)

We need not take Procopius too literally. His source was mainly malicious tittle-tattle, and the grave historian hated and feared Theodora. In fact she seems to have been a rather successful actress in the comic theatre of the time, a kind of *soubrette* with a talent for striptease. One of her most successful turns was a burlesque of the myth of Jupiter and Leda. Her morals were no better than those of her colleagues. The fashionable young men had to have girls for their parties. But it was a hard life, and one which could never, as it might today, lead to a measure of public esteem and affluence. Theodora looked for something a little more permanent, and she found it. She became the official mistress of a certain Hecebolus, holder of a high government post, and accompanied him when he left to be governor of a minor province in North Africa. She was not quite the governor's lady, but she had come up in the world. And if all went well she could count on being pensioned off discreetly when Hecebolus tired of her. But it was not to be. Perhaps her sharp wit was found out of place in government house. Perhaps her fidelity to her dull lover was not all that it might have been. At any rate there was a fierce row, and Theodora was sent packing.

Her situation was now desperate, a thousand miles from home. Procopius implies that she worked her passage as a common prostitute. He may be right. But she spent some time in Alexandria, and there are indications that she made the acquaintance there of some of the leading Monophysite clerics, including the Patriarch Timothy and the austere Severus of Antioch. It is probably from this time that her inclination towards the Monophysite faith dates; and it has been suggested that she underwent some kind of religious conversion and renounced her former way of life. She did not return to the stage but settled in a small house near the palace, where she made her living by spinning wool.

Justinian in later life was an abstemious and continent man. But it would be surprising if someone in his exalted position had not sown some wild oats in his youth. From the day he met Theodora, however, all this was over. His worst enemies – and he had many – could not find a single act of infidelity to charge him with. She became his mistress, and he showered her with all the wealth of the ruler of the Roman world. He was no doubt the father of a daughter born to her about this time, who died young.

She was still strikingly beautiful, by all accounts, though her countenance bore the marks of her eventful life. Nature and experience had given her a quick and ready wit, an unfailing memory, and a talent for public appearance. Her self-confidence was boundless, and she feared no man. Somewhere, somehow, she had acquired a wide, if superficial, culture; later, on a memorable occasion, she quoted the orator Isocrates with electrifying effect. Justinian when he met her was about forty, of medium height, with a rather heavy, somewhat florid face. On the surface rather a cold man, approachable but not sociable, he was a compulsive worker at state papers, with a meticulous attention to detail and a remarkable capacity for going without sleep. His ambition was boundless, his patience endless, his plans laid carefully for years ahead. Yet at crucial moments his courage sometimes failed him, and he floundered in indecision. Theodora was his ideal complement. She had every social grace, she lived for the present, and she never lost her head in a crisis. He was devoted to her, and their confidence in each other was absolute.

Soon he decided to marry her. Such a marriage would be highly unconventional, but Justinian was by now too powerful to care for convention. To make things more seemly, he persuaded his uncle to confer upon Theodora the dignity of the patriciate. There were, however, two more serious obstacles to their union. The old Empress Euphemia, who had never played any part in public affairs, was adamant: she would not have that hussy in the palace. And Roman law specifically forbade the marriage of a senator to a woman who had appeared on the stage. In 524, however, Euphemia died. And shortly afterwards Justin issued a most remarkable edict. In sonorous and circumlocutory Latin it ordains that henceforth actresses who have abandoned their former life may contract a legal marriage, and those upon whom a high dignity has been conferred may marry men of the highest rank. The law was clearly intended to deal with the special case of Theodora, for no other retired actress in the history of Rome had had a high dignity conferred upon her. In 525 the couple were married, doubtless by the Patriarch, and in the great church of Hagia Sophia built by Constantine two centuries earlier. At about the same time Theodora's elder sister Comito married the Master of Soldiers (commander-in-chief in one of the regions of the empire) Sittas, an old friend of Justinian. A little later, Justinian, now without a rival, was promoted to the new rank of *nobilissimus*. On 1 April 527 the old emperor, now mortally ill, proclaimed his nephew co-emperor. Three days later, in the great church, the Patriarch crowned Justinian emperor and Theodora empress. In solemn procession, escorted by the dignitaries of church and state, by the corps of palace guards, heralds and trumpeters, between the lines of soldiers holding back the crowd, the new rulers made their way to the Hippodrome and, standing in the Kathisma, or imperial box, received the acclamations of their joyful subjects. What were the thoughts that passed through Theodora's mind as she stood, stiff and hieratic in the glittering brocades and jewels of a Roman empress, in that very circus where she had begun her strange career? Did she exchange a wink of complicity with her brooding and unsmiling spouse? Or with her sister, Comito, soon to be a general's wife? We shall never know. But we may be sure that on this day she gave the finest performance of her life.

2 The men around Justinian

The old emperor Justin survived for a few months after the coronation of his nephew, though he played no part in public affairs. On 1 August 527 he died, leaving Justinian as his undisputed successor. In the years when he was the power behind the throne Justinian had gathered around him a group of men upon whom he could rely for the conduct of affairs. For a man who found delegation of responsibility difficult he had a surprising ability to enlist the loyalty and even the devotion of men of high ability, some of whom might have been dangerous enemies. He kept his own counsel and gave his full confidence to no one, perhaps not even to Theodora. But just as in his younger days he had been able to use the raffish ringleaders of the circus factions as his instruments, so now on the threshold of middle age he could count upon the unswerving support of talented soldiers and civil servants. Most of these men make their first appearance in the closing years of Justin's reign or early in Justinian's. For years before he must have been watching, choosing his men, grooming them for the great responsibilities that were to be theirs. In army messes, in government offices, in courts of law, the prince, distant and impenetrable behind his superficial affability, observed, listened, talked and pondered, as he put together the team with which he was to execute his great design. He cared nothing for birth and rank – indeed these were if anything negative qualifications: the great families of the empire were sullenly hostile to the upstart from Thrace. Though an educated, indeed an erudite man himself, with a taste for intellectual matters and learned discussion, he was unimpressed by elegant speech and refined manners. Experience had taught him how often these concealed a void of incompetence and muddle, or a spirit of hostility and intrigue. The men he sought had to be superbly good at their job, able to carry on in the face of unpopularity and virulent attack; men who could keep their heads in an emergency. This was the first qualification. The second was lack of ambition. Not that he rejected those who wished to rise to the top of the ladder in their career, and who enjoyed the fruits of success – indeed many of his ministers were justly criticized for enjoying them too much, for acquiring colossal fortunes from the exercise of their office. For Justinian the wealth of his subordinates and the splendour of their way of life merely increased their dependence upon him. So long as his power remained undisputed, a nod could divest them of their palaces, their lands, their private armies and their throngs of servitors and dispatch them in chains to a wretched exile in some dismal corner of his empire. Early Byzantine society was unlike the feudal world of the Middle Ages in which a tight network of bonds linked vassal and lord, and gave to a great baron independent power with which he could challenge his sovereign. It was a mobile and insecure society; men rose and fell at the whim of the ruler. And the ruler himself, though God's vicar on earth, had to justify his power by the success with which he exercised it.

Having picked his men, Justinian backed them through thick and thin. In the later Roman Empire tenure of high office, military or civil, had in general been short. There were too many groups manoeuvring for the ruler's favour, too many claims to satisfy. And men who retired after only a year or two of office were less dangerous than those whose hands had grown used to the reins of power. Justinian's principal ministers, on the other hand, often held office for decades. And when public pressure forced their dismissal, as happened in the great revolt of 532, he reinstated them again as soon as it was safe. If they were loyal to him, he too was loyal to them.

The generals

The most conspicuous group, though in the last analysis perhaps not the most important, were the generals. First, Belisarius. Procopius, who was his military secretary, recognized his weaknesses, but was clearly captivated by the magnetism of his personality and impressed by his achievements. The Byzantines too treasured his memory; minstrels, singing in the vernacular, passed from generation to generation a legend of his life which has little to do with historical reality, and he thus became the hero of a romance of which a fourteenth-century version in demotic Greek is extant.

He was a much younger man than Justinian. It is not known exactly when he was born – it was probably about 505; he was a native of Germania, now the village of Sapareva Banya near Dupnitsa, now Stanke Dimitrov, in western Bulgaria. His name appears to be Thracian. He belonged, as did Justinian himself, to the stratum of Romanized Thracians, much mingled with Gothic stock by this time. Yet he was hardly a peasant lad: he began his military service as an officer in one of the regiments of the palace guard, and he was most likely the son of some local landowner. But nothing whatever is known of his family. He did not bring with him to the capital, like Justin, a following of nephews and cousins eager to profit by his success. He was, according to the sources, tall, handsome and dashing, the very epitome of the young cavalry-officer. Constantinople was full of young cavalry-officers, but Belisarius had qualities which distinguished him among his colleagues and caused Justinian, when he was Master of Soldiers under his uncle Justin, to appoint him to his staff. By 526, when he cannot have been past his early twenties, he was put in command of the Roman army in Mesopotamia in the war against Persia. Belisarius hardly distinguished himself in this first command, in which he fought two rather indecisive campaigns. Probably the troops at his disposal were inadequate for anything more. Perhaps Justinian intended no more than a show of force on the frontier, for he was not at this stage anxious to embroil himself in a major war with the Persians. At any rate Justinian was satisfied with the conduct of his protégé. In April 529, now sole ruler, he appointed him Master of Soldiers in the east, commander-in-chief on the Persian front. The general whom he replaced,

Hypatius, was a nephew of the emperor Anastasius, an officer of long and undistinguished service – he had suffered a humiliating defeat at the hands of the rebel Vitalian in the closing years of his uncle's reign – and a man who might have become emperor. The young guard was taking over. But Justinian took no unnecessary risks. An older officer, Hermogenes, who had served under Anastasius and Justin, was posted as his chief of staff, presumably to curb any unpractical flights of strategic imagination. In this command too he achieved little to suggest the brilliance he was soon to display. But he defended the city of Daras against a much superior Persian force, by a combination of skilful field engineering and rapid choice of the right place and time to attack. It was, as Procopius observes, the first time for many years that a major Persian army had been defeated by the Romans. The next year, as he pursued a withdrawing Persian force, carefully avoiding engagement with it but hastening the pace of its retreat, he allowed himself to be provoked by some of his officers into an untimely attack at Callinicum, now Raqqa on the Euphrates. The Persians broke through the Roman ranks and sent them in headlong flight. Belisarius fought gallantly himself, ordering his staff-officers to dismount and fight on foot with him. In the end he held the Persian charges, and what might have been a disaster was averted. When he was shortly afterwards recalled to Constantinople, it was hardly because of this defeat, but because Justinian had greater things in store for him. During his stay in Constantinople the young general, probably still in his twenties, married. His wife, Antonina, was considerably older than he – it is not known by how much. She was a close friend of Theodora's, and like the empress she had been an actress. Whether she had been legally married before is unknown, but she had had several children, of whom at least one, a boy called Photius, was in her custody. Procopius, who knew Antonina well, hated and feared her; and in his *Secret History* he makes her out to be a magician, an adulteress and a murderess. That she was not as faithful a wife as Theodora seems beyond doubt. And she evidently had few scruples about how she used her great power. She led Belisarius something of a dance. There were searing quarrels in which the empress had to intervene, largely over a young man called Theodosius, whom Belisarius had adopted in a quasi-legal fashion, and with whom Antonina had a long and chequered affair. It was an uneasy household, racked by denunciations, tearful reconciliations, perhaps assassinations. It is hard to know what to make of Procopius' lurid stories. Belisarius seems to have yielded to his wife's every suggestion. He certainly took her with him on almost all his campaigns. Maybe she was less dangerous when he could keep an eye on her. Maybe he enjoyed her company in spite of her infidelities. Most probably he early fell into a relation of emotional dependence upon her – after all she was his senior in age and experience – which made a break impossible.

Another Thracian general was Sittas. He may have been a little older than Belisarius. At the close of Justin's reign he held a command in the east, as did Belisarius; and in 528, a year before Belisarius, he was appointed Master of Soldiers in Armenia and Pontus, with full responsibility for a sensitive sector of the front, where the Byzantine government, by a combination of military and diplomatic pressure, was trying to detach the Laz clans from their allegiance to Persia, and so block off the Persians from access to the Black Sea. It was shortly after this promotion that he received a very special token of imperial favour, in the form of the hand of Comito, elder sister of Theodora. In 530 he was again in command in Armenia, where he displayed great tact and skill in winning over the touchy and influential clan chieftains. In particular he insisted on their being given appointments in the Roman service, both to reward their loyalty and to engage them in a larger community than that of their quarrelsome mountain cantons. Indeed it was Sittas who began the Armenian diaspora. Without his insight into the character of their society, the Armenians would perhaps have remained confined to their upland valleys, and would not have played their conspicuous role in the life of Byzantium, of the Ottoman empire, and of the world at large. Thus far Sittas seemed to be ahead of Belisarius in the contest for power. Why, then, is his name today known only to a handful of specialists? Maybe he showed traits of character which aroused Justinian's mistrust. Perhaps even his political skill in dealing with Armenia counted against him. Most probably, however, the explanation must be sought in his absence from Constantinople in 532, the year of the Nika revolt. It was then that Justinian's friends were put to the test. Belisarius was on the spot, and never wavered. Sittas, as Master of Soldiers in the Presence – the highest military appointment – was conducting a successful campaign against steppe nomads on the Danube frontier. When he returned he was met with the emperor's respect and with popular acclamation, but he no longer belonged to Justinian's inner circle of confidants. In 538 a revolt by some discontented clan leaders in Armenia required his presence there. The prestige of his person soon calmed the situation. But in a casual skirmish he was killed. Belisarius was now left without a rival, for the time being.

A man who might have rivalled not merely Belisarius but Justinian himself was Germanus. A nephew of Justin and hence a cousin of Justinian, he had, like Justinian, followed his uncle to Constantinople. In the closing years of Justin's reign he was Master of Soldiers in Thrace. Germanus was a victorious general. Why, one may wonder, did Justin prefer as his successor his unwarlike cousin Justinian? Age may have something to do with it – Germanus seems to have been considerably younger than Justinian. And perhaps the old emperor distrusted the fine manners and aristocratic connections of Germanus. For he had married into the immensely rich and noble Anicii, a western Roman family which had moved to Constantinople when the Ostrogothic kingdom was established in Italy, and he seems to have been assimilated by the aristocracy. Procopius, who liked him, tells that he had the manners of a *grand seigneur*, that he was incorruptible, generous, the owner of palaces and estates all over the empire, contemptuous of the circus and its mob passions – and that Theodora detested him. The dislike seems to have been mutual. It needs little imagination to picture the feelings of Germanus' wife, whose pedigree was studded with emperors and consuls, when she had to bow the knee to the impossible ex-actress. And Theodora, who understood such matters, will not have relaxed protocol one iota in her dealings with her patrician cousin. As for Justinian, he got on well with Germanus and appreciated his steadiness, his military skill, and his lack of ambition. The relations between the two men had probably been established for some time – in the dirt of a Balkan farmyard – before either rose to prominence, and Justinian knew that he could dominate Germanus. He appointed him to a series of important commands: in Africa in 536, in the east in 540, in Italy in 550. After Theodora's death in 548 a conspiracy was formed to put Germanus on the throne, but it misfired, largely through Germanus' own lack of enthusiasm – he passed the information to an officer of the palace guard, who told Justinian. The emperor was furious that he had not been informed earlier and in person, but did not doubt Germanus' essential innocence. Two years later, when he went to take command in Italy, he was married with great solemnity – he was by now a widower – to the Gothic princess Matasuntha, widow of King Vitiges and grand-daughter of Theodoric. This marriage symbolized Justinian's project for a final settlement in Italy between the Byzantine government and the old Gothic royal family. And it marked out Germanus as Justinian's eventual successor; for the emperor was now sixty-eight. But like so many of Justinian's plans, this grand design was frustrated. The Gothic people fought on under new, popular leaders. And in any case Germanus died at Sardica (Sofia) in 550.

The man who really rivalled Belisarius as a general was very different from Germanus, though like him – and like Justinian himself – he was of humble origin. Narses was not even a Roman: he came from the Persian zone of Armenia; and he came as a eunuch slave, how and when is not known. Men believed that he had been born about 480. How he first entered the imperial service is a mystery. When he first appears, at the beginning of Justinian's reign, he is commander of the emperor's eunuch bodyguard and already in his forties. His position made him the emperor's confidant. And he would not have remained long in office had he not had the confidence of Theodora too. According to contemporary sources, he shared her Monophysite sympathies. If he had strong views on the theological controversies of the age, he probably kept them to himself. Life had taught him discretion. 'A slight, frail-looking man,' says the historian Agathias, who must have known him, 'he had unbelievable courage and competence.' Not an educated man, and with no training in formal eloquence, he could yet grasp a complicated problem with rapidity and insight; and once he had decided what must be done, he did it with thoroughness and energy. The dignity and humanity with which he behaved in every situation emerge strikingly from the accounts of his contemporaries. And it is significant that Procopius never mentions his name in his virulent and scandal-mongering account. A good man, an able man, an intelligent man; but hardly the stuff field-marshals are made of. However during the Nika revolt, when Justinian's power hung by a thread, Narses, in command of his personal bodyguard, was in a key position. His loyalty was unwavering, and he displayed unexpected military gifts. Advancement soon followed. He applied himself to the study of military science, and learned much from his close friend John the son of Vitalian, a soldier of long experience. In 538 he was sent to Italy to see whether the war could not be finished more rapidly. This was tantamount to making him sit in judgment over Belisarius, and the great commander was shocked and hurt. In any case he could not stand the grave, elegant, ageless eunuch. There was a continual series of disagreements, and one of the two men had to be withdrawn. In the event, to everyone's astonishment, Belisarius returned to Constantinople and Narses stayed. But Justinian knew what he was doing. Ultimately it was Narses – in command again in Italy from 552, and with vast resources, far greater than those put at the disposal of Belisarius – who brought the long Gothic war to its conclusion. He had not Belisarius' dash and style. But he was a careful architect of victory, and on 20 July 561 he took Verona, the last Gothic stronghold, and Justinian's dream was accomplished. At once Narses, by now nearing eighty if not older, put in hand the military reorganization of Italy. And in spite of the Pragmatic Sanction, by which civil government was restored in the peninsula, he was in effective control until Justinian's death. He was the only one of the men around Justinian at the beginning of his reign who outlived him. When he died in about 575, he was reputedly aged ninety-five.

There were other soldiers whom Justinian had picked from the beginning, and who served him well. John the Troglite held a command in Mesopotamia at the beginning of the reign, and followed it by a long career in Africa, until at least 552. He was a specialist in mopping-up operations and punitive expeditions, and his well-planned and dashingly executed campaigns restored the morale and the organization of the Byzantine army, shaken and dismayed by the gulf between victory in the field and pacification of the country. Strangely, he became the hero of the last Latin epic in the classical manner, the *Johannid* of Flavius Cresconius Corippus, a school-master from Carthage.

Another soldier whose career lay in Africa was Solomon, from Daras in Mesopotamia. He too was a eunuch, but as a result of an accident. How he got his military training is not known. He seems to have been at first a protégé of Belisarius, who took him to Africa as his chief of staff, and left him in command there when he himself went on to Sicily and Italy in 533. An inflexible man and a harsh administrator – his experience had hardly prepared him for the tasks he faced – he became unpopular with soldiers and civilians alike. An attempt to assassinate him in Carthage Cathedral on Easter Sunday 536 failed, but was the signal for a large-scale military revolt. Justinian, who had Italy in the forefront of his mind, realized that things were going wrong in Africa and recalled Solomon. It might have been the end of his career. But the emperor did not readily abandon his collaborators. In 539 Solomon was back in Africa with reinforcements and new directives, and began a campaign to establish Byzantine power among the Moors of the Aurès mountains, south of Constantine in present-day Algeria. It was crowned by a great victory. But hardly had the jubilation ceased when Solomon was faced by a graver challenge. In 543 a section of the Roman army mutinied, with support from the local population. Solomon acted with speed and decisiveness and won a series of local victories; but in spring of the next year he fell in battle. Inscriptions throughout Tunisia and Algeria bear witness today to the engineering works, roads and fortresses built by this eunuch from Mesopotamia.

There were Goths among Justinian's generals. Bessas was an Ostrogoth from Thrace, who had served in Anastasius' Persian war. He was still in a minor command in the east on Justinian's accession. Perhaps he attracted Belisarius' notice there. Or perhaps Justinian had earlier formed a favourable opinion of him. At any rate he was given a major command under Belisarius in Sicily and Italy, and was in charge of the troops in Rome during the desperate siege by Totila in 545. His inactivity and the harshness he showed to the civil population were severely criticized, and in the end he had to evacuate the city as a result of an agreement reached between Totila and a deacon of the Roman Church. Justinian however maintained his confidence in Bessas. He was raised to the rank of patrician and despatched to the sensitive Armenian frontier as commander-in-chief, although then in his seventieth year. Five years of tricky operations in the wild mountains of Armenia and Lazica followed. Bessas gained no great victories, but he maintained Roman control in a key area. Suddenly, it is not known how, Justinian's patience became exhausted. The old general was stripped of his rank, his property confiscated, and he himself banished to a remote village in Abkhasia, on the eastern shore of the Black Sea. Justinian was already in his seventies, and had been ill: perhaps he was losing his grip. This is one of the rare cases when he turned against a man who had served him well for thirty years.

John, the nephew of that Vitalian who had successfully rebelled against Anastasius and who was lured to Constantinople by a consulship and promptly assassinated by Justinian's orders, was either a Goth or a Thracian. He held a high command under Belisarius in Italy, but was at the same time a close friend of the eunuch Narses. When the two generals quarrelled, he took the side of Narses. Perhaps that is why he was sent back to Constantinople by Belisarius. Justinian discreetly ignored his great marshal's implicit condemnation of John. While in the capital he married a daughter of Justinian's cousin, the urbane and magnanimous Germanus, and soon he was back in Italy where he remained, a trusted general of both Narses and Germanus, until the final victory in 561.

There were many more generals whose names and exploits fill the pages of Procopius. Of them all only Belisarius and Narses had the talent for large-scale strategy which makes a great commander-in-chief. The others were brilliant tacticians, good administrators, brave men who soldiered on; and above all they were Justinian's men. The imperial armchair strategist, poring over maps and communiqués in his palace by the Bosphorus, impressed his will and his vision on this odd collection of military leaders. In return for loyalty and success he gave them wealth, prestige and protection.

The civilians

In the civil departments of state, leadership was perhaps less important. A civil service can function perfectly well, up to a point, without a minister; but an army is helpless without a general. The tradition of very short tenure of high office had given great autonomy to the civil service departments of the late Roman empire. Their antiquarian, precedent-loving atmosphere with its pervasive patronage is admirably conveyed by the treatise *On the Magistracies of the Roman People* written by John the Lydian in the 550s. John entered the staff of the Praetorian Prefect, with the help of a relative, and rose slowly through the hierarchy, often as the result of a well-timed push. A judicious marriage arranged by his superior helped him along. But finally one of Justinian's administrative changes prevented him reaching the highest office in his department and the perquisites it carried with it. John clearly enjoyed almost every minute of his long walk down the corridors of power. And even a blighted career and a penurious retirement did not dim his enthusiasm for the system, though he is blistering in his criticism of the changes effected by Justinian's minister.

This is a very different world from that of the nervy, quarrelsome, plundering soldiers with whom Belisarius and Narses had to deal. Hands did not spring to swordhilts at the shadow of an insult in the bureaux of the Master of Offices or the Quaestor of the Sacred Palace. And the cohorts of scribes, notaries, under-secretaries, chartularies and *castrenses* never teetered on the edge of armed revolt. Nevertheless a ruler who wished to carry out a policy, and not to be a mere representative head of state, needed to put men he could trust at the head of the great departments. Here too, Justinian picked his team early, and supported it through thick and thin. Less is known about these men, because the principal narrative history of the age, that of Procopius, is concerned with wars. Procopius, however, has something to say about them in his *Secret History*. Many of Justinian's civilian collaborators will be encountered in the narration of the story of his life. At this point three merit introduction, both for the key role they played from the beginning in the implementation of their master's policy, and because they are striking characters in their own right.

John of Cappadocia came from Caesarea in the heart of Asia Minor. A man of humble origin and little education, he had attracted the prince's notice by his personal qualities. These cannot have been easy to discern; for he had none of the graces of life, his speech was rude and unpolished, his Christianity seems to have been rather superficial, and contemporaries describe him as a drunkard, a glutton and a debauchee. What attracted Justinian to him was his single-minded efficiency, his ability to grasp and organize an inchoate mass of detail, and his contempt for the pressures exercised by the rich and powerful. He was outspoken, even to Justinian. So was Narses; but Narses enjoyed the protection of Theodora. What protected John the Cappadocian must have been his fundamental incorruptibility. He was not above enriching himself by selling small favours; but no amount of money would induce him to yield on a matter of principle. Even Procopius, who hated him, praises his energy, his clarity of mind, and his practical ability.

John began his career as a clerk in the office of the local military commander, and must have attracted the emperor's attention in some way. At any rate he was transferred to Constantinople and given accelerated promotion, and in 531 appointed Praetorian Prefect. This officer was responsible for the provisions and maintenance of the army, and raised taxes to do so; and he also had direct control over provincial governors. His was perhaps the key position in a government in which there was no prime minister. John at once began a long series of reforms, which it may be presumed had the general approval of Justinian. Some of this was mere tidying-up, such as the reforms directed against inflated staffs and inefficient tax-collecting. Others had as their target the pervasive corruption and the consequent purchase of offices. Still others were money-savers, designed to help meet the costs of Justinian's campaigns in the west: the cost of food provision was cut down, but the saving was not passed on to the producers; new taxes were imposed, including one upon the spaces between buildings illegally built over. Finally, and most important of all, there were the measures of centralization. The Roman empire had been and still was an assemblage of self-governing civic communities grouped together by the ruling power for certain purposes such as defence, roads and post, customs duties, public lands. Each of these functions was carried out by a different department of state with its own head. There was thus a series of parallel administrations, which caused constant clashes, and which could be exploited by the ill-intentioned. At the same time, as the cities grew less and less able to manage their own affairs and the provincial governor had more and more to intervene, his power grew, sometimes to menacing proportions. It was this series of interlocking problems which John the Cappadocian tackled in a lengthy series of measures.

Tax-collectors are never popular, and when they are both efficient tax-collectors and energetic reformers they make many enemies. John was heartily detested by the upper classes and doubtless by many of the lower orders too, especially in the capital. One of the demands of the Nika revolt of 532 was his dismissal, and Justinian had to remove him from office as part of the settlement of that crisis. But within a few months, when the heat had died down, he was back in office, continuing his programme of reform. He made enemies by meting out to the rich and influential tax-evader something of the barbarous severity which the poor and humble had always suffered. John the Lydian has many stories illustrative of this, which should be viewed with the scepticism due to one-sided statements. During a tour of inspection of the eastern provinces in 540-1 a plot was mounted against him by Antonina the wife of Belisarius, who insinuated herself into the friendship of John's daughter Euphemia and through her persuaded John on his return to attend a secret meeting at which the replacement of Justinian by Belisarius was discussed. Officers concealed on the premises rushed in and arrested John, but his bodyguard of armed mercenaries rescued him. Justinian evidently did not take the matter seriously. But in 541, yielding to the insistence of Theodora, he dismissed John and confiscated the vast wealth which he had accumulated. A little later, when Theodora's anger had cooled, the emperor returned to John his property, but exiled him to the pleasant and salubrious city of Cyzicus. But Theodora had a long memory, and a long arm, and when the next year the bishop of Cyzicus was found murdered, John was accused. An imperial commission sent to investigate the matter found him guilty; and the once all-powerful prefect was flogged, and deported in destitution to Antinoupolis in upper Egypt. Even there he continued to denounce the irregularities of local officials to the emperor. After Theodora's death in 548 he was allowed to return to the capital, was ordained priest, and died at an unknown date. John the Cappadocian was clearly 'framed'. It may be argued that Justinian should have protected him. But if the emperor was forced to choose between Theodora and his Praetorian Prefect, he had little freedom of choice. Many of John's administrative reforms were abrogated by his successors, and the centralized, uniform, tidy empire of his dream – and Justinian's too – was never realized. It was probably an impossible dream, given the structure of Byzantine society, in which more and more of the political power at a local level was passing from the cities, with their councils and magistrates, to the big landowners. Let there be no illusions: John the Cappadocian was a cruel and rapacious man. And while there is no need to believe all his enemies relate, his pleasures were scarcely refined. But he was a loyal, efficient and incorruptible servant. Justinian's judgment had been unerring when he picked him out from a roomful of clerks in a provincial office.

If John of Cappadocia's achievements perished with him, those of another of Justinian's closer collaborators still survive as an influential element in western culture. Tribonian was born in Side in Pamphylia, on the southern coast of Asia Minor. He first appears in the reign of Justin as a successful advocate in the court of the Praetorian Prefect. He was a man of deep and wide learning, who astonished his contemporaries by his erudition. In another respect too Tribonian was the very opposite of John of Cappadocia, for he was greedy and eminently corruptible. It is the duty of an advocate to present his client's case in the best light, but Tribonian exceeded the requirements of duty; and when he was later in charge of the emperor's programme of legislation, he made and unmade laws for gain. This trait earned him the hatred of the city populace, and he was one of those sacrificed for a time during the Nika revolt, but soon restored to office again. In the first year of Justinian's reign he was appointed Master of Offices, and in 529 Quaestor of the Sacred Palace, the highest judicial officer of the empire. He was the moving spirit in Justinian's great codification of Roman law in the 530s. In the preface to the first edition of the *Code* – a collection of imperial enactments then valid – he is mentioned along with the other members of the drafting commission. But in the prefaces to the *Digest* – a systematic compilation of the opinions of the authoritative Roman jurists – and in a multitude of other legal enactments, his name stands alone at the head of the list, as the inspirer and organizer of the great enterprise. The spirit which animated the codification and the way in which it was carried out will be examined in detail. For the moment it suffices to bear in mind only that it was no scissors-and-paste job. It involved constant modification, interpretation, interpolation – as well as organizing ability of a very high order: this was the work of Tribonian. It is odd to reflect that Latin cannot have been his native tongue. He must have learned it as a prerequisite for the study of the law. It was still in some measure, however, the language of the Roman state, of the army, the courts and the central administration; while Greek was the language of culture and art, of science, and of the local life of the cities.

That he was also the architect and probably the draughtsman of other sweeping innovations of Justinian's becomes clear when we observe that, after his death in 543, the stream of imperial legislation suddenly runs dry. These enactments, the *Novels*, are the work of a powerful legal mind, with a distinctive and personal manner of expression. There is mention of a body of poems, *belles-lettres*, and scientific treatises attributed to a certain Tribonian. These too are probably the work of the great Quaestor, but they have perished. He can only be judged by the corpus of law: yet that is sufficient monument for any man.

If John of Cappadocia was a lukewarm and superficial Christian, Tribonian was openly a pagan. That he should have held so high a position in a Christian, theocratic empire may seem strange. But paganism of a somewhat philosophical kind was still widespread in intellectual circles, though it would have been intolerable – and illegal – in a general or a Praetorian Prefect. Moreover Tribonian's paganism enabled him to be neutral in the theological disputes of the time. His personality, according to contemporaries, was charming and pleasant, and his eloquence graceful. If to these qualities are added the energy and drive which alone made the rapid accomplishment of his tasks possible, one can begin to see why Justinian chose him as collaborator in what has turned out to be the emperor's most imperishable monument.

Another collaborator of Justinian's whose handiwork still stands was Anthemius. He came from Tralles, in western Asia Minor, where his father Stephanus was a doctor. His five sons all distinguished themselves in learned professions: Anthemius became a mathematician and engineer. It is not known where he studied, but Alexandria is the likeliest guess. There the traditions of Greek mathematics and physics were maintained; the work of the classical masters was studied, and new researches undertaken. Both Anthemius and his brother Metrodorus, a teacher of Greek language and literature, became so celebrated in their native province that they attracted Justinian's attention and were summoned to Constantinople. This must have been at the end of Justin's reign, or soon after Justinian's accession. For in 532, when the old Church of the Holy Wisdom, built two centuries earlier by Constantine and his son Constantius was burnt down in the Nika revolt, it was to Anthemius that the emperor turned to build a great new church which would symbolize the power and might of the empire and its dedication to God. Anthemius was no mere master-builder, but a theoretician of first rank as well as an incomparable architect. His contributions to mathematical thought are less striking than his Great Church, but the one cannot be understood without the other. For instance, the problem of constructing so great a dome and of supporting it upon a rectangular base demands not only practical skill, but understanding of the mathematical principles of the vault. His colleague as architect – perhaps his teacher – Isidore of Miletus, had written a learned commentary on the treatise on vaults of the Hellenistic engineer, Heron of Alexandria. And it was to Anthemius that another pupil of Isidore's, Eutocius, dedicated his commentary on Apollonius of Perga's treatise on conic sections. All this is in the main creative stream of classical Greek mathematics. Anthemius' ability to unite theory and practice fruitfully manifested itself in lesser matters than the building of the Church of the Holy Wisdom. He shared a house in Constantinople with a rhetorician named Zeno. The two men quarrelled about the property, and Zeno's eloquence swayed the court in his favour in the ensuing lawsuit. But if Zeno could talk, Anthemius could act. He installed large cauldrons in a room beneath Zeno's flat, and connected them by leather pipes to the joists above. When he boiled the water in the cauldrons he caused the floor of the flat above to shake as if in an earthquake, and Zeno rushed out and hastened to the palace – for he was distinguished enough in his profession to be admitted – to enquire how the emperor and others had fared. It is a pity that it is not known exactly how Anthemius did this. The procedure described by the historian Agathias – a man of letters who had no contact with the science of his time – would not produce the effects he describes. Another of Anthemius' interests was optics. He wrote a treatise on concave burning mirrors, and gave demonstrations of their effects in Constantinople. The practical aim of his research was probably military – he was trying to produce a secret weapon for Justinian. What made the project impracticable was technical backwardness, the constant shortcoming of the ancient world. That Justinian should have picked upon a scientist who spanned the gap between theory and practice is a striking instance of his talent for finding – and keeping – the men he needed.

Anthemius saw his Great Church begun but not completed, for he died in about 534. When the dome collapsed in an earthquake some years later, it was the son of his colleague, Isidore of Miletus, who rebuilt it according to an improved formula, and it is Isidore's dome that stands today. But the majestic and harmonious conception of the whole belongs to Anthemius of Tralles, Justinian's engineer and minister of public works.

3 Roman law and riot

Justinian was sole ruler from August 527. For nine years he had been the power behind the throne; but his position had lacked security. The senile and ineffectual Justin might be overthrown. He might vacillate in his choice of a successor, and leave a battle for power to be fought on his death. He might make himself so unpopular with influential elements in society that the heir whom he designated would be rejected. Justinian had needed foresight, patience, and a steady hand and head. By nature inclined to keep his own counsel, he had learned to work with others. He had overcome his natural hesitancy, and learnt to act decisively. Fastidious and academic by character, he had learnt to use men who were at home in a brawl and who stopped at nothing. His marriage to Theodora had done little to strengthen his position, at any rate in the short term. But her connection with the Monophysite leaders, the blamelessness of her present life, and her undisputed talent for making the most of any public occasion were already turning her from a liability into an asset.

Slowly he had been familiarizing himself with the empire and its problems, and with the men upon whom he was to rely for their solution. When at the age of forty-five he found himself at last in complete and undisputed control, he knew what had to be done.

It was more than five hundred years since the Roman empire had reached its maximum extent. Throughout this time the Mediterranean had been a Roman lake, and the lands which bordered upon it had been governed by Rome. Men and goods and ideas had moved freely from end to end of this vast state, with its uniform system of law, its common culture, and its myriad cities which were growing increasingly like one another. Undoubtedly, the central administration impinged less upon the lives of its ordinary citizens than does that of a modern state. Much was left to local initiative: a man could satisfy all his ambitions within the bounds of his native city or province. Long-distance trade was confined to expensive luxuries, and to essential food-supplies for some of the great cities. But Roman armies manned the frontiers, and Roman magistrates sat in judgment upon a population which since AD 212 consisted entirely of Roman citizens. To the east lay a huge but rather ramshackle Iranian state, ruled first by the Parthians and from early in the third century by their more energetic successors, the Persian Sassanids. The boundary between the two super-powers was the scene of frequent incidents and skirmishes, as disputed territory was fought over. But negotiation rather than war was the pattern of Romano-Persian relations. And neither state had either the intention or the capacity to conquer the other. Elsewhere the frontiers of the empire were the frontiers of civilization itself. There were no durable states beyond the border, merely an ever-changing mosaic of tribal confederations, client princelings, and nomad peoples. Local threats might become menacing at this or that point of the frontier. A party of Goths had come down from the Danube frontier in 267 and devastated all in their path as far as Athens. Such episodes were alarming, but they did not threaten the security of the empire, or lead its citizens to anticipate its downfall.

When, in the early fourth century, Constantine was converted to Christianity – which soon became the dominant and then the official religion of the empire – a new dimension was added to the political idea of its citizens. The permanence of the Roman empire was seen no longer as a mere matter of fact, but as an essential part of the divine plan for the salvation of mankind. The first step had been the unification of the civilized world under Augustus at the time of the birth of Christ. This was now seen to have been the necessary condition for the rapid spread of Christianity. Now the Roman state, from being a passive vehicle for the spread of the truth – and sometimes, under bad emperors, striving to hinder its spread – had become its active champion, foreshadowing upon earth the Kingdom of God which was to come in the fullness of time. As there was one God, so there could be only one empire and one emperor. In the words of the preamble to one of Justinian's decrees, 'It is under the authority of God that We rule the empire which has been entrusted to Us by His celestial majesty, that We bring Our wars to a successful conclusion, and that We maintain the position of Our commonwealth.'

These were the ideas which Justinian, like every man of his time, had inherited. It would never have occurred, even to a humble man, to question them. And Justinian was anything but humble. In the years which had passed between his boyhood among the peasants of Bederiana and the day when, with Theodora by his side, he received the acclamations of the multitude in the Hippodrome at Constantinople, he had become convinced that he was the man of destiny. He knew what he had been called upon to do, and he was sure that he could do it.

As he looked round him, he could not fail to notice that things seemed to have been going wrong in the last hundred years. The empire itself was no longer coextensive with the civilized world west of Persia. Gaul had been lost to the Visigoths, who in their turn had been ousted by the Franks. Spain was the seat of a Visigothic kingdom. North Africa had been conquered by the Vandals, who had extended their power to Sardinia, Corsica and the Balearic Islands. And Italy itself, with the ancient capital of Rome, was an Ostrogothic kingdom, whose dependence on Byzantine suzerainty was only a polite fiction. To make matters worse, the rulers of these new Germanic kingdoms, most of whose subjects were Romans and Catholics, were themselves, with the sole exception of the Franks, Arian heretics. Along the northern frontiers of what remained of the empire, the movements of peoples had brought new enemies to the fore. Bulgars, Huns and Slavs now raided and infiltrated on an unprecedented scale. Were the eastern provinces to go the way of the western? Within the empire itself unity of belief was far from achieved. Apart from surviving groups of pagans and Jews, the dualist religion of the Manichaeans was gaining many adherents. Some Christian groups which had long ago broken with the church, such as the Montanists, continued to flourish. And worst of all the church itself, far from proclaiming unity of doctrine, was growing more and more divided. The western church under the bishop of Rome was separated from the eastern patriarchates by a tiresome schism of little doctrinal significance. And the Council of Chalcedon of 451 had failed to put an end to doctrinal disputes within the church. The Monophysites had gone from strength to strength. They were numerous throughout the empire. Under Anastasius they had obtained control of the official apparatus of the church. Even now their adherents had considerable influence in the capital. And in Syria, and in particular in Egypt, they were in a majority. Indeed the Monophysite church had to some extent become the vehicle of ethnic separatism. The mass of the Egyptian and Syrian peasantry, only superficially hellenized, and clinging to their ancient languages and traditions, found in a separate church the means of asserting their consciousness of being distinct peoples. A lively Monophysite literature in Syriac and Coptic fed the national pride of these regions. In Syria the orthodox Chalcedonians were known as Melkites, 'the emperor's men'. And In Egypt the whole organization of the church outside Alexandria was in Monophysite hands.

Had God's plan for the salvation of mankind gone astray? Where was the one ecumenical empire, united in doctrine and faith? Justinian, who in any case slept little, must have spent many a night pondering on such questions as these. Historians today tend to speak of a series of problems: the Persian problem, the problem of the Danube frontier, the problem of the western empire, the problem of the papacy, the Monophysite problem, and so on. And of course, in so far as they had to be tackled by different means, they were distinct problems. But it seems that for Justinian they were in essence aspects of a single problem, that of the restoration of the Roman empire to its proper place both in this world and in the transcendent order of being of which this world is but an imperfect reflection. A modern man, faced with a situation in which things seem to be going seriously wrong, would think in terms of reform, of fashioning something new. For a man of the sixth century, and especially for one as steeped in the traditions of the past as was Justinian, such an approach was impossible. 'Innovation' was a word with strongly pejorative overtones; in theological parlance it implied heresy. Neither the refinements of philosophical thought nor the clichés of popular expression had any room for the concept of progress or continuous change. Although Justinian, as shall be seen, introduced much that was new into the Roman world, he could only do so by convincing himself and others that he was restoring the past. His grand idea was to correct the errors of the past century and to rebuild, in even greater majesty and glory, the empire, the Christian empire of Constantine. Reconquest of the west, religious unity, codification of the law, moral reform, public works, art and letters were all for him part of a single programme, one whose realization he was to pursue with tenacity of purpose and almost fanatical devotion throughout his long reign.

However an overall aim is one thing, the practical measures by which it is to be attained are quite another. Justinian had by 527 long experience of the complexities of government. He knew that many things must be done slowly, that he was dependent on fallible human instruments, and that resistance and error cannot be conjured away by mere words. And a certain deviousness of character, whether natural or acquired, made him favour indirect approaches to obstinate problems. Did he ever discuss his aims with his ministers? There is no record of it. And the occasion would hardly arise, for he was no modern president or prime minister who has to carry a cabinet with him. He may have discussed them with Theodora. But even she did not always enjoy his full confidence. And one suspects that she did not always listen to what her august but long-winded husband said: her mind was intuitive rather than discursive. However, in the preambles to his enactments he sometimes outlines his policy. These were propaganda documents, designed to have the maximum of publicity, and they did not lend themselves to elaborate or finely nuanced declarations. Yet they are the nearest thing we have to a statement of Justinian's programme. For the rest, it has to be constructed by interpretation of his actions; and no man's motives are ever wholly clear, to others or to himself.

War with Persia

Persia was the first problem. It was essential to reach some kind of settlement of the many minor frontier disputes, always threatening to blaze up into local incidents, if troops were to be moved to the west. No sooner was Justinian sole emperor than he sent a special embassy to Persia. At its head were Hypatius, nephew of Anastasius and Master of Soldiers, together with a pro-Roman chieftain of the Lazes – a people dwelling in the wild mountains at the south-east corner of the Black Sea – named Pharesmanes. Pharesmanes had been serviceable to the Romans on many occasions, and had been rewarded with high military rank; at the same time he seems to have been *persona grata* at the Persian court. So this was no routine mission. Justinian was anxious to reach a real settlement. However, at the same time, he had given orders to Belisarius to build a new fort on the frontier. The Persians treated this as a provocation and broke off negotiations. The next spring – 528 – fighting broke out both in Lazica and in Mesopotamia. At first the Romans were heavily defeated on both fronts, and Justinian prepared to send reinforcements from Constantinople under Pompeius, Hypatius' brother. Arms were not his only resource, however. Much of the Caucasus was at this time in the hands of the Sabiri, a nomadic people akin to the Huns. They formed no unitary state, but were divided into a number of clans, often hostile to one another. Some of these were in the pay of the Persians, and fought on their side in Lazica. In their rear a confederation of clans was ruled by a woman, named Boa. To this barbaric princess Justinian and Theodora sent letters, accompanied by costly gifts and subsidies in gold. As a result her warriors fell upon their pro-Persian kinsmen and slew them to a man. At the same time the Roman army in Lazica, under a new commander Peter, attacked. The Persians fell back with heavy losses; and Lazica, the key to the Black Sea, remained under Roman control. By the autumn of 528 new negotiations led to an armistice with the chastened Persians.

Justinian may well have hoped that there would be no further incidents with Persia. And throughout the remarkably cold winter of 528-9 there were indeed none. But no sooner had spring begun than Al-Mundhir, ruler of one of the Arab principalities of Mesopotamia and long a vassal of the Persians, decided on a raid into the empire. Whether he had the authority of the Great King in Ctesiphon we do not know; this is the kind of measure of which heads of state prefer to remain in ignorance – until they are successful. Al-Mundhir's fierce Bedouin horsemen made a dash across the frontier, swept through northern Syria, pillaging, burning and raping as they went, and got as far as the walls of Antioch, the third city of the empire. Reports, which may well have been true, declared that Al-Mundhir, who was a pagan, had on a single day sacrificed to his gods four hundred Christian virgins. Justinian had to act. And within a month of Al-Mundhir's raid, Belisarius was promoted commander-in-chief in the east. There is no need to follow in detail his military measures, which included a punitive expedition against Al-Mundhir. They were marked by no great victories and no great defeats.

In the meantime Justinian was trying to obtain a settlement by a direct approach to the king of Persia. While the military advantage lay with the Persians, Justinian made no haste to present his compliments. But early in 529 Hermogenes, the Master of Offices, was despatched to the Persian capital Ctesiphon with an impressive retinue and splendid gifts. In July he arrived, and negotiations began. Neither side was willing to make concessions; and neither was strong enough to exact concessions from the other. The discussions dragged on.

The Persian government had its hands tied by the need to suppress a vast uprising of peasants inspired by the utopian egalitarianism of the Mazdakites. On the Roman side there were difficulties which Justinian had not foreseen. The Samaritans were a nation of peasants, living mainly around Neapolis (Biblical Shechem, modern Nablus) in northern Palestine. They had been separated for many centuries from the orthodox Jewish community. Until recently the schism was dated to the period of Assyrian occupation, when much of the Jewish population of Samaria was allegedly deported and replaced by colonists from other regions of the Assyrian empire. Later research suggests that the split may go back to the days of Eli, high priest and judge, and teacher of the prophet Samuel. Be that as it may the Samaritans, who recognized only the Pentateuch and not the later books of the Old Testament, were treated with hatred and contempt by the Jews. The Romans regarded them with suspicion and frequently persecuted them. In the eyes of the Christian Roman empire they were little better than pagans. Their low social status and lack of protection made them vulnerable alike to the rapacity of tax-collectors and to forced conversion. Yet they had a strong social cohesion based on the sure conviction that they and they alone were the Lord's elect, and that one day a Messiah would restore them to their rightful place in the scheme of things. Eighty years earlier they had risen in armed revolt and defended their arid hills in fierce guerrilla warfare. To Justinian, however, whose aim was the establishment of Christian orthodoxy and Roman loyalty throughout his empire, they were merely a tiresome and obdurate minority who had to be brought to their senses. So in 528 he issued an edict ordering their synagogues to be closed and forbidding them to transfer their property by sale or bequest to any but Christians. The response was immediate. The Samaritans took to arms. Their leader Julian, whom Roman sources naturally describe as a brigand, proclaimed himself emperor in Neapolis. The Roman garrison was massacred, and Julian, crowned by the Samaritan high priest, presided at chariot races in the Hippodrome there in imitation of the emperor in Constantinople. In the eyes of his fellow-countrymen he may have been the Samaritan Messiah rather than a Roman emperor. Troops had to be rushed to Samaria from other regions of the east. Village by village and hill by hill the land was reconquered during 529 and 530, and pacification was followed by savage punitive measures. In all more than a hundred thousand Samaritans were killed. For the time being the trouble was over, and Justinian could proceed with his plans. But Samaritan disaffection simmered on. Twenty years later the bishop of Caesarea was able to report that the Samaritans were now in a more cooperative frame of mind, and the restrictions imposed upon them were relaxed. Within a few years they were once again in revolt, this time – and most remarkably – aided by the local Jews. The Christians of Caesarea were put to the sword, and the governor of Palestine murdered. It took a long and bloody campaign of repression to reduce the remnant of the Samaritans to obedience. A man less sure of himself than Justinian might have been discouraged by the resistance offered to his policy by so insignificant a minority.

In 530 the Romans resumed their offensive against Persia. Sittas in the north and Belisarius in the south won considerable victories, though a Persian counter-offensive in Mesopotamia soon restored the balance. In the meantime Justinian's engineers, following in the wake of his armies, were building and repairing roads and fortifications throughout the frontier area. The confrontation with Persia was turning out expensive for Rome. Troops needed for the long-planned offensive in the west were pinned down in the east, and the vast financial reserves piled up by Anastasius were already becoming seriously diminished. But the Persians too were feeling the strain. They had, as we have seen, their own internal problems; and the nomads of the central Asian steppe were increasing their pressure on the north-eastern frontier. And the King of Kings, Kavadh, was an old man. He had been on the throne since 488, when Justinian was a child, and he was anxious to settle the succession in favour of his fourth and favourite son, Chosroes. So Justinian was relieved, but scarcely surprised, when in June 531 the Arab prince Al-Mundhir made cautious overtures to the local Roman official, suggesting the resumption of negotiations between the two sovereigns. Scarcely had the cumbersome diplomatic machinery been set in motion – it was a long journey from Constantinople to Ctesiphon – when a weary and travel-stained horseman brought Justinian the news he had been waiting for. The King of Kings was dead.

His son Chosroes, who had his hands full dealing with rival claimants to the throne, was anxious to come to terms. The emperor, eager though he was for peace in the east, knew that he must not appear too hasty. Hermogenes the Master of Offices and the patrician Rufinus were sent off to the Persian capital. After a succession of three-month truces, a peace treaty was signed in September 532. It was called the Everlasting Peace, and was to remain in force indefinitely. Needless to say, it did not. The Romans retained their control of Lazica, thus cutting off Persia from the Black Sea. Territory conquered by either side in the recent hostilities was returned. Persian suzerainty over Iberia – the modern Georgia – was recognized, thus putting an end for the time to the Roman attempt to turn Persia's flank on the north. And the Romans agreed to pay Persia the considerable sum of eleven thousand pounds of gold a year; ostensibly in fulfilment of a treaty obligation, dating back 150 years, to pay for the defence of the Caucasian passes against the steppe nomads; in reality a kind of tribute. It was a costly settlement, but it gave away no essential Roman interest; and above all it freed Justinian's hands for other enterprises.

Imperial munificence and religious minorities

While his armies had been fighting, Justinian had been turning his mind to other matters. On 1 January 528 he celebrated his second consulship. It was the custom in the late empire for a newly appointed consul to distribute largesse to the city populace. He had indeed no other duties. Justinian, eager to impress the image of the new reign upon the minds of his subjects, outdid all his predecessors as he threw handfuls of gold coins from a sack like confetti among the crowds who lined the streets of the capital. At the same time he had rebuilt from imperial funds several cities which had fallen upon evil days, adorning them with theatres, baths and porticoes. Some of these, perhaps all, he renamed Justinianopolis, the city of Justinian. The new ruler was determined that the Romans should share his own conviction that a new age had begun.

So far as is known, he never returned to his native village in western Thrace. But he certainly did not forget it. Among his first acts as sole emperor was to found an entirely new city at nearby Bederiana, designed and built by engineers and architects from the capital, and paid for by the imperial purse. He called it Justiniana Prima – the first city of Justinian. By 535 it was sufficiently flourishing to be the seat of an archbishop. Justiniana Prima was engulfed in the great Slavonic invasions of the Balkan peninsula early in the next century; it is last mentioned in 602. But the memory of it remained, and its name appeared in the titulature of certain Serbian archbishops down to 1718. It is not known with certainty where it was. The most likely situation is Caričin Grad, south of Nish, where archaeologists have revealed a large fortified city datable by coins to the sixth century. Not far off, at the present-day Lipljan, the ancient city of Ulpiana, founded by Trajan, was rebuilt and named Justiniana Secunda.

On 29 November 528 the great city of Antioch in Syria was severely damaged by an earthquake. Justinian and Theodora – she is expressly associated with her husband in contemporary accounts of the matter – hastened to send lavish aid for its restoration. In other ways too Theodora's striking personality was given full rein. In the summer of 528 she decided to take the cure at the mineral springs at Pythion, in north-western Asia Minor. Her journey there became a demonstration of imperial splendour. Accompanied by the Prefect of the City, palace guards and eunuchs and an entourage of four thousand, she made her progress through the countryside, distributing largesse and making princely gifts to the churches of the cities and villages on her route. Justinian may have been the prime mover in this demonstration. The initiative for another manifestation of imperial munificence more probably came from Theodora herself. One day she summoned to her quarters in the palace all the brothel-owners of Constantinople, read them a lecture on the evil of their ways, and demanded what price they had paid to the parents of each of their girls. When they declared on oath that the current rate was five gold *solidi*, she repaid to each his outlay and warned him sternly to seek another occupation. She then sent for the girls, gave them a gold *solidus* apiece and a new dress, and sent them home to their parents. Needless to say, the brothels did not long remain closed. Theodora was no sociologist, and the deep roots of prostitution in ancient society may well have been beyond her grasp. But she understood the indignities that it brought upon a girl with no resources, and this was only the first of many efforts she made to combat an institution with which she had a more intimate acquaintance than any ruler before or after.

Justinian was well aware of the distinction between civil and ecclesiastical power. As he puts it himself in the preamble to one of his laws,

> The greatest blessings of mankind are the gifts of God which have been granted to us by the mercy of Providence – the priesthood and the imperial authority. The priesthood ministers to things divine: the imperial authority is set over and shows diligence in things human; but both proceed from one and the same source, and both adorn the life of man. Nothing, therefore, will be a greater matter of concern to the emperor than the dignity and honour of the clergy; the more as without ceasing they offer prayers to God on his behalf. For if the priesthood be in all respects without blame, and full of faith before God, and if the imperial authority rightly and duly adorn the commonwealth committed to its charge, there will ensue a happy concord which will bring forth all good things for mankind. (Justinian, *Novella* 6, praef.)

The problem is, who is to ensure that the priesthood be in all respects without blame? Justinian, authoritarian by character and convinced of his mission to recreate the Christian Roman empire, was in no doubt about the matter. It was his duty to keep the church in order, as a part of his care for the empire and its citizens. Thus when in the first year of his reign two bishops, Esaias of Rhodes and Alexander of Diospolis in Thrace, were found guilty of homosexual practices and dismissed from their posts by the ecclesiastical authorities, Justinian at once had them arrested, castrated and paraded through the streets of Constantinople in ignominy. There ensued something of a witch-hunt, and many were condemned to savage punishments.

There was another side to the close interpenetration of church and state. For communities outside the empire, conversion to Christianity implied irreversible commitment to alliance with Rome. And the successful conclusion of diplomatic negotiations was often marked by the baptism of a foreign ruler. Justinian and Theodora knew how to make the most of these occasions. The candidate for baptism would be invited to Constantinople, shown the marvels of the city, baptized in the Great Church with the emperor and empress standing as his godparents, and despatched to his homeland with lavish presents and every mark of respect. In the first few years of his reign Justinian was host to a number of such state visitors. None of these ceremonies took place without long diplomatic preparation, in which the emperor himself was the moving spirit.

Within the empire life was made as intolerable as possible for deviant religious groups. The story of the Samaritans has already been told; the year which saw the closure of their synagogues was marked by a series of laws directed against pagans, Manichaeans and heretics. Manichaean beliefs and practices, even under the cover of orthodoxy, were to be punishable by death. For the other groups exclusion from the liberal professions, incapacity to inherit, or to bear witness in court, the obligation to perform civic duties without the status and rewards attaching to them, turned their members into pariahs, at any rate in the upper strata of society. This was all very just and logical. 'It is right,' observed Justinian, 'that those who do not worship God correctly should be deprived of worldly advantages too.' But the emperor was no narrow fanatic. An exception was made for Arian Goths, many of whom served as mercenaries in the Roman army. One result of Justinian's policy of enforced orthodoxy was the closure of the university of Athens. For a thousand years the city had been a centre of philosophical and literary study; and for six or seven centuries its schools, and above all the Academy, had attracted students from all over the Greek-speaking world and from the Latin west as well. The schools had become enriched over the centuries by endowments, and their prestige was enormous. The head of the Academy when Justinian came to the throne, Damascius, was a sober, dedicated and somewhat dull commentator on Plato. His colleague Simplicius, whose subject was Aristotle, was an honourable and worthy representative of the millenary tradition of Greek philosophy. Justinian himself was a cultivated and well-read man, with a taste for learned disputation. He certainly had no personal grudge against Damascius and Simplicius. But they were odd men out in the empire as he saw it. Their intellectual eminence gave a factitious prestige to pagan doctrine. And, perhaps, the rich endowments of the Academy were a tempting prize to a ruler always short of money for his grandiose projects. At any rate they were brought under the general ban on pagans in public teaching appointments, the Academy was dissolved, and its estates seized. For men of this distinction there was to be no personal humiliation. They were treated with courtesy by imperial officials, and permitted to settle in any city they chose, no doubt with an imperial pension. To Justinian's surprise, after a few years they chose to accept the invitation of Chosroes, the newly enthroned Persian king, and set off for Ctesiphon. Chosroes was a man of intellectual interests, he was anxious to keep abreast of the Romans, and the chance to snub Justinian was not to be missed. An ambitious programme of translation from Greek to Pehlevi – the medieval Persian tongue of the Sassanian court – was set on foot, and every facility given to the seven professors who had chosen to emigrate: Damascius, Simplicius, Eulamius, Priscian, Hermeias, Diogenes, and Isidore. But within a few years they grew dissatisfied. Perhaps they missed the cut and thrust of controversy. At any rate they all returned, with Justinian's permission, to Roman territory, where they ended their days. Whether Justinian's orders were executed with less than full rigour, or whether they were later modified, recent research has shown that the teaching of philosophy and rhetoric continued in Athens after 529, though doubtless on a more modest scale.

The measures against religious non-conformists were no dead letter. A number of Manichaeans, including men and women from the highest ranks of society, were put to death, often by burning at the stake. Justinian, who had no taste for gratuitous cruelty and who prided himself on his talents as a disputant, sometimes engaged in a personal attempt to convert them before sentence was carried out. Dismayed and astonished at their failure to listen to the voice of reason, he felt he had no alternative to letting justice be done. But he did not himself attend at the painful spectacle of their execution. In autumn 529 a number of highly placed officials were charged with pagan practices. They included Thomas, Quaestor of the Sacred Palace, the principal legal officer of the empire, Asclepiodotus, an ex-prefect, and the patrician Phocas. Thomas was dismissed, Asclepiodotus committed suicide, but Phocas seems to have been acquitted – only to be charged once again sixteen years later, when he too committed suicide.

Justinian realized that the Monophysites could not be treated in this fashion. They were too numerous, and in the eastern and southern regions of the empire too influential. They had, too, their spokeswoman in court; for Theodora, whether she fully understood the theological points in dispute or not, was emotionally deeply committed to the Monophysite cause, and was on terms of close friendship with some of its most respected leaders. Indeed she harboured many of them in a monastery in Constantinople which she founded and maintained. Justinian was convinced that the division between Monophysites and Chalcedonians was all due to a misunderstanding, that a formula could be found which would satisfy both sides, and that he was the man to find such a formula. So although the harsh measures against Monophysites passed under Justin remained on the statute-book, they were administered with much less severity than before. Exiles were allowed to return. Monophysite leaders were invited to the palace, where Theodora treated them with lavish hospitality, while her husband argued theology with them. Finally in 532 a formal debate was organized in Constantinople, with six bishops participating on either side. The first two sessions were presided over by a high court official, himself an Egyptian. At the last the emperor himself took the chair. The pressures to reach agreement were enormous, but little was attained. One Monophysite bishop proclaimed himself converted. Justinian, however, was well pleased. He thought he saw his way to a unifying formula. On 15 March 533 he issued, in the form of an imperial edict, a profession of faith which made no mention of any of the ecumenical councils, avoided the phrase 'two natures', and declared that one person of the Trinity suffered in the flesh. Anathema was pronounced upon the followers of Nestorius, 'who divide our one Lord Jesus Christ, and do not admit that the blessed Virgin Mary was in very truth the Mother of God', and upon the extreme Monophysites, 'who deny that Jesus Christ was connatural with the Father in his divinity and connatural with us in his humanity'. This, believed Justinian, was a profession in accord with the Catholic faith, and at the same time one to which few reasonable Monophysites could take exception. It is easy to speak of him as an 'amateur theologian', as some church historians have done. But there were no professional theologians in Constantinople, in the sense of men who had pursued a systematic course of study and passed an examination at the end of it. And Justinian was no mere dilettante dabbler. He was as familiar with the vast and forbidding literature as were most of the bishops present. And he was sharply aware of the divisive effect of ideological differences. What he failed to grasp were the deep social discontents which found expression in religious difference. And it probably never occurred to him, as it does to us now, that an imperial decree was unlikely to change deeply held religious convictions. His new 'Theopaschite' doctrine in the end contributed nothing to the religious unity of the empire.

The reform of the law

Another unifying enterprise which he undertook at the beginning of his reign was more successful. Next to religion, Justinian felt that law was the greatest force for cohesion in society. It was also, along with military strength, one of the sources of Roman power. As he says in the preamble to an enactment of 529, 'The greatest security of the state comes from two sources, arms and the law. Drawing its strength from these, it has enabled the fortunate race of the Romans to overcome and rule over all peoples in the past, and with the favour of God will enable them to do so for ever.' This is only one of many passages in which the interrelation and interpenetration of military power, religious legitimation, and legal order are seen to confer a special status on the Roman empire. In the Latin west Augustine had a century earlier declared that the Roman state was, like all other human institutions, a product of history, which had come into being and would pass away. In Constantinople such ideas found little echo. Their legal system was something of which the Romans had every right to be proud. In its finesse, its logical construction, and its exhaustive scope it far surpassed anything the Greek world had produced. But by the sixth century things were getting very confused. The main sources of the law were imperial decrees and the opinions of distinguished jurisconsults on particular cases. These were by now so numerous that it was impossible for the most diligent lawyer to possess let alone to read, all the necessary texts. And among authorities dating from over half a millennium there were inevitable contradictions and obscurities. Furthermore, some of the conceptions inherited from the past were at variance with the requirements of a Christian society. Marriage, for instance, was treated as entirely a matter for the civil law, without any religious legitimation or sanction. The law of property was cluttered with ancient usages which had no relevance to the conditions of the sixth century. All in all, Roman law had become a jungle through which a skilful lawyer could cut a path which might not lead in the end to justice. Previous attempts to codify the law -- the last had been made by the emperor Theodosius II a hundred years earlier – had not gone beyond mere mechanical compilation of imperial edicts, and in any case they were now quite out of date. These matters had exercised Justinian much before his accession. What was needed, he believed, was a radical reform which would restore Roman law to its pristine purity, with all uncertainties and contradictions removed, and all irrelevant antiquarianism dropped. Only such a body of law would be fit for the restored Christian empire which he, the heir of Augustus and of Constantine, was about to inaugurate.

In Tribonian, the pagan advocate of impressive erudition and intellectual powers, he found a man who shared his grand concept and had the energy, technical skill and organizing ability to see it through. The first task was to be a new compilation of all imperial enactments still valid. But they were not to be set mechanically side by side. Repetitions and contradictions were to be removed by changing the wording. Decrees were to be cut down or extended as required. Several might be conflated into one. And the work was to be done quickly. On 13 February 528 Justinian issued an edict setting the project on foot:

> What many previous emperors saw must needs be rectified, but none has ventured to put into effect, we have decided to grant now to the world, with the help of Almighty God, and to cut short the prolixity of lawsuits by pruning the multitude of enactments contained in the three Codes of Gregorius, Hermogenes and Theodosius, as well as those promulgated after the publication of his Code by Theodosius of divine memory, and the emperors who succeeded him, and by Our own Clemency, and by compiling a single Code which shall bear Our own name, and shall contain the enactments of the above-mentioned Codes and the new laws promulgated after them. (Justinian, Constitution *Haec quae necessario*, praef.)

Justinian goes on to set up a commission to compile his new *Code*, which accomplished its task with exemplary speed. On 8 April 529 a further imperial edict validated the new *Code*. Henceforth no imperial enactments, other than those embodied in it, were to be cited in the courts, and grants in favour of individuals, cities or corporations were to be valid only in so far as they conflicted with none of its provisions. The Praetorian Prefect Menas was ordered to prepare copies of the *Code* for the imperial signature and to dispatch them to all the provinces of the empire so that the new *Code* might come into force on 15 April.

The next step in the legal reform was to compile all the responses of the jurisconsults of the classical period, arranging them according to subject-matter and dividing them into fifty books. This vast undertaking was launched on 15 December 530 by an edict addressed to Tribonian, by now Quaestor of the Sacred Palace, who was himself to choose a commission to help him. They were to make excerpts from all the works of jurisconsults to whom former emperors had granted the right of interpreting the law, removing all repetitions and contradictions, and modifying the original texts where necessary. All that was obsolete was to be excised. Tribonian chose sixteen colleagues: Constantine, Count of the Sacred Largesses; Theophilus and Cratinus, professors at Constantinople; Dorotheus and Anatolius, professors in the school of law at Berytus; and eleven distinguished advocates. The task was immense. Two thousand books by thirty-nine authors, amounting in all to three million lines, were read by the commission and reduced by them to one hundred and fifty thousand lines, or close on a million words. As well as the commissioners themselves, a staff of hundreds of clerks, copyists and shorthand-writers must have been engaged in the work. But their names were not thought worthy to appear in the proud edict with which, on 16 December 533, the new compilation, the *Digest*, was presented to the world:

> So great is the favour of divine Providence towards Us, that it ever deigns to sustain Us with its everlasting kindness. For now that the Parthian war has been ended by the Everlasting Peace, and that the race of the Vandals has been destroyed and Carthage, or rather the whole of Africa has been restored to Our empire, it has permitted the ancient laws, bowed down by age, to be brought by Our vigilance to a new beauty and a measured abridgement. (Justinian, Constitution *Tanta*, praef.)

All commentaries on the new *Digest* were forbidden. In the emperor's view they could only lead to fresh ambiguities and uncertainty. Only short summaries of passages and references to parallel passages were permitted: these, and literal translations into Greek. For the corpus of law was in Latin, the traditional language of law and administration in the empire – and incidentally Justinian's native tongue – while Greek was the language of most of its citizens. Students of Roman law, eager to reconstruct the classical law of the early empire, have laboured long to detect the interpolations and modifications introduced by the commission. That they have had on the whole so little success is a tribute to the powerful intellect and tireless capacity of Tribonian, and to the sound principles worked out in advance by Tribonian and approved by his master Justinian.

The great edifice of the law had been rebuilt anew. The next task was to ensure that lawyers were trained to make use of it. Tribonian and his colleagues Theophilus and Dorotheus addressed themselves to the compilation of a new text-book for students of law, the *Institutes*, which was published on 21 November 533, accompanied by an imperial decree giving it the force of law. It remained in use as a text-book in many European countries until the present century. In arrangement, and often in its actual words, the new *Institutes* closely followed those of Gaius, jurisconsult of the second century. But a long section on procedures which had become obsolete was removed, new chapters on the duties of a judge and on criminal law were added, and a multitude of minor changes were introduced, some of them referring to Justinian's own legislation. At the same time the course of legal studies at Constantinople and Berytus was extended from four to five years, and the curriculum for each year minutely laid down by imperial edict. Even the names by which the students of each year were to be known merited the emperor's attention. The freshmen, hitherto known as *dupondii* – an obscure but doubtless pejorative term – were henceforth to be called *novi Iustiniani*.

Meanwhile a stream of legislative enactments had been issuing from the Chancellery, inspired by Justinian and drafted largely by Tribonian. The *Code* had thus become an unreliable guide to the law. No sooner had the *Digest* been completed than a commission of five, Tribonian, Dorotheus and three advocates who had been members of the commission for the *Digest*, was instructed to prepare a second edition of the *Code*. On 16 November 534 it was published. It is this second version which we still possess.

Though in intention a work of conservation, Justinian's legislation was in many ways innovative. The old Roman family, an autonomous collective existing side by side with the populus Romanus, and with powers not derived from the populus Romanus, was virtually swept aside, and its place taken by the nuclear family of parents and children. New and simpler ways of conveyancing property were introduced. The complex laws of inheritance were simplified. The Canons of the first four Church Councils – and eventually of the fifth, which Justinian himself convoked – were given the force of law. As in many other fields, in seeking to conserve or recreate the Roman past Justinian in fact paved the way to the Middle Ages.

The story of the great legal reform has run a little ahead of the main narrative. For in January 532 an event occurred in Constantinople which nearly brought Justinian down from his throne.

Financial problems

The Persian War was costly. The Everlasting Peace was if anything more costly. Apart from the pay and supplies of the troops and the annual payment to the Persians, the network of fortifications, roads and bridges by which Justinian attempted to strengthen the defences of the eastern frontier demanded vast expenditures, in particular when heavy building materials had to be transported over long distances. The policy of buying the support or the neutrality of nations beyond the frontier led to ever-increasing charges upon the budget. Once paid to keep quiet, the barbarians always came back for more. Justinian, too, was a man of grand concepts. The economies of an Anastasius were not to his taste. He was eager to impress upon his subjects the magnificence of the new age over which he was to preside. Hence the lavish imperial subventions in cases of disaster. Antioch, after the earthquake in 528 in which 4,870 persons lost their lives, was exempted from all taxes for three years, as well as receiving gifts in money and in kind from the emperor. The next year it was the turn of Laodicea – where some 7,500 perished in an earthquake – as well as of Amasea and Myra. In 530 there were extensive droughts and a series of minor earthquakes. To all these disasters Justinian and Theodora responded with truly imperial munificence. After the pacification of Samaria, all the churches were rebuilt at imperial expense. Then there were the new buildings in the capital and elsewhere. A great new underground cistern to conserve water during the dry season was built early in the reign. Already during the reign of his uncle Justinian had built or rebuilt a number of churches in Constantinople, including the great church of the Mother of God at Blachernae, on the Golden Horn just outside the walls of Theodosius. And it was probably in the closing months of Justin's reign that work was begun on the church of SS. Sergius and Bacchus. This building represented a departure from the traditional basilica style. Instead of a long rectangular building with an apse at one end, and one or more aisles on either side, an octagonal structure supported by piers and arches supported a round dome and was surrounded by an outer shell, between which and the main piers were a series of ambulatories. The technical problems were formidable, and they were not all solved satisfactorily. Yet it was a remarkable achievement. All these factors amounted to a strain on the financial resources of the empire. The reserves accumulated by Anastasius had already been partly dissipated under Justin. A few years later they were rapidly running out.

The problem was not insoluble. The resources of the empire were great, and there was plenty of slack to take up. Basically, three things needed to be done. The efficiency of the state's own enterprises had to be increased. Waste in the collection of existing taxes had to be reduced. And the tax system itself had to be so reformed as to extract a proportionate contribution from those classes and groups which had hitherto escaped lightly. This above all meant the urban population and the better-off classes. For taxation in the ancient world always bore most heavily on the peasants, whose assets were visible to the assessor – unlike those of the merchant or shopkeeper – and who could not pull any strings. From the beginning of Justinian's reign measures directed to these ends can be traced. The various departments of the privy purse, which owned and exploited immense estates throughout the empire, were reorganized and tidied up, and their revenue brought under stricter control. But it was most of all upon the Praetorian Prefect that the burden of balancing the budget lay, for his department, as well as being a big spender, produced a large part of the revenue. In 531, after a series of short tenures by ephemeral prefects, John of Cappadocia was appointed to this office. Shortly before – and even more so after – his appointment a serious attack was begun on the vested interests and legalized rake-offs which drained much of the revenue before it reached the imperial coffers. The custom had evolved of paying fees to all kinds of officials. For instance the enormous sum of thirty-seven gold *solidi* had to be paid to the staff of the Praetorian Prefect before a case could be heard in his court. Another line of approach was to cut down the swollen staffs of many government departments, weed out the holders of sinecures, and remove dead men's names from the payroll. Then certain very expensive services were drastically cut, such as the imperial post. Only along the main route to the Persian frontier was the apparatus of staging-posts with changes of horses every thirty miles maintained. Elsewhere it was either suppressed, or maintained only in skeleton form. Finally a serious attempt was made to exact taxes from those best able to pay for them, the rich. This involved attacks upon a whole series of entrenched positions, including the general immunity of the upper classes from corporal punishment, as well as the corrupt agreements made between their members and the local officials. Contemporary sources, who mostly belong to the upper classes, regale us with lurid tales of the iniquities of John of Cappadocia's subordinates, who actually dared to imprison and flog men of high social position for non-payment of taxes. The very names by which some of the tax officials were known – Alexander the Scissors and John Leaden-jaws – were ominous. No doubt there were excesses of zeal. And many of John's officials were as ready to line their own pockets as had been their predecessors. But revenue was raised, and leaks were plugged.

A short-term result of all this was the gathering in Constantinople of men with a grudge. Dismissed civil-servants, officials of the post, minor landowners who had not only been ruined but also humiliated in the eyes of their fellows, evicted squatters on imperial estates, dependents and hangers-on of men who could no longer afford a retinue – all flocked from the provinces to the capital, both because life was easier there and because they still hoped to have their wrongs redressed by the emperor or his highest officials. In the meantime the disorganization of transport and the economic uncertainty of life in the provinces caused temporary difficulties in the food supply of the capital. The quality of the bread distributed to registered householders had to be reduced. It was an explosive mixture.

In the last years of Justin's reign vigorous repressive measures in Constantinople, Antioch and elsewhere much reduced the power and influence of the Blues and Greens. Justinian needed them no longer. But, as we have seen, they were organizations which engaged the emotions and loyalties of the masses. Their leading charioteers were true folk-heroes. And when the factions were gathered together in their tens of thousands in the Hippodrome they provided a genuine means of direct mass pressure upon the rulers. In the growing disquiet and uncertainty of Justinian's early years, men turned to them once again for encouragement and support. The long-established rivalry between them, for all its outward fierceness, had a factitious character. There was sometimes more to unite them than to divide them.

In the early days of January 532, in the depth of the cold and damp Constantinopolitan winter, everyone's nerves were on edge. The Greens put on a demonstration in the Hippodrome in which they complained of the arbitrary action of the authorities, and did not spare even the emperor himself. 'Would that

Sabbatius had never been born,' they cried, 'that he might not have a murderer for a son.' 'You are the only murderers here,' replied the Blues; and the demonstration turned into the usual slanging match between the factions, ending with the departure of the Greens in high dudgeon. During the next few days there were scuffles and fights in the streets, and the City Prefect's police arrested a number of faction activists. Several were condemned to death. The crowd which gathered to watch the executions, on a hill on the other side of the Golden Horn, was in an ugly mood. The nervous hangman bungled the job, and two of the condemned men, a Blue and a Green, fell from the scaffold still alive. The crowd began chanting: 'To the church, to the church.' Some monks from the nearby monastery of St Conon rushed out, seized the two victims and, protected by the crowd, transported them in a boat across the Golden Horn to the Church of St Lawrence, which enjoyed the right of sanctuary. The Prefect posted an armed guard outside the church, while the people continued to demonstrate in the streets, demanding that they be acquitted.

When three days later, on Tuesday 13 January, the races began in the Hippodrome, the vast concourse began chanting slogans calling for the release of the two men; but the authorities remained adamant. Suddenly, towards the end of the afternoon, the two factions made common cause against the government. Their traditional rivalry forgotten, both factions surged from the Hippodrome, chanting their new slogan, Nika (win!). This was the cry with which they urged on their favourites during the races, 'Nika, the Greens', 'Nika, the Blues'. But this time there was no question of Greens or Blues: they were all in it together. They forced their way into the palace of the City Prefect, killed such of the police as offered resistance, set free all the prisoners from the cells, and set fire to the building. The sight of the flames incensed them all the more, and they swept across the square to the great gateway of the imperial palace, and set fire to that too. The flames soon spread, and before night came on the Church of the Holy Wisdom, begun by Constantine, completed by Constantius II, and rebuilt by Theodosius II, was a heap of smoking ruins, and many of the public buildings along the Mesé were ablaze. The crowd dispersed at night, but its leaders were busy. When the races began again the next morning Justinian no doubt hoped that their passion would have spent itself and that they would return to their ritualized shouting of mutual insults. But he was disappointed. Their solidarity was unbroken, and their demands had become openly political. While some groups rampaged through the streets setting fire to buildings, the rest gathered in the Hippodrome and demanded the dismissal not only of Eudaimon, the City Prefect, but also of John of Cappadocia and Tribonian. The emperor, who saw that his only chance to regain mastery of the situation was to make speedy concessions, at once announced the dismissal of the three officials.

But the citizens of Constantinople had tasted power, and would not lightly relinquish it. While fires raged all over the city, the crowd besieged the imperial palace. Justinian and the ministers and senators who were with him were in a quandary. There were plenty of troops in the city, mostly units recently withdrawn from the eastern front, as well as the regiments of palace guards. But who knew whether they could be trusted? Belisarius and another general, Mundus, were in the palace, with their private detachments of German mercenaries; but an attempt by these to restore order proved fruitless, since the Roman troops would not support them. And what of the senators inside the palace? Two of them, Hypatius and Pompeius, were nephews of Anastasius, and had been Justin's rivals for the empire. Could they be trusted not to make a second attempt? And how many of the senators might be hedging their bets and preparing for the advent of a new ruler? By the evening of 15 January the crowd was proclaiming as emperor the third nephew of Anastasius, Probus. But he had discreetly left the capital – as had indeed many of the wealthier citizens – and the crowd avenged themselves by setting fire to his house. Justinian was now in morbid fear of an attempt on his life from those within the palace. On 17 January he ordered most of the senators to leave at once. Hypatius, who knew what would happen, begged to stay. But Justinian, although he liked him, was taking no chances. With the other senators, he was let out privily through a postern gate.

The next morning Justinian had recovered his confidence. He determined to follow the example of Anastasius – at which he had no doubt been present – and appeared in the imperial box, carrying the gospel in his hands, declaring that he alone was to blame for what had happened and promising a complete amnesty. But he was less of an actor than Anastasius, and the situation was far more dangerous. For by now a group of prominent men had decided to exploit the disorder for their own ends and get rid of Justinian. Some of the crowd which filled the Hippodrome on the news of the emperor's appearance acclaimed him. But the majority greeted his oration with cries of, 'You lie, you swine.' Justinian hastily withdrew to the palace, while the crowd went in search of the hapless Hypatius, who had not managed to slip out of the capital. When they found him they carried him shoulder-high to the Forum of Constantine and crowned him with a gold necklet which someone happened to be wearing. At first the old general was almost dead from fear. But as he saw many of the leading citizens and senators rallying to his cause, his spirits rose. When a rumour began to spread that Justinian had fled the city in secret, he allowed himself to be conveyed to the Hippodrome and seated in the throne in the imperial box, dressed in the purple robes of an emperor. The crowd chanted acclamations to Hypatius and insults to Justinian and Theodora.

Meanwhile, behind the doors leading from the imperial box to the palace, Justinian and his closest associates were in earnest debate. A fast galley was waiting at the private harbour of the palace, and the emperor was resolved to flee to Herakleia in Thrace. Belisarius thought that if Hypatius could be captured, the passions of the crowd would soon fade away. Unenthusiastically, Justinian let him try. With a hand-picked force of his private Herule mercenaries he made his way along the corridor leading to the Kathisma, the imperial box. But some of the palace guards themselves opposed him. Unwilling to risk a fight which might turn the rest of the guards against Justinian, he returned without accomplishing his mission. Justinian was now desperate, and ordered immediate flight to the harbour. Then Theodora, who had sat silent as the men argued this way and that, rose to her feet:

Whether or not a woman should give an example of courage to men, is neither here nor there. At a moment of desperate danger one must do what one can. I think that flight, even if it brings us to safety, is not in our interest. Every man born to see the light of day must die. But that one who has been emperor should become an exile I cannot bear. May I never be without the purple I wear, nor live to see the day when men do not call me 'Your Majesty'. If you wish safety, my Lord, that is an easy matter. We are rich, and there is the sea, and yonder our ships. But consider whether if you reach safety you may not desire to exchange that safety for death. As for me, I like the old saying, that the purple is the noblest shroud. (Procopius, *History of the Wars* I 24. 33-37.)

She sat down. The men looked at one another nervously. Belisarius and his fellow-general Mundus were the first to move, and began hastily discussing military plans. They were to leave the palace separately, each with his mercenaries, and approach the gates of the Hippodrome by a roundabout route. In the meantime *agents provocateurs* mingled with the crowd. From here and there on the benches came cries of 'Long live Justinian'. Fighting broke out between the rival factions. At this moment, at a predetermined signal, Belisarius and Mundus burst in through two of the gates and fell upon the rear of the squabbling crowd. Their German mercenaries cared nothing for Greens or Blues, but cut down every civilian within reach. The benches flowed with blood, and the Hippodrome re-echoed this time to the screams of the wounded and the groans of the dying. Narses had meanwhile led a detachment of armed palace guards to another entrance, where he slaughtered the fugitives who streamed out. Suddenly the doors behind Hypatius were broken in, two of Justinian's cousins, Justus and Boraides, dashed into the Kathisma and dragged the terror-stricken man, purple robes and all, back into the palace.

It was soon over. Some thirty thousand men were killed in the Hippodrome before Belisarius and Mundus called off their weary soldiers. As for Hypatius, he was brought before Justinian, now icily cold and sure of himself. Why, asked the emperor, had he allowed himself to be crowned. Hypatius replied that his only aim was to lure the crowd to the Hippodrome, where Justinian's men could deal with them. Why, then, was the next question, did you wait until half my city was burnt to the ground before doing it? Hypatius could only grovel before the emperor and beg for his life. Justinian, who had little stomach for personal cruelty and who had known Hypatius for twenty years, was on the point of yielding, but a sign from Theodora halted him. The next day Hypatius and his brother were put to death and their bodies thrown into the sea. Their property was confiscated as was that of a number of senators who were sent into exile. Justinian needed no more bloodshed to confirm his position. And he knew whom he could trust – Belisarius, Mundus, Narses, and above all Theodora.

4 Hagia Sophia and the reconquest of Africa

As the last of the corpses was carted away from the Hippodrome for burial, and the last of the smouldering fires along the Mesé was extinguished, Justinian and his advisers were already busy with plans for the future. The citizens of the capital were cowed and distraught; their master, recovered from the panic and vacillation which for a time had seized him, was once again inspired by his mission. There were the immediate tasks of tidying up and repair: they could be left to the City Prefect and his subordinates. But some of the destruction in the city was a challenge to Justinian himself. The Great Church of the Holy Wisdom of God, facing the bronze gateway of the palace across the Augusteion, was reduced to rubble. Begun by Constantine, the first Christian emperor and founder of the city, and completed by his son Constantius II, it symbolized the place of the empire in the divine scheme of things. Evidently it had to be rebuilt.But this was to be no mere reconstruction. The new church would surpass every other building ever erected to the glory of God and proclaim the greatness of Justinian, its builder, to all nations to the end of time. Perhaps, reflected the emperor, its destruction had been foreordained, so that the new Constantine might outdo his predecessor.

There were plenty of master-builders in Constantinople, and Justinian knew the best of them, whom he had employed on the church of SS. Sergius and Bacchus. But they built traditionally, and by rule of thumb. They could not do what Justinian wanted. Since Constantine most churches had followed the pattern of the basilica – the large hall for the transaction of public business which the Roman empire had inherited from its hellenistic predecessors. Such a church would be rectangular, with a pitched or occasionally a vaulted roof. More often than not it would have a rounded apse at the east end. And often the main rectangular area would be flanked by two or four aisles, whose pitched roof, at a lower level than that of the nave, was supported by a row of columns and arches. This was the plan followed by the most magnificent churches of the time: Constantine's Church of the Holy Wisdom, now in ruins, and his church of the Nativity in Bethlehem, the original plan of which can still be distinguished among the later accretions; the church of St Demetrius in Thessalonica; of S. Apollinare Nuovo, in Ravenna, begun by Theodoric and completed in 519; of Sta Sabina in Rome, built on the Aventine after the sack of the city by Alaric in 410; of the immense Basilica of S. Paolo fuori le Mura, by the gates of the city on the way to Ostia, completed about 440; of Sta Maria Maggiore in the heart of Rome, built by Pope Sixtus III in the middle of the fifth century. It was also the pattern of innumerable smaller churches throughout the empire and beyond its territories in the barbarian kingdoms of the west: the episcopal Church of St Peter in Vienne, the basilica at Tebessa in Tunisia, the church of the White Monastery (Deir al-Abyad) at Sohag in Egypt, the little church at Kufer in northern Syria, the basilica at Qalblozé on the desert fringe, the church of St Symeon the Stylite, built about 480 on a ridge overlooking the Orontes, the monastery church at Alahan in the Taurus mountains, to name only some buildings still standing.

These rectangular buildings, themselves the culmination of a long architectural tradition, could be in a high degree aesthetically satisfying. But with their firm outlines and their cartesian space they belonged unequivocally to this world. They appealed to the intellect rather than to the spirit.

There was another pattern of church architecture in late antiquity, the round church. Its origins went back to certain types of tomb in the ancient world; and it was above all over the tombs of martyrs that such churches were built. For technical reasons they were mainly small. A variation on the same plan, somewhat easier to construct, had a hexagonal or octagonal ground plan, such as the two baptisteries – Orthodox and Arian – at the Gothic capital of Ravenna, or the mausoleum which Theodoric had built for himself in the same city. These buildings mainly had pitched roofs; and the space which they enclosed was clearly defined, with nothing mysterious about it. Both the rectangular basilica and the round martyrium belonged firmly to the rationalist tradition of the classical world.

Yet to Justinian and the men of his age the church was the meeting-point of this world and the transcendent world in which God's purpose was unfolded, a gateway from the known to the unknowable. And this was especially true of the Great Church of Constantinople, in which patriarch and emperor met in the elaborate ritual of feast-days. The building should be adapted to its function. It should give to those who enter it the illusion of being on the threshold of another world. This required a radically new treatment of spatial relationships. Already before 532 there had been attempts to build churches in a new way. Justinian's and Theodora's own church of SS. Sergius and Bacchus in Constantinople was a move in this direction, with its eight central piers supporting a vaulted dome, set within a rectangular framework. In far-off Ravenna, where in the 420s Byzantine influence was paramount, an even more striking and successful step was taken in this direction. A wealthy local banker, Julianus, financed the building of a new church dedicated to St Vitalis, which was begun under Bishop Ecclesius (521-32). Unlike the earlier churches of the Ostrogothic capital, which were either basilical or round in plan, the new building consisted of an octagonal core resting on eight piers and arches, surrounded by an ambulatory, into which project niches from the central core. The combination of inner and outer zones interpenetrating one another – further complicated by the existence of a gallery – make it difficult for the visitor to find his bearings at first: the ordinary geometry of visible space seems inadequate. The church of S. Vitale was not completed for some twenty years. By that time Ravenna was in Byzantine hands; the church was finished under imperial patronage, and decorated with mosaics of Justinian and Theodora, as a symbol in reconquered Italy of the magnificence of the empire. Even when it was begun, in what was then the Gothic capital, its conception was inspired from Constantinople. The design recalls that of SS. Sergius and Bacchus in its creative break with tradition. Even the bricks of which it was built were of a standard Byzantine shape, quite unlike the high, short bricks used in other buildings in Ravenna.

These were first steps. The Great Church of the capital called for a more radical solution to the problem of spatial relationships, and for a greater scale and magnificence of execution. Justinian did not turn to the master builders, but to Anthemius of Tralles and Isidore of Miletus, engineers and mathematicians whose training and social standing put them in a different category altogether from that of the ordinary architect/master-builder of antiquity. The problems they had to face could not be solved empirically: rigorous theory was needed. The decision to employ a new kind of architect must have been Justinian's own. The matter was too important to be left to a subordinate. He had doubtless made the acquaintance of Anthemius and Isidore in connection with some of his military works on the eastern frontier, or with his improvements to the water supply of Constantinople, and learnt to respect their intellectual and technical ability. In the meantime column drums and marble slabs were brought from all over the Aegean and even from as far as the Atlantic coast of France – for the emperor's arm was long, and his diplomats maintained friendly relations with the distant kingdom of the Franks. Masons and sculptors and workers in inlay were assembled from the cities of the empire. Justinian spared no expense – it appears that he spent twenty-three million gold *solidi* on the project – and his powerful patronage and personal drive may have simplified the architects' task. Nevertheless it is a tribute to the organizing skill of Anthemius and Isidore that the building was ready for consecration by the end of 537.

Justinian had often inspected the work; and Anthemius had explained his designs to him. Yet a building site is not an easy place for a layman to understand. It was only just before the formal consecration that the mass of scaffolding was removed, the clutter of workshops and stores cleaned up, and the building ready to be seen as a whole, Justinian crossed the augusteion from his palace in the company of Isidore, the doors were thrown open, and the emperor passed through the narthex or porch into the ambulatory and thence to the vast central space crowned by its stupendous dome. All around him polished marble of every hue glittered in the light which entered by the ring of high windows round the base of the dome.

The elaborate patterns of coloured marble in apse and dome were like a second set of windows, opening into a transcendent world. On every side there were complex, bewildering vistas of space receding into space. For a long time Justinian stood in stunned silence. When he recovered his composure all he could murmur was: 'Solomon, I have surpassed thee.' Whether he surpassed Solomon we cannot know. But he certainly outdid Juliana Anicia, the blue-blooded builder of the ornate but undistinguished church of St Polyeuctus, which until 537 was the largest ecclesiastical building in Constantinople. Her son Olybrius was one of the senators exiled after the Nika riot.

And indeed the architects had created a building whose form surpassed any preconceived idea. The visitor is still overwhelmed. The structure is simple enough in conception. Four immense piers rise at the corners of a square whose side is 100 Byzantine feet. They are joined, at a height of 70 feet, by four great arches. Those to north and south are embedded in the walls of the nave; those to east and west are free-standing, opening into semicircular prolongations of the central square. The arches are linked by pendentives. And from the apex of the arches and the pendentives there rose – we do not possess the church as it was completed by its architect – a flattish dome 100 feet across. Semi-domes resting on the main piers and on pairs of subsidiary piers abut the main dome at a lower level to east and west. And smaller conchs fill in the four spaces between the main dome and the semi-domes.

Surrounding this bold construction, and enclosing ambulatories and galleries as well as the narthex, is a rectangular wall. It plays no part in supporting the main structure. And the vaults and pendentives with which the aisles, narthex and galleries are roofed rest on free-standing columns and piers. They are linked to main piers and walls alike by diminutive groin-vaults and barrel-vaults.

The design is meant to be perceived from the centre. The first impression is of a vast, formless space filled with light. Gradually its form becomes clear. The huge niches on east and west form an elliptical space, which is itself extended in four directions by the conchs. Vertically the space is delimited by the dome in the centre, sloping down to the two semi-domes in east and west, and further to the vaults of the conchs. But the differences of height are hard to estimate by eye. To north and south the space is bounded by vertical walls. But between the piers and beyond the semi-domes and conchs the eye glimpses further spaces of unknown form. There are no firm planes, no easily measurable distances, as the central space penetrates the surrounding arcades and returns again from them. As a modern architectural historian, Richard Krautheimer, has written: 'Within the inner shell, both the spatial volumes and their sequence are all intelligible. But beyond this core, space remains enigmatic to the beholder who is restricted to the nave. The form and interplay of spatial shapes is first established, then denied.'

Slabs of coloured marble encased the massive piers and concealed their bulk. Columns of veined green marble and of deep red porphyry support the arcades. The piers and walls of the nave are sheathed in green, red, yellow and blue marble. The dome, the half-domes and the pendentives glittered with non-figurative marble mosaics. Silver and gold gleamed in the apse and chancel, and golden lamps hung between the columns. Justinian's comparison of himself to Solomon was no idle boast. Rome was the new Israel, and Justinian its ruler, anointed by God. And he had completed the most magnificent house of worship the world had yet seen. To enter it today, stripped as it is of most of its decoration, is still a deeply moving experience.

Contemporaries sang the praises of the great new church. When in 563 the church was reconsecrated after being damaged in an earthquake, a young poet, Paul, the son of Cyrus, whose literary talent had won him a place as a gentleman-usher at court, recited to the white-haired old emperor a long poem describing, with a wealth of florid imagery, the church which stood as his greatest claim to fame. True, Justinian could not have built Hagia Sophia without Anthemius. But equally Anthemius could not have built it without Justinian, who provided not merely money, but a lively interest in every detail and the encouragement to try something which had never been done before – and which has never been done since on a remotely comparable scale.

Justinian may have begun Hagia Sophia as a thanksgiving for his victory over the Nika revolt, or to lighten his conscience in the matter of the thirty thousand corpses which had lain piled up in the Hippodrome. By the time it was completed he had forgotten the corpses, and he had greater victories to celebrate.

War with the Vandals

When Belisarius was recalled from the east, it was because Justinian had work for him to do. He was to command an expedition against the Vandal kingdom in north Africa. The Vandals had left Scandinavia in the second century A D. By the late fourth century they were settled north of the Sea of Azov. Then, under

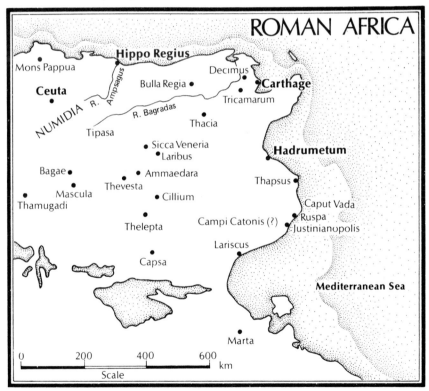

pressure from nomadic peoples of the steppes, they trekked across Europe, outside the northern frontiers of the Roman empire, as far as the Rhine, crossed into Gaul, and later passed over the Pyrenees to Spain, where once again they settled. On the way they had become converted to Christianity, but of the Arian variety. They were not long left undisturbed in their new Spanish home. The Visigoths were pressing in upon them from the north, and a Roman expeditionary force harried them. In 429, led by their young king Gaiseric, the Vandals crossed the straits of Gibraltar and swept through Roman north Africa. By the next year they were besieging Hippo (Bône), whose aged bishop, St Augustine, lay dying within the walls. After a temporary agreement with the western Roman authorities which kept them out of Carthage, they went on to seize the city and to establish a kingdom stretching from the Atlantic to the desert east of Tripoli. Unlike the other barbarian kingdoms of the west, the Vandal state acknowledged no shadowy Roman sovereignty. And unlike the Goths of Italy and Spain they were fanatical Arians, persecuting the Catholic church and seizing its property. At first they practised a kind of apartheid, in which the Romans and Romanized Africans were second-class citizens. But in time the attraction of Roman civilization and their own small numbers led to closer relations. There was another respect in which the Vandals were unique among contemporary barbarians: they understood sea power. The Vandal fleet was no professional force like that of the Roman empire in its heyday, but in the fifth century it dominated the western Mediterranean. Sicily, Sardinia, Corsica and the Balearics fell to them – though Sicily was subsequently taken from them by Theodoric and his Ostrogoths. The corn supply of Africa was no longer available for Rome and the cities of Italy. In 455 King Gaiseric landed at the mouth of the Tiber and captured and sacked Rome itself. It was their behaviour on this exploit which earned for the Vandals their reputation for reckless pillage and destruction. In 468 the eastern Roman emperor Zeno sent a great naval expedition from Constantinople against the African kingdom. The fleet was utterly destroyed in a naval battle, with terrible losses to the Romans. When Gaiseric died in 477, he could look back upon a half-century of unbroken success.

Fifty years later things had changed. Their king was now Hilderic, a grandson of Gaiseric. But Hilderic was also the descendant of a Roman emperor, for his mother the princess Eudocia, daughter of Valentinian III, had been one of the choicest pieces of booty brought back to Carthage by the grim old king Gaiseric after his sack of Rome. Hilderic was proud of his Roman ancestry, and rejected Vandal traditions and values. He even gave up the Arian faith and became a Catholic.

Justinian saw in Hilderic the man who might bring Africa back to Roman allegiance. And long before the death of Justin he had entered into correspondence with him, sent him lavish presents, and cultivated his friendship. The Vandal kingdom swung towards alliance with Rome and hostility to the Goths of Italy. The dowager queen, Amalafrida, a kinswoman of Theodoric, was thrown into prison, and her Gothic entourage massacred to a man. For a time it looked as though Africa might be restored to Roman sovereignty without a blow being struck. But Hilderic was overthrown by a conspiracy among the Vandal nobility, who elevated to the throne in his place his cousin and designated successor Gelimer, a man more after their own heart. Justinian, who was now sole emperor – it was in 530 that Hilderic was displaced – intervened diplomatically on behalf of his friend, only to receive a sharp rebuff from Gelimer.

Plans had to be changed. The Vandal kingdom could no longer be used by Justinian as a stepping-stone to Italy, but had to become the objective of his first attack. Justinian decided to mount an expedition against Africa. The pretext was to restore Hilderic to his rightful throne. The true aim was the conquest of Africa.

The memory of the terrible disaster of 468 was still fresh in men's minds, and many in Constantinople were terrified at the prospect of its repetition, no less than by the cost in money and material of such a long–distance naval operation. A great fleet was got ready in the ports of the empire. In the meantime Justinian's secret service was also at work. A Roman of north Africa, one Pudentius, raised a revolt in Tripoli, the Vandal city nearest to Roman territory, and Justinian sent a small garrison to support him. Godas, the governor of Sardinia, a Goth in the Vandal service, was encouraged to revolt and promised Roman assistance. Gelimer fell into the trap and concentrated his fleet in Sardinian waters to put down the rebel.

In late June 433 the expedition set sail from Constantinople after a ceremony of blessing by the Patriarch Epiphanius, and watched by Justinian from the palace walls. There were five hundred ships in all, of which ninety-two were war galleys. There were sixteen thousand soldiers and thirty thousand sailors and marines, mostly from Egypt or the west coast of Asia Minor. The commander-in-chief was Belisarius, accompanied as usual by his wife Antonina. His immediate subordinates were Dorotheus and the eunuch Solomon. The other generals, whose names Procopius lists, were all Thracians with the exception of Aigan the cavalry commander, who was a Hun. These were men from Justinian's own homeland, men whom he understood and could trust. The admiral of the fleet, Kalonymos, was from Alexandria. The army itself was a motley band. Apart from the regular Roman units there were companies of barbarian mercenaries from beyond the frontiers – the so-called *federati* – and several thousand *bucellarii*, mercenaries in the personal service of Belisarius.

Calling at Herakleia, Abydos, Sigeion, the fleet then crossed the Aegean to the tip of the Peloponnese, thence to Methone and Zakynthos. Diplomatic negotiations had guaranteed them the right to put in to Sicily, which was part of the Ostrogothic kingdom. They were lucky with the weather, crossed the often stormy stretch of open water to Sicily without mishap, and anchored off a beach south of Taormina to take on water. They no doubt took on fresh food too, for the biscuit which had been issued to them by John of Cappadocia turned out to be mouldy and many of the men were sick. As they lay off the beach, Belisarius sent his military secretary, who was none other than the historian Procopius, to Syracuse to ascertain if the Vandals had found out about the approach of the fleet. Procopius had a stroke of luck: he ran into a boyhood friend of his from Caesarea in

Palestine, who was settled as a merchant in Syracuse. This man had a slave agent who had arrived from Carthage, the Vandal capital, only three days before. He reported that the Vandals knew nothing of the expedition, that all was quiet in Carthage, and that the main body of the Vandal fleet was still concentrated against Godas in Sardinia. Pretending to go for a walk in the city with his friend's slave, Procopius led him down to the waterfront, where they were picked up by a pinnace from the Roman fleet; and a few hours later the slave was being interrogated by Belisarius on his flagship.

The man's story held. Belisarius, scarcely able to believe his luck, ordered his fleet to weigh anchor at once for Malta. After a brief rest they continued their journey towards Africa, every eye alert for any sign of the dreaded Vandal fleet. But the bulk of it was still in Sardinian waters, and the rest tied up in the port of Carthage. The north wind carried the Romans further south than they intended, and they made landfall at Caput Vada (Ras Kaboudia) midway between Sousse and Sfax. Belisarius called a council of war aboard his flagship. It was decided to disembark the land forces, which would then march north keeping as close to the sea as possible, while the fleet kept pace with them offshore. The disembarkation went off without incident – a tribute to Belisarius' organization and discipline, when one recalls that some ten thousand horses had to be got ashore on an open beach. Once the army was landed, Belisarius' first concern was to warn his soldiers against alienating the feelings of the local inhabitants. 'We came here to fight the Vandals,' he said, 'and to liberate the Africans, who are Romans. If you do not keep discipline, we shall end up by driving the Africans into the arms of the Vandals.'

Meanwhile the news of the Roman landing had been brought to Gelimer, who was conducting a punitive operation against Moorish tribesmen west of Carthage. He at once ordered his brother Ammatas, whom he had left in charge of the capital, to put Hilderic and his imprisoned supporters to death. Belisarius' hands were thus untied, and the pretence of restoring legitimate Vandal rule was quietly dropped.

As the Roman army and fleet advanced side by side up the African coast, Gelimer made plans to entrap them between three Vandal armies. But his staff work was not up to that of Belisarius. One Vandal detachment, under Ammatas, arrived too soon and was cut to pieces by the Roman advance guard, and Ammatas himself was killed. The second was routed by a cavalry charge by six hundred Huns, which took them unprepared. But the main Vandal force, under Gelimer himself, drove back the advance guard of Belisarius' force; and for a moment the Roman cavalry – the infantry had been left behind – was in disorder. This was Gelimer's chance, and he missed it. As he was about to fall on the Roman force, he came upon the body of his brother Ammatas, whom he believed still alive, and his nerve broke. Belisarius had time to get his own troops in order, and to charge the much larger Vandal force, which was still only half deployed for battle. The Vandal ranks broke, and in a few minutes Gelimer and his army were in headlong flight westward towards Numidia, bypassing Carthage. But it had been a close-run thing.

1. The Barberini ivory – an idealized portrait of an emperor, either
Anastasius or Justinian, riding in triumph. On the left a general bears a
statuette of victory, while at the bottom defeated Scythians and Indians offer
tribute. A female figure representing earth supports the emperor's foot.

VIR INL·COM·DOMESTIC·EQVIT·
ET CONS·ORDIN·
FL·ANASTASIVS·PAVLVS·PROBVS·
SABINIAN·POMPEIVS·ANASTASIVS·

2. (left) The Empress Ariadne, widow of Zeno and wife of Anastasius, depicted on the leaf of an ivory diptych.

3. (above) Anastasius Paulus, a relative of the Emperor Anastasius, portrayed twice on an ivory diptych as commander-in-chief of cavalry and consul (517) at the games. In his right hand he holds the *mappa* with which he gave the signal to start the races. Below are shown actors and a scene at the circus.

4. Consular diptych of Justinian, 521. The text reads: 'These gifts, small in value but kindly in esteem, I as consul offer to my fellow senators.'

5. (above) Head of a sixth-century empress, probably Theodora.

6. (left) A sixth-century portrait head, probably of Queen Amalasuntha, daughter of Theodoric.

86

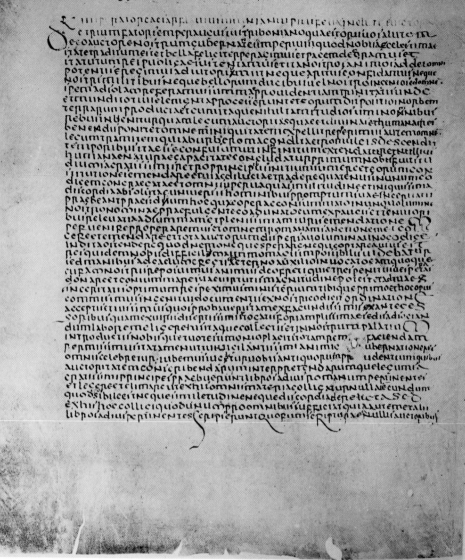

7. (left) Boethius in prison visited by Philosophia; from a tenth-century manuscript, now in Munich.

8. (above) A sixth-century manuscript of Justinian's *Digest*. This page shows the beginning of the constitution *Deo auctore* of 15 December, 530.

9. Gold solidus of Anastasius.

10. Gold coin of 527 showing Justin I and Justinian as co-emperors.

11. Gold medallion of Justinian, probably about 534.

12. Verso of the same coin, showing the emperor triumphing over the Vandals.

13. Coin of Theodahad, King of the Goths, 536.

14. Coin of Totila, last King of the Goths.

15. Icon of Bishop Abraham, sixth or seventh century, from Middle Egypt.

16. Chariot race in the circus, a fourth-century mosaic from Carthage.

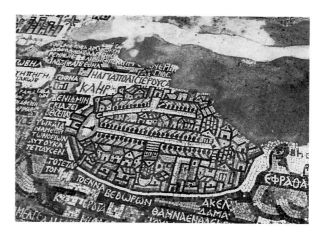

17. (right) Jerusalem, a sixth-century mosaic map at Madaba, Jordan.

18. (below) Sixth-century mosaic showing street scenes in Antioch.

19. (bottom) Fourth-century mosaic from Carthage showing a fortified country house surrounded by scenes representing the seasons.

20. (above) St Irene, Constantinople, built by Justinian about 532.

21. (left) Detail from SS. Sergius and Bacchus, Constantinople, showing part of an inscription of Justinian and Theodora.

22–24. Church of S. Vitale, Ravenna, completed in 547. In the general view (left) we are looking from the octagonal nave into the chancel, where the two large mosaics of Justinian and Theodora with their court (above) face each other.

25. Inscription on the roof beams of the monastery of St Catherine, Mount Sinai, built by Justinian. It reads: 'For the commemoration and eternal rest of our late Empress Theodora.'

26, 27. Exterior and interior of Justinian's great church of the Holy
Wisdom (Hagia Sophia). The exterior clearly reveals how the huge dome is
supported – on the east and west by semi-domes over apses and on the north
and south by mighty buttresses. (The minarets are Turkish additions). Inside,
the space seems miraculously free of supports and the dome floats above it,
'as if suspended by a golden chain from heaven'.

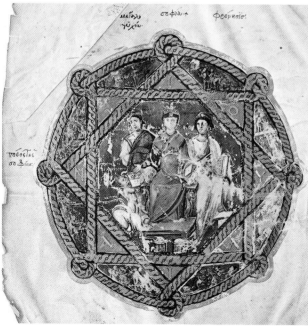

28. The cross of Justin II (565–78) in silver gilt set with precious stones. The praying figures on the arms are Justin and his consort Sophia; Christ is shown twice at the head and the foot, with the Lamb of God in the centre. The cross originally contained a fragment of the True Cross.

29. Detail from a manuscript of the Herbal of Dioscorides made in 512, with a portrait of Juliana Anicia, a member of a leading Roman family settled in Constantinople.

The battle took place on 13 September 533, at the tenth milestone on the road south from Carthage, on the coast of the Gulf of Tunis, somewhere in the suburbs of present-day Tunis. The next day the Roman army encamped before the walls of the city, while the fleet sailed into the Gulf of Tunis. Belisarius could have entered Carthage. The Vandals left in the city had fled to sanctuary in the churches. The Catholic clergy were taking possession of the churches sequestrated by the Arians, including the great basilica of St Cyprian. The gates stood open, and the joyful population strung lanterns along the walls to welcome the Romans. But Belisarius feared a trap in the narrow streets of the city. So it was on the next day, Sunday 15 September, that he made his solemn entry into Carthage, amid the acclamations of the jubilant crowds. He went straight to the royal palace, where he received the leading men of the city, seated on the throne of King Gelimer. The lesson was obvious: Vandal power was ended, and Africa once more united to the Roman empire.

The troops were kept under the sternest discipline – they even paid for what they needed in shops, remarks an observer – and the goodwill of the citizens carefully cultivated. In the surrounding countryside things did not go so well. The peasants, Punic or Berber in language and culture, had less emotional attachment to Rome and feared the chilling efficiency of Roman tax-collecting. Gelimer and his Vandals, encamped at Bulla, four days' journey west of Carthage, offered a bounty for every Roman soldier's head brought in. The pile of heads soon grew high. However, Gelimer had other things to think about. He had lost a battle, and he had lost his capital, but he had not lost the war. The Roman lines of communication were dangerously long, and winter was approaching, when men sail the sea at their peril. He hastened to recall his brother Tzazon and his forces from Sardinia. And he cultivated, not without success, the friendship of the Berber tribes, most of whose chiefs had hastened to Carthage to proclaim their loyalty to the new rulers. Soon he was able to approach the city, whose neglected walls Belisarius was hastily repairing. Although he cut an aqueduct, he could not altogether stop the water supply. His agents were busy inside the city, where not all were as well-disposed to the Romans as they appeared. Even Belisarius' Hunnic cavalry were bribed by the Vandal king. All Belisarius could do was to promise them bigger rewards, make them swear an oath of loyalty, and hope for the best.

The Vandals were regaining the initiative; and before the winter was out the small Roman force might be worn out by guerrilla warfare, desertion and despair. Belisarius decided that he must force a pitched battle. His troops were better trained, and he knew he could outmanoeuvre and out-think the mediocre Vandal commanders. In mid-December he led his cavalry out into the countryside and forced Gelimer to give battle by threatening his camp. The engagement took place at Tricamarum, thirty miles west of Carthage. Tzazon was killed. The Vandals fell back towards their camp. Only then did Belisarius' Huns, who had been mutinously awaiting the outcome of the battle, decide to follow their leader, and their thunderous charge completed the rout of the Vandals. About eight hundred

Vandals had fallen, against only fifty Romans. After a swift reconnaissance, Belisarius attacked the Vandal camp. Gelimer did not attempt to defend it, but fled westwards into Numidia. The rest of his army followed their king's example, abandoning their families and all their possessions. The Vandal force no longer existed. Indeed the Vandals as a people vanished from the face of the earth, killed or absorbed by the surrounding Romans or Berbers. Belisarius seized the camp, rounded up the Vandals who had taken refuge in the churches, and pressed on to Hippo, which he entered without resistance. There he captured the royal treasure, as well as many Vandal notables, who awaited his arrival clinging to the altars of the city churches. Gelimer, however, gave him the slip. With a few faithful followers he fled to the inaccessible mountains of southern Numidia, where the local Berber people gave him shelter. But he no longer counted: he was a king without subjects. Blockaded by a Roman force, he spent his time composing a Latin poem on his own misfortunes. When it was completed he sent a messenger under a flag of truce to Pharas, the Roman commander, to ask for a lyre on which to accompany himself, a sponge to wipe away his tears, and a loaf of bread. Finally, towards the end of March 534, he surrendered under terms to Belisarius. In the meantime Roman detachments had occupied Sardinia, Corsica, the Balearics, Caesarea in Mauretania (Cherchel), and the distant fortress of Septem (Ceuta). Within six months of landing, Belisarius had restored a continent to Roman rule. Or so at any rate it seemed.

Communications between Africa and Constantinople were not easy. Justinian probably received dispatches from his commander-in-chief by sea to a Peloponnesian port, and thence by relays of horses. We do not know when he received the first news of victory. Until it came, he lived in suspense. Failure now meant abandonment of all his hopes for the future; and failure could not be ruled out. But by 21 November he had heard of the victory at the tenth milestone and the capture of Carthage, and he judged that the issue was decided. For on that day he issued the decree introducing his *Institutes*. In that decree he says: 'Our warlike labours barbarian nations who have passed beneath Our yoke know; and Africa, as well as countless other provinces which, thanks to the victories vouchsafed Us by Heaven, have after so long a space of time been restored once again to Roman dominion and added to Our empire, bear witness to them.' And in the preamble to the decree he adds to the titles Alamanicus, Gothicus, Francicus, Germanicus, Anticus, which, in imitation of earlier emperors, he had conferred upon himself, those of Alanicus, Vandalicus, Africanus. He was not only the new Augustus and the new Constantine, but the new Scipio too.

The spoils of victory

As soon as the news of the final victory at Tricamarum reached the capital, the emperor promulgated two long edicts, setting out the civil and military organization of the conquered territories. A third praetorian prefecture was established for Africa, in which were included Sardinia, Corsica and the Balearics. Seven new provinces were set up. The establishment and salary of every official, down to the humblest clerk, were laid down in detail, beginning with the Praetorian Prefect himself, who was to have a staff of three hundred and ninety-six and an annual salary of a hundred pounds of gold.

In summer 534 Belisarius was recalled. Justinian had other tasks for his great marshal. Solomon, a capable and experienced officer, could deal with the pacification of Africa. There had been a tiresome rising of the Berbers of Byzacene, who had annihilated a small Roman garrison. But it would be quickly dealt with. Justinian had as yet no conception of the agonizing gap between military victory and final pacification. He was to learn of it, in Africa and elsewhere.

When Belisarius returned, accompanied by Gelimer and his fellow-captives and loaded with the spoils of Carthage, which included much of the booty taken from Rome by Gaiseric in 455, he was granted an honour without parallel, and one which bore witness to Justinian's own view of what he was accomplishing. He celebrated a triumph according to the ancient Roman custom. Emperors themselves had for centuries let the custom lapse. As for subordinate commanders, the last to enjoy a triumph had been Lucius Cornelius Balbus under Augustus, for his victory over the Garamantes, 553 years earlier. Belisarius marched at the head of his soldiers, followed by Gelimer dressed in royal purple, and the tallest and handsomest of the Vandals, and by wagon after wagon loaded with the opulent spoils of Africa, to the Hippodrome. There Justinian and Theodora, surrounded by the grandees of the empire, waited in the Kathisma. As Belisarius and his royal captive approached, soldiers tore the purple robe from Gelimer's shoulders and forced him to prostrate himself in the dust before the imperial pair. Murmuring 'Vanity of vanities, all is vanity,' the last king of the Vandals grovelled before the rulers of the world; and at his side his conqueror knelt in obeisance to his master. As a further reward, Belisarius was appointed consul for the next year, and his inaugural procession on 1 January was a repetition of his triumph.

As for Justinian, he had accomplished more in seven years than men had thought possible. God favoured his designs.

Gelimer was settled on a rich estate in Galatia, where he could do no harm, and allowed to practise his Arian religion without hindrance. Such able-bodied Vandals as had been rounded up were formed into five regiments of *Vandali Justiniani* and despatched to the Persian frontier. Nothing was to be wasted. The spoils brought by Justinian were indeed rich, and more than paid for the expenses of the expedition. Among them was the Menorah, the seven-branched candlestick from the Temple of Herod taken to Rome by Titus in AD 71, and removed from there by Gaiseric in 455. The news of its presence electrified the Jewish community of the capital. One of their most influential members approached a high official, believed to have the ear of the emperor, and pointed out that it would be unwise to keep it in Constantinople. It had always brought ill-luck. Jerusalem had been captured by Titus, Rome by Gaiseric, and now Carthage by Belisarius. Perhaps the best thing would be to return it to Jerusalem, whence it came. The suggestion was conveyed to the emperor. Justinian had no desire to quarrel with the Jews, whom he regarded as a feature, albeit a regrettable one, of the divine dispensation. And like all men of his age, he was superstitious, and a little frightened. The Menorah and the other Temple vessels were hastily sent to Jerusalem, and lodged in various Christian churches there, where they remained until the Holy City was sacked by the Persians in 618.

5   Belisarius in Italy

The restoration of Roman power in Africa was a triumph for Justinian's policy. But it was only a beginning. Far more central to the emperor's plans was the Ostrogothic kingdom of Italy. Whoever held Italy could threaten east Roman power in the Balkan peninsula. And indeed most of the Dalmatian coast was already in the hands of the Ostrogoths. But to Justinian tradition and the sense of history were more important than strategic calculations. Rome, the Eternal City, was the cradle of the empire. It had been founded nearly thirteen centuries earlier, and for seven hundred years it had been the paramount power in the Mediterranean. It was also the seat of the bishops of Rome, the successors of St Peter. While the question of papal supremacy was still one for the future, the prestige of the popes was immense. They were *primi inter pares*. That such a city should be in the hands of a foreign power was galling to Justinian, and might become dangerous. For his ideal of a uniform, autocratic church, working hand-in-glove with an equally autocratic state, could hardly be realized so long as the most prestigious of all churchmen lived outside the emperor's reach.

The Ostrogoths, seen from Constantinople, were a more complicated problem than the Vandals. The founder of the kingdom, Theodoric, ruled not only as king of the Goths, but as viceroy of the emperor and commander-in-chief of the imperial forces in the west. This relationship had been confirmed by Zeno's successor Anastasius in 497, and never repudiated by either side. Like many constitutional arrangements, it did not reflect the reality of power; the Ostrogoths were in practice independent of Constantinople. But it did help to make Gothic rule more palatable to the Roman population of Italy, and in particular to the influential and traditionalist Roman senate. And it meant that the rulers in Ravenna could not simply be branded as illegitimate usurpers. Then the Ostrogoths, though they were Arians like the Vandals, never persecuted the Catholic majority. Theodoric, perhaps the most outstanding man of his age, took care to cultivate good relations with the popes and with the leading members of the Roman community. His ultimate aim – not, of course, to be realised in his own time -- was some kind of fusion of Goth and Roman, in which the best features of each community would be embodied.

So Justinian could not count on the automatic support of the Roman population of Italy, or indeed of the Pope, who might prefer to live under the rule of a heretical monarch in Ravenna who let him run the church in his own way. Military intervention might therefore be very hazardous, and there were no quick and easy victories to be snatched. Justinian had long come to the conclusion that the best way to restore Roman power was to exploit the constitutional situation. Italy was theoretically under imperial suzerainty. If this suzerainty could be made a reality by constant extension of precedent and by seizing every opportunity for the assertion of his authority, Italy could well be brought under his effective control without a costly and dangerous confrontation with the Ostrogoths. In a sense this was Theodoric's policy too. He had no male heir, and was anxious to secure his succession. So he was ready to make considerable concessions to Justinian in return for a guaranteed succession. It was this mutual readiness to seek a peaceful, if somewhat vague, solution which was reflected in the arrangements made in 518. Eutharic, the husband of Theodoric's daughter Amalasuntha, and his heir presumptive, was designated by Justin consul for the following year, and entered upon his office with great solemnity and splendour. At the same time the imperial ambassador Gratus assured Pope Hormisdas that Constantinople had abjured the Monophysite tendencies of Anastasius and returned to the Chalcedonian faith. Thus the schism that had separated pope and emperor for fifteen years was ended. Had everything gone according to plan, Eutharic would have succeeded in due course to the Ostrogothic throne, but as the subordinate and representative of the emperor in Constantinople. And the Roman church would have been under no temptation to play an independent role. The fact that Eutharic was something of a Gothic nationalist and an anti-Catholic was a discouraging circumstance. But his wife Amalasuntha had had a Roman education and shared her father's admiration for the Roman way of life; and she was a forceful character. She also was, or would be when Theodoric died, a very rich woman indeed. And in the male world of the Gothic tribal nobility there was little room for rich and forceful women. So Amalasuntha could be counted upon to steer her countrymen towards accommodation with Constantinople, whatever her husband's views. As it turned out the plan was never put to the test, for Eutharic died in 522, leaving a four-year-old son Athalaric as heir to the now venerable Theodoric.

The death of Eutharic began a period of worsening relations between Ravenna and Constantinople. Theodoric grew suspicious of Justinian's long-term designs. The accession of the pro-Roman Hilderic to the Vandal throne in 523 led to close cooperation between Constantinople and Carthage, which seemed menacing to the Ostrogoth monarch. Hormisdas' successor as pope, John I, lacked his predecessor's tact and identified himself openly with pro-imperial factions among the aristocracy of Rome. It is this background, plus the suspicion of old age, that explains Theodoric's break with the Roman senate and the arrest and execution in 524 of Boethius, Symmachus and other leading Romans on a charge of plotting to restore imperial power in Italy. During these difficult years Justinian must have despaired of a peaceful restoration of Roman power in Italy. But on 30 August 526 the old king died, leaving relations between Ravenna and Constantinople at a low ebb but opening the door to a reassessment of the situation by both sides.

The eight-year-old Athalaric was now king of Italy, under the regency of his mother, Amalasuntha. The regent at once began a policy of *rapprochement* with Constantinople, both from conviction and to strengthen her own position against the turbulent Gothic nobility, to whom the rule of a woman was an abomination. Towards the end of 527 there was a *coup d'état* in Ravenna, directed against

Amalasuntha and her pro-Roman ministers. The education of the young king was taken out of the hands of his mother and left to the Gothic nationalists, who made a hopeless mess of it. Amalasuntha, now alienated from her son, was driven into the arms of Justinian, and soon began to conduct a secret correspondence with him. Once again a peaceful restoration of Roman power in Italy seemed to be the order of the day. By 532, when Justinian, victorious over the Nika riots, had signed the Everlasting Peace with the Persians, Amalasuntha had reached the end of the road. Seeing power slipping from her hands, and realizing that her life was in danger from the constant intrigues and plots among the leading Goths, she came to a secret agreement with Justinian. She was to flee to Dyrrhachium (Durazzo in Albania) – the nearest port in imperial hands – where a palace was made ready for her – and to call on Justinian to restore her to power. At the same time she sent a ship containing

her personal fortune of nearly three million gold *solidi* to Dyrrhachium with orders not to unload it until she arrived. With the daughter of the great Theodoric and the legitimate ruler of the kingdom of Italy as a suppliant at his court, Justinian would have been in a very strong position indeed. Many Goths would take his side, and he could in his own good time march his armies into Italy with every hope of a bloodless victory. Amalasuntha, however, unexpectedly succeeded in getting some of her principal enemies among the Gothic nobility assassinated, and in finding support from other leading Goths. So she decided to stay in Ravenna and rule on her own. There was probably another factor behind Amalasuntha's decision. Justinian, she had heard, was not the only power in Constantinople. There was also Theodora to reckon with. She had a mind of her own, and since the Nika revolt her influence had increased. Justinian and Theodora might sometimes pull in different directions; but in the last resort they would stand together, and anyone or anything which stood between them would be sacrificed without a thought.

Amalasuntha was a woman of great beauty and charm, cultivated and sophisticated. Moreover she was the daughter of the king of Italy, not of a bear-keeper in the Hippodrome. In 532 she was about thirty – somewhat younger than Theodora. It needed little feminine intuition – and Amalasuntha had no lack of that – to imagine what would happen if she turned up in Constantinople as an honoured guest of Justinian. If the emperor were moved by lucid calculation of his own interest – and Amalasuntha had no reason to suppose that he was not – what better course for him than to get rid of Theodora by one means or another and marry the daughter of Theodoric? She would have to renounce the Arian faith, of course; but this could be arranged. In this way the Gothic problem would be solved at a single stroke, since the young king Athalaric, worn out by depravity, was unlikely to survive long. Appreciation of the dangers of such a situation may well have contributed to the Gothic princess's reluctance to throw herself on Justinian's mercy.

When a courier from Dyrrhachium reached the capital with the news of Amalasuntha's change of plans, Justinian was disappointed but not dismayed. The fundamental weakness of Amalasuntha's position, which made her dependent on Justinian, was not changed. He had only to wait for the next crisis at Ravenna. In the meantime he had other plans afoot. Amalasuntha's only male kinsman, the only surviving member of the ruling Amal family, was her cousin Theodahad. Theodahad had no taste for power, and no military experience. He combined a dilettante interest in Platonic philosophy, which he must have acquired through contact with the circle of Symmachus and Boethius at Rome, with a cupidity which had twice provoked the anger of Theodoric. Seeing that the course of events might push him into the centre of the stage, and desirous above all to pursue a life of philosophical leisure supported by a princely private income, he too had been in contact with Justinian. By 533 things had reached the point where Theodahad had offered to transfer his property – or at any rate the liquid portion of it – to Constantinople, in return for a position of dignity at the imperial court. Justinian welcomed this overture, but was in no hurry to accept it since Amalasuntha herself, as he had foreseen, was once more in secret communication with him. It was during this period, when all the cards seemed to be in his hand, that Justinian issued a curious edict. It was dated 1 June 534, and it dealt with a dry, technical matter, the disposal of property for which no owner could be found. But it was addressed to the senates of Constantinople and Rome. This was a clear attempt to assert his sovereignty in Italy. It apparently provoked no reaction from Ravenna. A precedent had been established.

In the same summer Justinian's ambassador, Alexander, arrived in Ravenna to continue discussions with Amalasuntha, under cover of negotiating compensation for a frontier incident of some years back. During the Vandal war, the Gothic government maintained a neutrality that was more than benevolent towards the Romans. This, as well as the generally pro-Roman attitude of Amalasuntha, provoked hostility among the Gothic nobility. Once again Amalasuntha found herself in danger. Justinian expected that she would turn to him for help, and give him an occasion for intervention in Italy to restore the legitimate government. But when on 2 October 534 her son Athalaric died, Amalasuntha needed to act decisively. For the only basis for the power that she exercised was that she was the mother and guardian of the king of the Ostrogoths. The new king Theodahad had already been in covert negotiations with Justinian. Amalasuntha, knowing that if she let power slip from her hands she would be at the mercy of her many enemies in Ravenna, persuaded Theodahad to make an agreement with her, whereby sovereignty would be divided between them. In November 534 Theodahad was proclaimed king and Amalasuntha queen. The understanding was that Theodahad would enjoy all the perquisites of monarchy but leave the conduct of affairs to Amalasuntha. This, however, was too much for the royal Platonist. He at once made approaches to the anti-Roman Gothic nationalists, whose greatest enemy he had hitherto been. There was a new *coup d'état* at Ravenna, and power was snatched from Amalasuntha's hands.

While waiting at Valona for favourable weather to cross the mouth of the Adriatic, Peter the Patrician, Justinian's ambassador sent to continue discussions with Amalasuntha, heard that she had been deposed, but that she was being treated with all the respect due to her position. At the same time a member of the embassy approached Peter privately and told him that in fact Amalasuntha was being held in captivity on an island in Lake Bolsena, and that her life was in danger. Justinian ordered Peter to protest most forcibly to the Goths against their treatment of Amalasuntha, and to indicate that if she was not restored to her former position the Byzantine government would be forced to intervene in Italy. But there was another message from Theodora, ordering Peter to assure the Goths privately that the emperor would do nothing, and that Theodahad need not fear to get rid of Amalasuntha.

What had happened in Constantinople? Procopius, who had no love for Theodora, says that she was prompted by jealousy, and by fear of Amalasuntha's influence upon Justinian, should she come to Constantinople, and that the emperor knew nothing of the second message. He may be right. Theodora would certainly have objected strongly to the installation of the Gothic princess in the Great Palace, and she had no scruples about having those she found inconvenient murdered. But Amalasuntha was not on this occasion thinking of coming to Constantinople, nor did Justinian want her there. There are other considerations too which allow Procopius' story to be treated with some scepticism. When Peter's despatch reached the capital, the Vandal war had been successfully concluded. Belisarius had been recalled to Constantinople and granted a triumph. He was now free to assume another command. Justinian had learnt that an apparently powerful Germanic kingdom could be destroyed by resolute military action on a relatively small scale, largely because the Roman population gave it no support but welcomed the Byzantine armies. For more than fifteen years he had been trying to establish Byzantine power in Italy by diplomatic means but had been continually frustrated. It seems likely that in the autumn of 534 he decided to seek a military solution, hoping for as rapid and easy a victory as in Africa. What he wanted now was a *casus belli* which would unite the Roman population of Italy on his side and divide the Goths. If Theodahad had Amalasuntha murdered, this would provide just the occasion which Justinian wanted. This is not to say that he and Theodora put their heads together and composed the double set of instructions for the ambassador. It is more than likely that Theodora acted on her own, out of spite. But that the message got through and was acted upon suggests that Justinian knew about his wife's step and welcomed it. If it produced the desired effect, so much the better. If not, it could always be disowned as the whim of a capricious woman.

Shortly after Peter disembarked in Italy on his way to Ravenna, he learned that Amalasuntha had been strangled in her prison in Lake Bolsena by the kinsmen of three Gothic nobles whom she had had murdered earlier. As soon as he received the news, Peter told the Goths this would mean war. In the meantime Amalasuntha's murder caused a revulsion of feeling against the Ravenna government among the Roman population, and many of the Goths too felt that Theodahad had gone too far: Theodoric's daughter could not be killed like a common criminal. When Peter's courier brought the news to Justinian, the emperor at once ordered Mundus, the Master of Soldiers in Illyricum, to invade Dalmatia, and Belisarius to sail with an expeditionary force to Sicily. The Gothic war had begun.

Sicily fell to Belisarius without a battle. As he was preparing to take his tiny army – he had brought only some ten thousand troops from Constantinople – he received disastrous news from Africa. There had been a large-scale mutiny of the Roman army, whose pay was in arrears and who were demoralized by the guerrilla operations of the Berbers. The mutineers were now making common cause with their enemies, and were threatening Carthage itself. A brief visit by the great marshal averted the threat to Carthage, and Solomon was left to subdue the mutinous forces. But Belisarius had to spend some time in Sicily raising the morale of his own troops, who threatened to follow the example of their colleagues in

Africa. It was not until summer 536 that he was able to disembark in southern Italy.

In the meantime Justinian was continuing to negotiate with Theodahad, hoping that under pressure of a military threat he would concede what he had been unwilling to grant before. In fact Theodahad bitterly regretted his truculent attitude. He caused the Roman senate to send Justinian a humble letter, composed by his Roman secretary of state Cassiodorus, and induced Pope Agapetus I to go to Constantinople in person. By the end of 535 Peter the Patrician was again at Ravenna, where he succeeded in negotiating a secret agreement with Theodahad, according to which Sicily was to be ceded to the emperor, the Goths were to pay an annual tribute to Constantinople, all senatorial appointments in Italy were to be approved by the emperor, and Justinian's name was to be acclaimed before that of Theodahad at all public ceremonies. The wily ambassador contrived to suggest to the terror-stricken king that this might not be enough. 'What then?' demanded Theodahad. 'If my lord the emperor is dissatisfied,' replied Peter, 'there will be war.' Theodahad then agreed to hand over the government of Italy to Justinian in return for an indemnity of twelve hundred pounds of gold a year and a position of dignity at the Byzantine court. Justinian was delighted with the news, but had no confidence in Theodahad. His reply to the king was that he accepted his terms and was sending Belisarius at the head of an army to implement them.

A few local victories by the Goths in Dalmatia, where Mundus had been killed in battle, together with the news of the revolt in Africa were enough to make the royal Gothic philosopher change his mind again, afraid as he was of the reaction of his fellow Goths if they discovered his secret negotiations with the emperor. When Peter returned to Ravenna in the spring of 536, he was treated with contumely. Theodahad began having coins struck with his own effigy in imperial garb. And the new Pope, elected in June 536, was Silverius, son of Pope Hormisdas and a partisan of Gothic rule. At the same time Theodahad ceded Provence to the Franks in return for an undertaking to give him military aid. Diplomacy had failed, though it had left Justinian in a strong position.

This was the situation when Belisarius crossed to Italy. Only when he reached Naples did he meet resistance. There was a strong Gothic garrison in the city, and the Romans began siege operations. Theodahad, once again paralysed by fear and indecision, made no move to relieve the besieged city, and in a few weeks Belisarius captured it. This was the moment to set an example which would discourage the other cities of Italy from offering resistance. The Roman troops were allowed to pillage the city, and pro-Gothic elements among the citizens were rounded up and massacred.

Too little and too late

The news of the fall of Naples produced a surge of hostility towards Theodahad among the Gothic soldiers. At Regata, near Terracina, the army declared him deposed and proclaimed as king Vitiges, a Gothic general who was not of royal Amal blood. Theodahad tried to flee to Ravenna, but was caught on the way and killed. Vitiges was in no position to meet the redoubtable Belisarius in a pitched battle, and withdrew north of Rome leaving a small Gothic garrison in the city. Pope Silverius, whose Gothic sympathies were not deep and who was anxious to save Rome from the fate of Naples, began secret negotiations with Belisarius; and on 9 December 536 the Roman army entered the city by the Porta Asinaria as the Gothic garrison marched out by the Porta Flaminia. When the news, together with the keys of the Eternal City, reached Justinian in the early days of January 537, he felt that his cup was overflowing.

He at once nominated a Praetorian Prefect for Italy, one Fidelis, a Roman senator who had held high office under the Goths and who had negotiated the surrender of the city to Belisarius. The units which were sent north and east to seize further strong-points met firm resistance; and soon Vitiges, his forces reorganized, was advancing on Rome, mopping up Belisarius' outposts as he went. Belisarius set his men to work repairing the walls built by Aurelian 250 years earlier, and stocking up the city with supplies. He knew that his forces would be greatly outnumbered by the Goths, that he would be hard put to it to man the long *enceinte* of the walls, that he was likely to be cut off from the sea, where the imperial navy ruled unchallenged, and that the citizens, who had surrendered their city to avoid a siege by the Byzantines, were unlikely to welcome a siege by the Goths. By late winter Vitiges had concentrated the Gothic armies from Italy and Provence against Rome. It was a formidable force, though not quite large enough to invest the city completely. Against it Belisarius had a garrison of barely five thousand men, since half his army was dispersed in fortresses throughout southern Italy.

The siege lasted one year and nine days. There were sixty-nine engagements between the besiegers and parties making a sortie from within the walls. Belisarius himself was everywhere: defending the walls, leading armed patrols, organizing civilian working parties, anticipating the enemy's intentions, and inspiring his own men by the example of his gallantry. The siege of Rome, rather than any of his many victories in the field, was his greatest military achievement, recounted in graphic detail by his military secretary Procopius. Water supply was a difficulty, for the Goths cut all the aqueducts leading to the city, thereby closing for ever the great public baths constructed by the emperors from Augustus to Diocletian. The civilian population soon became discontented and mutinous. Many of the women and children were evacuated to Naples, and the men organized in companies to guard the walls.

In the spring Justinian, who was still lost in dreams of a bloodless conquest, received a despatch from his marshal, which Procopius, who probably drew it up, summarises in these terms:

We have come to Italy, as you commanded, and have got control of a large part of it, and have taken Rome, repulsing the barbarians here whose leader, Lenderis, I recently sent to you. But it has come about that we have appointed a large part of the soldiers to garrison the forts in Sicily and Italy, which we have been able to conquer, and that we have left an army of only five thousand. The enemy are coming against us to the number of one hundred and fifty thousand. First, when we came to spy out their dispositions beside the river Tiber, we were forced, against our better judgment, to come to grips with them, and the outcome was that we were nearly buried beneath the multitude of their spears. Later, when the barbarians made an attempt on the wall with their entire army and attacked it over its whole length with machines, they came very near to taking us and the city at first blow. It was some fate that saved us, for supernatural deeds should be attributed, not to human valour, but to God. Thus far we have done well, whether by fate or by our own courage; but as for what is to come, I would wish for better things for your cause. What I ought to say and what you ought to do, I will not conceal; for I know that although human affairs proceed as God may wish, the leaders in any venture win praise or blame from their own actions. Let weapons and soldiers be sent to us in sufficient quantities to establish us in future in this war on a basis of equality with our enemies. We ought not to entrust all to fate, for it is not wont to follow the same course permanently. Think of this, my Lord: if the barbarians defeat us now, we shall be driven out of your Italy and lose the army as well, and in addition shall bear the great shame of our failure. I refrain from mentioning that we should give the impression of having abandoned the citizens of Rome, who have thought less of their safety than of their loyalty to your empire. And so even our successes will turn out but the prelude to disaster. Had it so happened that we had been repulsed from Rome and Campania and, much earlier, Sicily, our misfortunes would be light – we should have failed to enrich ourselves at the expense of others. This too you should reflect on: it has never been possible to defend Rome for long, even with many tens of thousands of soldiers, for it is surrounded by a vast area, and since it is not on the coast it is cut off from all necessary supplies. At the moment the Romans are on our side. But if their sufferings are prolonged, as is likely, they will not hesitate to choose what is best for themselves. Those who show good will on the spur of the moment do not retain their loyalty when they are faring ill, but only when they are doing well. Besides, hunger will force the Romans to do many things which they would rather not. I know that it is my duty to die for your empire, and for this reason no one will be able to remove me from here alive. But consider what kind of reputation Belisarius' death in such circumstances would bring to you. (Procopius, *History of the Wars* 1. 24. 33-37).

Justinian was shocked. He realized that it was not a question of temporary setbacks in a distant theatre of war, but that his whole project for reconquest of the west and restoration of the empire was in danger. Hastily he began collecting land and sea forces. And he gave orders to a detachment under the generals Valerian and Martin, which had been wintering in Greece, to proceed to Italy forthwith. Belisarius was relieved to be informed of these measures. But he had many anxious days of attacks and skirmishes before Valerian and Martin reached Rome, twenty days after the Goths had captured Porto, at the mouth of the Tiber, and so cut the main supply route. The reinforcements were mostly Slavs and Bulgars from north of the lower Danube, tough fighting-men trained and disciplined in the traditions of the Roman army. Their arrival changed the balance of forces. Vitiges suffered a series of tactical defeats, and his losses began to mount.

In the meantime Theodora too had been active in Roman affairs. It was largely due to pressure from Pope Agapetus, then in Constantinople, that her protégé Severus of Antioch, the leader of the Monophysites, had been anathematized and expelled from the capital in 536, and that severe measures were being taken against the Monophysites throughout the empire, even in their stronghold of Egypt.

Theodora, sincere though her religious convictions no doubt were, saw every conflict in personal terms, and her hatred of the bishop of Rome was bitter. No matter that Agapetus was dead. His successors continued his religious policy, and in Theodora's eyes they were evil incarnate. A leading Roman cleric, the deacon Vigilius, had curried favour with Theodora during a long sojourn in Constantinople, promising to follow a policy more favourable to the Monophysites should he ever become pope. From this moment it was Theodora's eager desire that he should. On the death of Agapetus she sent him post-haste to Rome, liberally supplied with money. But he arrived too late. Silverius had already been elected – the same Silverius who a few months later negotiated the bloodless surrender of the city to Belisarius. The empress did not readily accept the *fait accompli*, and bided her time, her anger undiminished. No sooner was Belisarius installed in Rome than she began sending messengers to her creature Vigilius and to Antonina, Belisarius' wife. Between them they arranged to lay against Silverius false charges of plotting to hand over the city again to the Goths.

Belisarius had enough trouble on his hands already, and did not believe a word of the accusations. Summoning Silverius, he told him that the simplest way of exculpating himself would be to issue a statement supporting the anti-Chalcedonian views of the empress. Belisarius cared little for theological niceties, and was surprised when the Pope refused to compromise. Negotiations were broken off and the Pope retired to his residence. Once more the harassed marshal tried to persuade him, again in vain. Finally, under intolerable pressure from his wife and from the agents of Theodora, he consented to act, though he realized that what he was doing would gravely weaken the morale of the civil population. On 21 March 537 Silverius was summoned to Belisarius' palace on Monte Pincio. At the entrance his escort was dismissed, and it was in the ominous company of Vigilius that he was introduced to the general's presence. He can scarcely have been reassured by finding Antonina there, with Belisarius sitting like a lap-dog at her feet. It was Antonina who addressed him, reiterating the old charges. As she spoke, a sub-deacon took the pallium from his shoulders. When she had finished he was rushed to a cell, which he left, tonsured as a monk, to board a ship for the east. A week later Vigilius was consecrated Pope, after Belisarius had taken vigorous measures to suppress opposition among the clergy of the city. Theodora's vengeance was complete. Justinian, informed of the squalid background of the affair by an honourable prelate, the bishop of Patara, made a feeble attempt to have Silverius restored. But Theodora's agents saw to it that he died of privation on an island off the Italian coast before the emperor's will could be accomplished.

By November the tide was beginning to turn. Three thousand infantry – mountaineers from Isauria in southern Asia Minor – and two thousand cavalry consisting mostly of Thracians arrived by sea in Campania under the command of an experienced general, John, the nephew of Vitalian. Belisarius made a sortie in force to draw off the enemy, and the long column of reinforcements entered the city safely. The Romans could now keep their lines of communication open, while the Goths went short of supplies. Soon disease began to spread in the Gothic camp. By the end of the month the Goths asked for a truce. In the negotiations which ensued, the Gothic envoys maintained that Theodoric's rule, and hence that of his successors, was legitimate. The Goths had entered Italy at the invitation of the government in Constantinople, to put down the usurper Odovacar; therefore the present Roman invasion was naked aggression. Belisarius replied that in that case Theodoric should have handed over Italy to the then emperor once he had deposed Odovacar. Italy was an integral part of the empire, and he, Belisarius, would never hand over the emperor's property to another. The Goths then proposed to cede Sicily to the Romans. Belisarius replied by offering the Goths Britain – a province which had been lost to Roman rule for a century – the implication being that it is easy to concede what one has no longer got. The Goths then added Campania and Naples to their offer, to which Belisarius replied that he had no authority to dispose of the emperor's territory. A further offer of tribute from the Goths evoked no response. Finally a truce of three months was agreed upon, while the whole matter was referred to Constantinople. Neither side observed the truce faithfully. Belisarius, confident of his strength, sent John to cut the enemy's lines of communication by seizing Ariminium, on the road to Ravenna. By March Vitiges was in despair, and withdrew from Rome. His retreating army, a shadow of the great force which had invested the city a year before, was harried constantly by Belisarius' men.

Vitiges, frightened and discredited, tried to consolidate his position in north Italy. Belisarius, who knew well by now how great were the powers of recovery of the Goths, intended to advance slowly, occupying strong-point after strong-point and making sure of his lines of communication. Ancona was captured in March, and a series of fortified positions in the Appennines protected the route overland from the Adriatic. John was now dangerously exposed in Ariminum, and Belisarius ordered him to withdraw southwards to the safety of Ancona. But John, whose uncle had aspired to the throne, had high ambitions; and his agents were already in negotiation with Matasuntha, grand-daughter of Theodoric and wife of Vitiges, who was ready to betray her hated husband. He refused to leave Ariminum. Vitiges, quick to see the enemy's weak point, invested the city, but the matter was settled for him by the arrival of a new Byzantine army, nine thousand strong, under the command of the eunuch Narses, a man of limited military experience but of infinite prudence, who enjoyed the full confidence of Justinian and Theodora. Narses, who was a friend of John, advised Belisarius to relieve Ariminum, which he did in a brilliantly executed manoeuvre. But for the first time Belisarius' will had been challenged, and ultimately overruled. Henceforward subordinate commanders could play off Narses and Belisarius against one another. A heritage of dissension and mistrust was left in the high command, which confused and delayed efficient conduct of operations for years.

During the same spring of 538, after the abandonment of the siege of Rome, Belisarius sent a small force to Liguria to harry the Goths from the rear. It succeeded in crossing the Appennines by the easy pass followed by the Genoa-

Milan *autostrada* today and captured Milan, the most populous city of north Italy. The invading force was welcomed by the Roman inhabitants. Soon Vitiges arrived to besiege the city, accompanied by an army of Franks whose king, Theudebert I, a grandson of Clovis, was eager to extend his territory, in spite of the treaty which bound him to an alliance with Justinian. Belisarius, who had just succeeded in relieving Ariminum, wished to mount a similar operation to relieve Milan. But Narses had other plans. A shameful row blew up in the Roman headquarters, operations were launched and then cancelled, and backbiting and intrigue became the order of the day. In the end, in March 539, the Roman garrison in Milan was starved into submission. The Gothic and Frankish soldiers made an example of the civilian population and three hundred thousand were put to the sword – men, women and children alike. When the terrible news reached Justinian, he withdrew Narses, leaving Belisarius once again in sole command.

Belisarius proceeded cautiously. The remaining Gothic outposts in central Italy were captured one by one, until only Auximum (Osimo, in the hills south of Ancona) remained. Against Auximum Belisarius concentrated the full weight of his attack and laid siege to the city. North of the Appennines a small force under John and Martin prevented the Gothic forces there from coming to the relief of their threatened kinsmen. During these operations a large Frankish army suddenly appeared in the plain of Lombardy. The Goths, thinking they had come as allies, opened the gates of Pavia to them and let them cross the Po. No sooner were they across than they turned on their Gothic hosts. The Gothic commander, disconcerted and demoralized, fled with his men towards the safety of Ravenna. Meanwhile the Franks, having massacred the women and children of Pavia and pillaged the city, directed their attack, with impartial treachery, against the Byzantine army. John and Martin were alarmed but managed to take up strong defensive positions. Before the Franks, who were out for quick booty, could mount an attack, their men began to fall sick from an epidemic that was raging in Italy. They hastily returned across the Alps to their homeland, laden with spoils and accompanied by a long train of wretched captives.

When the news of these events reached Justinian, it found him beset by new and serious anxieties. On the eastern frontier the Everlasting Peace with Persia had on the whole been observed by both sides. But recently the situation had been growing more tense. Quarrels over pasture-land between the pro-Roman and pro-Persian Arab principalities led to a regular war between the two. Al-Mundhir the Lakhmid, who enjoyed Persian protection, seized the opportunity to make a raid into imperial territory. In itself the matter was trivial; but any incident in which protégés of Persia were involved had to be taken seriously. Justinian sent one of his senior officers of state, Strategius, Count of the Sacred Largesses, to investigate the incident and to mediate between the Arab principalities. Strategius was accompanied on his mission by Summus, Master of Soldiers and commander-in-chief in Palestine. The negotiations were involved and confused. At one point Summus made proposals to Al-Mundhir which the latter believed, or feigned to believe, were incompatible with the obligations of his loyalty to Persia. The zealous officer, who ought to have known better since he came from a family experienced in diplomacy, had probably exceeded his instructions. But the damage was done. Al-Mundhir reported the matter to the Great King, who let it be known that he was gravely displeased and regarded the Roman move as a breach of the Everlasting Peace. At the same time heavy-handed and unimaginative administration in Roman Armenia led to active disaffection among the clan chieftains. For centuries the first rule of survival for Armenia, crushed between two great powers, had been never to commit itself irrevocably to either. Sittas had understood the situation and had seriously tried to give the Armenian leaders a stake in the empire. His successors could see nothing but oriental double-dealing. In 538 there was a revolt, headed by descendants of the ancient Armenian royal house of the Arsacids. A pro-Roman leader was murdered, and his assassins granted asylum in Persian territory. By now seriously alarmed, Justinian sent Sittas to Armenia to deal with the situation. Sittas began by negotiating with the leaders of the revolt; he knew that he could soon divide them. But the emperor was impatient, and ordered him to use force. In one of the first military engagements Sittas was killed. His successor Buzes pursued an active military policy, and succeeded in capturing the rebel leader and putting him to death. The immediate result was that the rebels crossed over to Persia and begged the Great King to attack while the bulk of the Roman army was still committed in the west.

This was in autumn 539; meanwhile, in Italy, Vitiges had been inspired by the same thought. With great difficulty he managed to get a message through to the Great King. His agents were two Italian clerics, who could traverse the empire without attracting too much attention. This they did in the guise of a bishop and his chaplain, travelling on ecclesiastical business. The letter which they carried from Vitiges warned Chosroes that the security of Persia would be threatened if Justinian succeeded in adding Italy to his realm. Now was the time to strike. The Great King made no direct reply but his resolve to reopen hostilities was strengthened.

The 'bishop' and his 'chaplain' stayed on in Persia and died there. But a Syrian whom they had taken on as interpreter decided to return to his home and his family. Caught crossing the frontier in suspicious circumstances, he was sent to Constantinople for interrogation and the whole story came out. Justinian was seriously alarmed. As he paced the silent corridors of the Great Palace before the wondering eyes of his sleepy courtiers, he pondered whether to press on in Italy and risk a Persian invasion of the eastern provinces, or to settle with the Goths for the best terms he could get and strengthen his eastern defences. It was a hard decision, because it seemed to compromise his ideal of restoring the empire to its ancient glory. Finally, by autumn 539, he made up his mind: total victory in Italy must be renounced. Belisarius was by this time investing the Gothic capital of Ravenna. Protected by its marshes, the city was impregnable to direct attack. It could only be taken by negotiation, by treachery, or by hunger. The imperial fleet blocked all access by sea, and Belisarius' army surrounded the city on the landward side. It was only a matter of time until the Goths would be forced to surrender and Belisarius could enter Ravenna in triumph, as six years before he had entered Carthage.

The renewed presence in north Italy of Theudebert and his Franks was as alarming to Vitiges as it was to Belisarius, and no doubt encouraged the king to open negotiations with his besieger. As these were proceeding, plenipotentiaries arrived from the emperor in Constantinople, authorized to sign a treaty by which the Goths would abandon Italy south of the Po and hand over half the royal treasure to the Romans. The Gothic leaders welcomed the proposals, as did most of Belisarius' staff. The great marshal, however, felt that he was being cheated of his final victory, and that the emperor was making needless concessions. When the Goths announced that they would not regard the treaty as valid unless it bore his signature as well as those of the imperial envoys, he refused to sign. Only Justinian's direct order would make him sign such a treaty. While Belisarius sulked and the deadlock continued, someone at the Gothic court had a bright idea. Why not abandon the ineffectual Vitiges and surrender to Belisarius, on condition that he proclaimed himself emperor of the west? In this way the solidarity of Goth and western Roman in independence of Constantinople, which had been the goal of the great Theodoric, might be attained. The plan won wide support among the Gothic leadership, and was communicated to Belisarius by a secret agent. The marshal had no political ambitions and never wavered in his loyalty to Justinian, though he might criticize his diplomacy. But seeing an opportunity to gain total victory without bloodshed, he feigned to agree with the proposals. Soon Vitiges, who had learnt what was afoot, made similar secret proposals to Belisarius. These too were accepted. Belisarius then called a meeting of his senior staff and the emperor's envoys and formally asked their approval for a last attempt to capture Ravenna. He naturally revealed nothing of his own secret negotiations with the Goths. The approval was given. In May 540, after some final secret assurances on both sides, the gates of Ravenna were thrown open and Belisarius marched in at the head of his soldiers. Only then did he reveal to the Gothic leaders that he had no intention of becoming emperor, that he was occupying Ravenna in Justinian's name, and that the Ostrogothic kingdom had ceased to exist.

In March 540 the Persian king Chosroes had invaded Roman Mesopotamia at the head of a large army. So Belisarius was recalled to Constantinople immediately after the capture of Ravenna. He returned with all haste, accompanied by Vitiges, Matasuntha and those Gothic nobles who had surrendered, and taking with him the royal treasure of King Theodoric.

But no triumph awaited him, as when he had returned from Carthage. No cheering crowds lined the streets of the capital. The news of the fall of Ravenna was overshadowed by another report which had just reached Constantinople. In June 540 Chosroes and his Persian army had captured and pillaged Antioch, capital of the eastern provinces, massacred those of its inhabitants who had not fled before them, and were now demolishing the splendid city stone by stone.

6   The years of hope deferred

The Persian king Chosroes Anoshirvan ('of Immortal Spirit') was a younger man than Justinian, and he outlived him by fourteen years. The two men never met. But for more than thirty years neither was ever far from the other's thoughts as they played their macabre game of chess over the mountains and plains of western Asia. Unlike Justinian, Chosroes took the field at the head of his army. He had, too, an ironic sense of humour which his rival lacked, and a streak of cruelty which was likewise absent from Justinian's make-up. Both monarchs were tireless and far-seeing organizers. And both conceived the reforms which they introduced as a return to the glorious past of their respective peoples.

Profiting by the Everlasting Peace and Justinian's preoccupation with the west, Chosroes had weakened the power of the great territorial magnates of Persia and created a new standing army, owing direct allegiance to himself. Now Chosroes was ready to reopen the war with the Romans. This was to be no war of conquest, such as Justinian had waged in Africa and Italy. Minor frontier adjustments were certainly sought; and in particular Chosroes was anxious to get a footing on the coast of the Black Sea. But his main aim was plunder. The opulent cities of the Roman east could be pillaged; and the Romans could be made to pay heavy indemnities.

The Roman pressure on his vassal Al-Mundhir and the appeal of the Armenian refugees gave Chosroes the *casus belli* he sought. The desperate call for help from the Gothic king Vitiges confirmed his resolve. At the beginning of 540 a Roman envoy, Anastasius of Daras, brought Chosroes a letter from Justinian, sternly reminding him of his treaty obligations and calling on him to cease his warlike preparations. The letter went unanswered. So too did one from Theodora to the Persian minister Zabergan, whom she had met on an embassy to Constantinople, and whom she now urged to dissuade his master from war: 'For I pledge,' she wrote, 'that by so doing you shall receive great rewards from my husband, who will do nothing without consulting my judgment.'

In March 540 the Persian army crossed the frontier and took Sura on the Euphrates. There were only weak Roman forces in Syria, and their commander Buzes wisely withdrew rather than risk a pitched battle with the Great King. As soon as news of the attack reached Constantinople, Justinian despatched his cousin Germanus to Antioch. The presence of a member of the imperial family would be good for morale. But Germanus had only three hundred soldiers with him: his mission was to buy off Chosroes, not to fight him. Chosroes was quite ready to play the game this way. He had already spared Hierapolis in Syria for a payment of two thousand pounds of silver, and he offered to spare Berrhoea (Aleppo) for twice that sum. But the citizens could not raise the money, so he captured and burned the city. The small Roman garrison, whose pay was long in arrears, offered no resistance but hastened to enlist in the Persian service. It was the bishop of Berrhoea, Megas, whom Germanus sent to Chosroes with the offer of a thousand pounds of gold, if he would refrain from attacking Antioch. The king was ready to accept the offer. But a high official who had just arrived from Constantinople upbraided Germanus for cowardice, and forbade him, in the emperor's name, to ratify the agreement. Justinian had evidently changed his mind. No doubt the imminent end of the war in Italy and the projected recall of Belisarius made him take a more sanguine view of the prospects in the east. Germanus, who knew only too well what would happen, announced that he would not give Chosroes the glory of capturing a kinsman of the emperor and withdrew to Cilicia. By June the Persian army closed in on Antioch. A Roman force of six thousand men, the first of the reinforcements sent by Justinian, was already in the city. But it fled at the first attack, the Persians opening their ranks to let it through. The citizens of Antioch, on the contrary, manned the walls and hurled insults at the besiegers, while their civic militia, organized by the circus factions, fought with the utmost bravery. But the issue was not long in doubt. The immense circuit of the walls could not be defended by a handful of civilians. The Persians broke in and began a systematic massacre. Those of the citizens who survived were transported by Chosroes to a site near Ctesiphon in Persia, where he built a new city for them and gave it the name of Antioch.

After demolishing the city, Chosroes informed Justinian's ambassadors of his terms for peace: five thousand pounds of gold at once, and an annual payment of five hundred, ostensibly for the maintenance of the fortifications in the Caucasus to protect Roman and Persian alike from the nomads of the steppes. While the ambassadors took his message back to Justinian, the Persian king marched through northern Syria, exacting tribute from city after city. In early autumn the ambassadors returned with a message from the emperor that he was prepared in principle to accept the peace terms proposed. Chosroes returned to Persia, well pleased with his first campaign against the Romans.

The blow struck by Chosroes to Roman prestige in the east had one immediate result. The people of Lazica were discontented with Roman rule, and in particular with the efficiency of Roman tax-collectors. The military governor, Tzibus, had concentrated all foreign trade – and Lazica lay on one of the great east-west trade routes of the ancient world – in the new fortified port of Petra on the Black Sea, and established a state monopoly in many spheres of commerce. Inter-clan warfare and pillage were discouraged. The turbulent mountaineers and their king Gubazes felt all the disadvantages and restrictions of firm government.

So during the autumn of 540 Gubazes sent envoys to Ctesiphon to ask the Great King to re-establish his sovereignty in Lazica. In the spring of the next year a Persian army swept through the heart of Lazica, defeated the Byzantine forces in a pitched battle and took Petra. A Persian garrison replaced the Roman garrison in the city. This gave the Persians once again an outlet on the Black Sea. In the same spring of 541 Belisarius returned to the east as commander-in-chief, bringing with

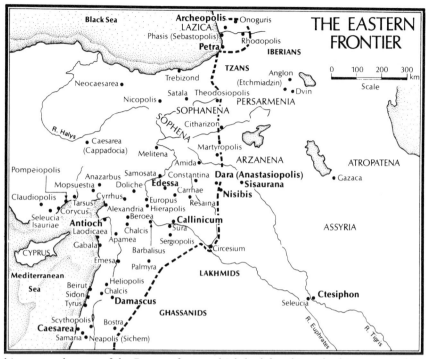

him not only part of the Roman forces which had fought under his command in Italy but also a large force of Ostrogothic soldiers. As the summer wore on he led his army across the frontier into Persian Mesopotamia. After approaching, but not attacking, the heavily garrisoned city of Nisibis, he took the fortress of Sisaurana, between Nisibis and the Tigris. There an epidemic struck his army, and his Arab allies became uneasy about possible Persian reprisals. To general surprise, Belisarius broke off his campaign and withdrew to Roman territory.

It is impossible to believe that personal considerations did not influence his unexpected decision. His wife Antonina, who usually accompanied him on his campaigns, had this time chosen to remain in Constantinople. Theodora had need of her friend to help engineer the downfall of John of Cappadocia. But it seems that Antonina had private reasons for remaining behind. She and Belisarius had no son, and Belisarius had some time ago adopted a young man called Theodosius. Antonina had fallen in love with her husband's adoptive son, and their behaviour during the African and Italian campaigns had caused something of a scandal. This time Antonina had decided that the liaison could be more conveniently pursued in the absence of Belisarius. The great marshal himself either was ignorant of what was going on or chose to close his eyes to what he could not prevent. But Antonina's son by a former marriage – if indeed it had been a marriage – Photius, who had accompanied Belisarius on his Italian campaign and admired and sympathized with his stepfather, now decided to take a hand in the affair. He was in

117

the east with Belisarius, and took the occasion of his mother's absence to put his stepfather fully in the picture about her relations with Theodosius. Belisarius was indignant; and Photius thereupon undertook to get rid of Theodosius, and persuaded Belisarius to swear a solemn oath to support and protect him, if need be, in what might turn out to be a perilous enterprise. For Antonina enjoyed the protection of Theodora, and Theodora was not to be trifled with. In the summer of 541 Antonina announced her intention of joining her husband in the east. It was this news, as much as the uncertain morale of his forces, which caused Belisarius to break off his campaign so indecisively.

He made haste to meet Antonina on the way, and immediately had her put under arrest. In the meantime the loyal Photius dashed to Ephesus, where Theodosius had been left, took possession of his person and his property, and sent him off under guard to a fortress in Cilicia, the location of which was known only to himself and his stepfather. Antonina, however, had managed to get a message through to Theodora in Constantinople. The empress put pressure on Justinian to make Belisarius release Antonina and to treat her with the respect due to her situation. At the same time she had Photius seized and confined in one of the dungeons which for long had formed part of her establishment. Although put to the torture, the upright young man would not reveal the whereabouts of Theodosius. Theodora's secret agents found him nevertheless, released him, and returned him to the arms of Antonina. Photius languished for three years in Theodora's oubliettes. When he finally escaped, he knew better than to rely on Belisarius again. He made straight for Jerusalem and entered a monastery. However, he can scarcely have had a lasting vocation for the religious life, since he was appointed by Justinian's successor Justin II to suppress a Samaritan revolt. He carried out his mission with bloodthirsty efficiency according to a contemporary witness, who writes that 'the earth trembled before him'.

If the morale of the army was low in 541, that of its commander can scarcely have been higher. However, this was but one of Justinian's worries. His finance minister, John of Cappadocia, had fallen a victim to Theodora's hatred. It was precisely because the reforms which he introduced made him many enemies among the richer classes that the empress's personal animus became a political force to which Justinian in the end had to yield against his better judgment. This was a major defeat for the emperor, and it meant in particular that the enormous financial resources needed for his campaigns, his fortifications and military works, his buildings and his diplomacy, became less easy to obtain.

The great plague

The northern frontiers, which had been quiet for a decade and a half, were once more under pressure; and the forces which might have defended them were committed in Italy, in Africa, or in the east. In the spring of 541 the Bulgars, a nomadic people of Turkish stock who had long supplied mercenaries to the Romans, crossed the Danube and swept through the Balkans, burning and ravaging. One horde ravaged central Greece as far as the Isthmus of Corinth, another laid waste the Gallipoli peninsula and sent raiding-parties across the Dardanelles to the Asian shore, a third reached the suburbs outside the walls of Constantinople. Panic reigned in the city, and those who could fled to the safety of Asia Minor. In due course the Bulgars withdrew to their homeland north of the Danube, taking with them one hundred and twenty thousand prisoners.

Justinian was alarmed, realized how he had neglected the long northern frontier of the empire, and set in motion a long programme of fortification in the Balkans, the traces of which are still visible, and impressive by their magnitude and solidity. He had more than the Bulgars to alarm him, however. When Belisarius was withdrawn from Italy, no new commander-in-chief was appointed. The Gothic offer to make Belisarius emperor underlined the danger of putting all the Roman forces in the west under a single command. It was not so much a question of what the Goths might do – they seemed in 540 no longer to represent a danger. But many of the western Romans, and in particular many of the influential senatorial landowners, would much prefer to have a western emperor, whom they could control, than to be subject to distant Constantinople. So although civil affairs were centralized under the Praetorian Prefect of Italy Athanasius, the military command was split up under a number of generals each reporting independently to the emperor. The result was as might be expected. Those of the Goths who had not surrendered were allowed to concentrate around Pavia, where they chose one of their own number, Hildebad, as king, while the Roman generals were paralysed by disagreement and indecision. Before long Hildebad had built up a considerable force. The Roman general Bessas hung about ineffectually at Piacenza while the Gothic kingdom was reconstituted north of the Po.

In spite of this early success, Hildebad's rule did not last long. Rivalry between the Gothic leaders – abetted by even more bitter rivalry between their wives – led to his assassination in May 541. He was succeeded by Eraric, leader of a small Germanic people, the Rugians, who had accompanied the Ostrogoths on their wanderings but had remained distinct from them. Unsure of his own position, and realizing well that it was easier to win a battle than to win a war against the Romans, Eraric hastened to open negotiations with Justinian. Publicly he offered to make peace on the terms originally offered by the emperor before the capture of Ravenna but repudiated by Belisarius. Privately he proposed to deliver the whole Gothic kingdom over to Justinian in return for a large sum of money and the dignity of patrician.

By autumn 541, Eraric had been assassinated in his turn. The successor upon whom the choice of the Goths fell was Totila, a nephew of Hildebad, who had recently been in secret negotiations with the Roman generals for the surrender of Treviso. Justinian had by this time decided to send reinforcements to Italy, in spite of the uncertain situation in the east. But he had no reason to believe that the unknown Totila would be a more formidable adversary than his two ineffectual predecessors. A rude shock awaited him.

In the spring of 542 Chosroes invaded northern Syria again. Belisarius was sent with all speed from Constantinople – where he had spent the winter in forced reconciliation with his wife – to take command of the Roman forces. After a complicated series of negotiations and a few skirmishes, the Persians withdrew before the summer was over. Both sides agreed in principle to discuss peace terms. This sudden change in attitude was brought about by the emergence of a new factor, equally menacing to Romans and Persians alike. A pandemic of bubonic plague, on a scale which had not been seen for nearly four centuries, swept through Europe and the near east. It first appeared in Egypt in 541, imported, so men said, from Ethiopia. With the reopening of navigation in the spring, it was not long in spreading to Syria and Asia Minor; and by May 542 it had broken out in Constantinople. A little later it had spread to the Balkans, Italy, Africa, Spain and Gaul. In the cramped and insanitary conditions of the capital the toll was frightful. Five thousand persons died a day, later ten thousand. On one day the number of deaths rose to sixteen thousand, as many as the total strength of the Roman army in Italy. The normal arrangements for the burial of the dead broke down completely. Justinian established a special burial service, directed by a high palace official, which carted off the corpses and piled them in empty buildings in the nearby countryside, or loaded them into ships which were sent to drift down the current into the Sea of Marmara. But many died unattended, and their bodies were left to rot in their empty houses. The regular food supply to the city was disrupted; the corn mills and the bakeries ceased to work. Thus to the scourge of disease was added that of famine. By the time the epidemic had run its course in the autumn, three hundred thousand are said to have died in Constantinople, perhaps two out of every five inhabitants of the city. The effect of this visitation upon public morale was disastrous. Some bolted and barred the doors of their houses, refusing to open them even to their closest friends and relatives lest a spectre should slip in along with them. Others spent days and nights in the churches in confession, prayer and supplication. Spread as it is by rats and fleas, bubonic plague is principally a disease of the poorer and worse-housed elements of the population. But the hygiene of even the richest left much to be desired. Many senior civil servants and ministers succumbed, and the emperor himself caught the plague. The functioning of the central departments of state was gravely hindered. And for a time the daily decision-making in which Justinian passed so much of his time was left in the experienced but unpredictable hands of Theodora.

Meanwhile in Italy things had taken an unexpected course. Totila proved himself a skilful strategist and a resolute and inspiring leader, and the Goths began to take heart. They had always been few in number compared with the Roman inhabitants of Italy, and they needed Roman skill and Roman tradition to administer and exploit their kingdom. Hence, since the beginning of Theodoric's reign there had been a continuous, if occasionally somewhat uneasy, cooperation between the wealthy senatorial class and the Gothic leaders, both of whom were equally interested in maintaining the system of large estates with tenants tied to the soil. Now the senators had abandoned the Goths to take the side of the victorious emperor; and the old Gothic nobility were either dead or discredited. The basis for the old class collaboration was ended. Totila scarcely formulated the matter in these terms; but his quick intelligence seized upon the radically new social situation and turned it to his profit. There was no question of replacing Romans by Goths. The civil administration of Italy was still to be left in the hands of the Romans, who alone had the necessary skills. But Totila sought the support and collaboration of a new element in the Roman population – the merchants, the urban middle classes, and the peasants. It was precisely these elements who were caught between the cold-blooded greed of Alexander the Scissors and the haphazard rapacity of the demoralized soldiers. What Totila promised, and what he carried out wherever he established his power, was nothing less than a social revolution. The great estates were divided up among their tenants, and the burdensome *corvées* and rents in money and kind swept aside. The slaves, and particularly those who cultivated the demesnes of the landowners, were freed and enrolled in the Gothic army, where they fought with the desperation of men who had everything to lose. The complex machine of administration was staffed by Romans of humble origin, jealous of the great landlords and disillusioned with the 'liberation' which the imperial armies had brought them.

The tables were now turned. In the spring of 542 Totila marched south from his base by the Po, outmanoeuvring the Byzantine army under Artabazus which tried to block his way, and annihilating it in the first pitched battle of the new Italian war at Faenza. A few weeks later he exploited the confusion and backbiting which reigned among the imperial generals to win a second decisive victory at Mugello, a day's march from Florence. Leaving his enemies bottled up in the fortresses of central Italy, he marched south with all speed and captured Beneventum. Next he turned to Naples. If he could take the city, he would cut off Roman sea communications with the north. And while his army was encamped before Naples he set to work to build a fleet in the smaller ports of Campania. Meanwhile, although Totila treated with the utmost respect various noble ladies who had fallen into his hands – for he still hoped to reach a *modus vivendi* with the senatorial class – he followed the logic of the situation. All over south Italy landlords were expelled or killed and slaves set free. Apart from Ravenna, Rome, and a number of towns on the coast, the whole of Italy was now in Gothic hands.

Stalemate on all fronts

Such were the reports which reached Constantinople while Justinian hovered between life and death, and during the long months of convalescence which followed. There were two courses which might have led to success. One was to find out what were the minimum terms on which Totila would acknowledge imperial sovereignty, accept them, and withdraw the scattered and vulnerable garrisons. The other course would have been to cut losses in the east and send a large army to Italy under the supreme command of Belisarius, the only general whose prestige in the west was still untarnished. Theodora – for most of the decisions made in summer and autumn 542 must have been hers – chose neither course. Her pride would not allow her to discuss terms with a barbarian whom she despised. As for Belisarius, she had always disliked him; and now her dislike had turned to fury. The emperor's grave illness brought to the forefront the question of the succession. Justinian and Theodora had no son. The emperor's closest kinsman, Germanus, was hated by Theodora, who did all she could to keep him in the background and had even prevented his by now adult children from marrying. But with the emperor perhaps on his deathbed, the question could not be avoided. Secret discussions were held between Theodora and some of the principal ministers. Meanwhile the generals in the east were discussing the problem on their own. In the course of the summer a confidential message reached Theodora from Peter, one of Belisarius' subordinate commanders, that Belisarius and Buzes, the second-in-command, had declared that if Justinian died, they would not recognize any successor who might be appointed in Constantinople. Whether this message was a faithful reflection in all respects of Belisarius' attitude we shall never know. He knew that any such successor could only be a nominee of Theodora, in whose judgment he had little confidence. And he realized that if he did not throw his hat in the ring himself, it would certainly be thrown in for him. Unpolitical though he might be, he also understood that the appointment of an emperor without the concurrence of the principal army commanders might well be the prelude to civil war. Nevertheless, Theodora took it as a personal insult. She summoned the commanders in the east to the capital and dismissed Belisarius and Buzes. Buzes she threw into prison, from which he was not released by Justinian until more than two years had elapsed. Belisarius was too powerful and too popular to be treated in so cavalier a fashion. But Theodora confiscated a large part of his private fortune and dissolved the corps of retainers, his *bucellarii*, who were the most highly trained and professional element in the forces which he commanded. At the very moment when Totila was undoing the work of ten years in Italy, the one man who might have rallied the Roman troops, restored the morale of the civilians and defeated the brilliant Goth in a pitched battle was skulking in disgrace in Constantinople, shunned by his former friends and in daily fear for his life.

In due course, when Justinian had recovered control of affairs, Belisarius was restored to favour. Theodora took care to let him know that it was only thanks to the intervention of his wife Antonina. This was in 543. The reconciliation was celebrated by the betrothal of Belisarius' and Antonina's only daughter Joannina to a grandson of Theodora. For the empress seems to have had a daughter, and possibly a son too, before her liaison with Justinian began.

While Belisarius was in disgrace, Justinian had at last decided to appoint a supreme commander in Italy. His choice fell upon a civilian official named

Maximinus, whose ineptitude and indecision led to the newly built Gothic fleet winning a naval victory and seizing the supplies destined for the beleaguered garrison of Naples. By the spring of 543 the city had surrendered to Totila. The king, eager to establish a favourable image, treated the inhabitants with unexampled magnanimity.

A little later in the same year a major revolt by the Moorish tribes wrested much of the province of Africa from Roman control. Fortunately, things were going better in the east. Many of the Armenian leaders, fearing the growth of Persian power, made their peace with Justinian. Chosroes massed an army on the frontier, but the threatened invasion never took place. Fear of the plague stayed the Great King's hand. And soon a rebellion led by his eldest son forced his return to his capital at Ctesiphon. Thereupon Justinian, in spite of the threatening situation in the west, decided to launch a campaign against Persian Armenia. No doubt he hoped to be able to negotiate peace terms with Chosroes from a position of strength, and so free his forces for the west. The army which marched across the frontier was far larger than any ever seen in Africa or Italy – thirty thousand fighting men. It was unlike Justinian to stake so much on one campaign. At first the soldiers were welcomed as liberators by the Christian Armenians. But divided command brought its usual results: there was no coordination between the various columns. The Romans suffered a stinging defeat at the hands of a much smaller Persian force and withdrew in disorder. For the first time since he mounted the throne, Justinian was faced with military disaster on all fronts. He was now in his sixties, and his dream of a restored empire seemed as far from realization as ever.

The spring of 544 began badly. In Africa not only were the Romans beaten in battle by the Moors, but the commander-in-chief Solomon, a tough and steady officer who had gone to Africa with Belisarius ten years before, was killed. Justinian, who seems during these grim years to have lost his flair for choosing men, appointed as commander Solomon's nephew Sergius, who combined lack of experience with a quarrelsome and uncooperative temperament. As the year wore on more and more of Roman Africa fell under the control of the rebels, who were joined by mutinous Roman troops whose pay was in arrears.

Totila takes Rome

Information is scarce on Italian affairs during the year after Totila's capture of Naples. Sure of wide support in the countryside, the Gothic king continued to mop up Roman outposts in central Italy. The absurd Maximinus seems to have been withdrawn from the peninsula, and with him his chillingly efficient finance officer Alexander, nicknamed the Scissors. But more was needed than that. Constantianus, the senior general in Italy, sent Justinian an appreciation, signed by all his colleagues, in which they declared that with the forces they had it would be impossible to defeat Totila. It was probably this serious warning that induced the emperor to appoint Belisarius once again commander-in-chief in Italy. Whatever Justinian may have thought of the loyalty of Belisarius – he could scarcely have had more assurances of it – Theodora distrusted him. He took no troops with him from the capital, and there were insufficient funds in his war-chest. So he spent some time during the summer raising troops in his native Thrace, largely at his own expense. It was late autumn before he arrived by sea in Italy, and relieved the siege of Otranto; he sailed into Classis, the port of Ravenna, shortly before the end of the year. Meanwhile Totila had sent a letter to the Roman senate, calling on it to throw in its lot once again with the victorious Goths. The Roman commander in the city, John, nephew of Vitalian, forbade the senate to reply. Thereafter proclamations signed by Totila, declaring that the Romans had nothing to fear from the Goths, began to appear mysteriously in the streets and public places of Rome. There was clearly a well-organized pro-Gothic faction in the city. All that the terrified commander could do was to expel the Arian clergy, as the most obvious target for suspicion.

At the same time the Bulgars once again invaded the Balkan peninsula, and took many captives, including the wives and families of the Illyrian soldiers serving in Italy. When the news reached Italy there were mass desertions, as the men set off to tramp back to their native villages. The programme of fortifications could hardly be speeded up – engineers and masons were in short supply. But as an interim measure Justinian invited a Slavonic people, the Antae, to instal themselves near the mouth of the Danube to serve as a buffer against the Bulgars. This was the old Roman technique of turning burglars into policemen, for the Antae themselves had been among the marauders who periodically raided Roman territory from across the Danube.

In the east Chosroes had dealt with his rebellious son, and the plague seemed to have spent itself. The campaigning season of 544 began with a Persian attack on Edessa, the principal city of northern Mesopotamia. One of the most treasured possessions of the city was a letter purporting to have been written by Christ to its then king Abgar, promising that, as a reward for his faith, Edessa would never be captured by an enemy. In selecting Edessa as his target, Chosroes may well have had in mind the propaganda effect of proving this promise false. Whatever the citizens may have thought of the impregnability of their city, the Roman general, Martin, had put the walls in a good state of defence. And during the two months of siege he responded vigorously to every move of the Persians. Finally, as so often happened in Romano-Persian hostilities, Chosroes withdrew in return for five hundred pounds of gold. A few minor Roman victories in Mesopotamia did nothing to change the balance of power. However, during this curious military shadow-boxing, messengers had been moving to and fro between Constantinople and Ctesiphon. Both sides were now ready to discuss peace terms. The bargaining was tough, and the treaty was not signed until the beginning of 545. The peace was to last five years, and was to include the tributary Arab states on either side: these turbulent principalities could thus no longer embroil the great powers in their own quarrels. No agreement was reached over Lazica. The Romans undertook to pay four hundred pounds of gold a year for the upkeep of the notional garrisons in the Caucasus, the payment for the whole five years to be made in advance.

The price was high, but Justinian had succeeded in freeing his hands in the east and in temporarily halting raids from the north – whose gravity neither he nor any of his contemporaries seems to have fully understood. He could now turn to the west and repair the damage there step by step: it was high time. A member of the old nobility, Areobindus, who was married to Justinian's niece Praejecta, was sent to Africa as joint commander with Sergius. He did his best, but Sergius' unwillingness to listen to anyone but himself led once again to a disaster for the Romans at Thacia in western Tunisia; and Justinian withdrew Sergius. Meanwhile Areobindus found himself faced by a conspiracy among his own officers. A Roman general of Vandal origin, Guntarith, hoped with the aid of the rebellious Moors to become king of an independent Africa. Plot succeeded counter-plot until finally Areobindus, assured by Reparatus the bishop of Carthage of safe conduct, agreed to meet Guntarith. The cunning rebel received his commander-in-chief with every mark of respect, but had him murdered the following night. A few weeks afterwards Guntarith himself was dead, stabbed at a banquet by one of his fellow-generals, Artabanus, who had remained in secret contact with loyalist troops. Justinian at once appointed him Master of Soldiers in Africa.

Belisarius on his arrival at Ravenna issued a proclamation calling on the Goths to submit to their lawful sovereign the emperor. There was no response. In fact some Roman garrisons, unpaid and ill-supplied, went over to the Goths. And the desertion of most of the Illyrian troops in consequence of the Bulgarian invasion of their homeland left the general Vitalis, whom Belisarius sent to recover Emilia, without an army to command. In central Italy the Goths reduced one by one the fortresses still remaining in Roman hands. Belisarius sent John, nephew of Vitalian, to Constantinople to represent to Justinian the urgent need for reinforcements and money. John remained for months in the capital, where he married a daughter of the emperor's cousin Germanus. This to the great chagrin of Theodora, who had so far prevented any of Germanus' children from marrying. Meanwhile Belisarius, who intended to take the new troops to western Italy by sea, was impatiently awaiting their arrival at Dyrrhachium. For towards the end of 545 Totila, having cleared out the Roman garrisons in his rear, had laid siege to Rome.

Though the imperial troops still held Porto, at the mouth of the Tiber, they were cut off from the city by the Gothic army. And supply-ships trying to reach Porto had to run the gauntlet of the Gothic fleet. The situation inside the walls soon became grim, as rations were cut to the minimum. Bessas, the Roman commander, exploited the famine to line his own pocket. Soon there was a strong movement among the starving civilians in favour of surrender to Totila. The deacon Pelagius – Pope Vigilius was in Sicily – used the wealth of the church and his own to relieve the sufferings of the citizens, and even entered into quasi-official negotiations with Totila. Such was his prestige within the city and such his influence in

Constantinople that Bessas did not dare to interfere with him. To lose Rome would be a terrible blow to imperial prestige, and Belisarius realized that the relief of the city must be his first priority. His first plan was to sail directly to Porto with the bulk of the new forces and fall on the rear of the besieging army. But John, when at last he arrived, insisted on the need to insure his position by reconquering southern Italy province by province. The outcome was a fatal division of forces. Belisarius went to Porto with an army insufficient to face Totila, while John dallied in the south, mopping up Gothic detachments instead of marching with all speed to Rome. It was now high summer of 546. Belisarius despaired of getting any help from John, and decided to try to break through to Rome on his own. The plan was well conceived: two hundred ships laden with supplies and with the best troops aboard were to sail up the river; meanwhile Belisarius was to march the rest of his army up the south bank. Their first objective was a chain barrier which Totila had thrown across the river, their next a wooden bridge a little upstream from it. Bessas was to pin down the enemy by making frequent sorties. Belisarius' second-in-command Isaac was to stay in Porto with Antonina and to leave on no account. In the outcome Bessas, preoccupied with his own lucrative trade in food, made no sortie. Yet Belisarius, profiting by every tactical slip of the Goths, managed to remove the chain and was about to attack the bridge – the last obstacle between himself and the city – when he received a message that Isaac had been taken prisoner by the Goths. Thinking that the Goths must have attacked and taken Porto in his absence, that his communications with the sea were cut and that Antonina was a prisoner, he broke off the combat and dashed back. In fact Isaac, as insubordinate as Bessas, had attacked a small party of Goths in Ostia and been taken prisoner by them. It was now too late to mount another relief expedition, and Rome's fate was sealed. It was not to be taken by storm. But hunger was a more effective weapon. On 17 December 546 a group of Isaurian soldiers opened the Porta Asinaria, through which Belisarius had entered the Eternal City nine years earlier almost to the day, and the Goths rushed in. Bessas and his senior officers slipped away in the confusion. The handful of civilians – not much more than five hundred – who were all that was left of the Roman people, took shelter in the churches until Totila managed to restrain his soldiers. The treasures of the great palaces of the senators and the vast sum of money accumulated by Bessas alike fell to the Gothic king.

As a military objective Rome was without significance. But, as a symbol of that very Christian Roman empire which Justinian hoped to rebuild, it had a powerful hold upon men's minds. The news of its capture by Totila brought gloom and despondency to court circles when it reached Constantinople in the first days of 547. The emperor, however, was not dismayed. He had at last secured a settlement in the east. His new commander in Africa, John the Troglite, was slowly but surely pacifying the province, enrolling the Moorish tribesmen in the Roman service, and building a network of great forts, reminiscent of medieval castles, in which permanent garrisons could be based and the civilian population could take shelter in times of trouble. And he was confident that Belisarius, given time, could deal with Totila.

The Gothic king, after haranguing what remained of the senate and reproaching it with ingratitude and treachery to the Goths, at once sent the deacon Pelagius and a Roman teacher of rhetoric, Theodorus, to Justinian in Constantinople. They bore a letter, the gist of which was this:

> What has happened in Rome I have decided to pass over in silence, as I am sure you know it all. Why I have sent these envoys I shall explain. It is our desire that you should both welcome the blessings of peace yourself and grant them to us. We have examples and reminders of this policy in Anastasius and Theodoric, who reigned not long ago, and who filled their age with peace and all the good things it brings. If this is your desire, I shall look upon you as my father, and you will henceforth have the Goths as your allies against any foe. (Procopius, *History of the Wars* 7. 21. 21–24.)

The ambassadors spelt out the implications of Totila's proposals. They amounted in fact to a return to the status quo before the war, and would have been an admission of the failure of the policy of reunification of the empire by military action. Justinian dismissed the two Romans politely, referring them to Belisarius, who possessed plenipotentiary authority and with whom all discussion of affairs in Italy had to be conducted.

Early in the same year another diplomat arrived in Constantinople. He was Izadh-Gushnasp, chamberlain of king Chosroes, who came to offer his master's compliments to Justinian and to settle a number of questions arising out of the peace treaty signed two years earlier between Persia and the Roman empire. Priceless presents were exchanged, elegant speeches were made in Greek and Pehlevi, as banquet succeeded banquet in the Great Palace overlooking the Bosphorus. Observers noted with amazement that the emperor condescended to admit Izadh-Gushnasp's interpreter Bradoukios to share the couch on which he himself and his distinguished guest reclined. They also did not fail to observe that during the ten months that Izadh-Gushnasp passed in Constantinople no less than a thousand pounds of gold were dispensed by the treasury in presents to him and to his royal master, and this at a time when Belisarius was reduced to virtual inactivity in Italy through shortage of money and men. Justinian had clearly decided to buy peace in the east at almost any price, so that he might have his hands free in the west. The policy, in the light of the circumstances of the time, was a rational one; although later historians have criticized him for preparing, by his neglect of the eastern frontier, the loss of half the empire to the Arabs a century later. But it was not the Persians who conquered Syria, Palestine and Egypt in the seventh century. Neither they nor the Romans ever entertained the idea of a radical and permanent revision of the frontier. But Romans and Persians alike, by the money, weapons and resources which they lavished on their client principalities in Mesopotamia and the Arabian peninsula, helped to spread in the Arab world the military skill and experience which the followers of Mohammed were later to use with such devastating effect. That neither Justinian nor Chosroes foresaw this development is scarcely to their discredit as statesmen. Justinian's own sense of tradition no doubt made diplomatic negotiations with Persia more to his taste than those with states of more recent origin and more doubtful durability. The Romans had dealt with the Parthians and their successors the Sassanid Persians on equal terms for more than six centuries. On the Persian side too men had long memories. So the ten months passed in a mood of nostalgic grandeur. And it may be that preoccupation with protocol prevented Justinian giving affairs in the west the attention they deserved.

Belisarius did his best with the material he had. It was a very good best: by a combination of bluff and speedy manoeuvre he succeeded in retaking Rome without offering the Goths a chance to resist. Totila had threatened to demolish the walls of the city, as he had done those of lesser towns. Belisarius had warned him that so sacrilegious a deed would make his name abhorred by all civilized men. Totila may have been impressed by this argument; and in any case he had already sent Pelagius and Theodorus to Constantinople, and hoped to force peace on Justinian. He halted the demolition which had already begun, and went off to south Italy to recover a number of towns which had fallen into Roman hands. So when in April 547 Belisarius re-entered Rome, he was able to make the city defensible at the cost of a few hastily executed fortification works. Totila realized his mistake and hastened back. His attempts to take the city by assault – which were costly in Gothic lives – failed miserably; and he withdrew his army to Tibur in some dismay. A Gothic attack on Perugia was equally unsuccessful. And soon Totila found himself forced to march up and down Italy to meet Roman threats. Though still desperately short of troops, Belisarius was beginning to regain the initiative.

The death of Theodora

As 548 dawned, there was more and more reason for optimism in the capital. The slow and painstaking measures of John the Troglite in Africa were bearing fruit. More and more of the warlike Moorish tribesmen were incorporated in the Roman army. This was the only possible solution to the problem of holding with a few thousand Roman troops a huge and populous province, many of whose inhabitants were used to bearing arms. The growing network of fortified positions made movement more and more difficult for the rebels. In the summer of 548 they fought and lost a last bloody battle at Campi Catonis near the Tunisian town of El Djem. Thereafter the fighting was confined to mopping up pockets of resistance. Africa had been terribly devastated during these years of civil war. Many of the settled urban and agricultural population had fled to Sicily and elsewhere. Millions of olive trees had been uprooted or burnt – and olive trees take twenty-five years to bear their first fruit. Nevertheless the recovery of Africa was remarkably rapid. Economic and social life soon began to flow in the old channels, and prosperity to return.

In Italy fresh troops continued to arrive, but the reinforcement was too little and too late. All that Belisarius could do was to sail from one Roman strong-point to the next, delivering local attacks on the Goths, who still enjoyed the passive acquiescence – if not always the active support – of the mass of the rural population. Then he had to dash to Rome to deal with an awkward situation. The garrison had killed its commanding officer, who was following the precedent set by Bessas and profiting from the shortage of rations. It then sent a message to Justinian threatening to go over to the Goths if it did not receive its arrears of pay and a free pardon. The emperor had no choice but to agree. Belisarius took charge of the city himself, established an efficient and uncorrupted system of supply and replaced as many as possible of the discontented garrison with soldiers from Sicily.

He was under no illusion that he was making any headway in recovering control of Italy. Hoping that the humiliation of nearly losing Rome once again, and to his own troops, might make Justinian more receptive to his demands, he determined to make a last request for troops and money which would enable him to defeat Totila in the field. The envoy he chose for this delicate mission was his wife Antonina. Her long friendship with Theodora would enable her to bring pressure on the emperor from that quarter. Duly briefed with Belisarius' appreciation of the military situation and his estimate of what was required to change it, she set off by sea from south Italy in the middle of June, while her husband awaited the outcome of her mission with high hopes. Belisarius was not a humble man, and it must have cost him something to appeal to the woman who had nearly ruined him a few years earlier.

The appeal never reached Theodora. For on 28 June 548, before Antonina completed her journey, the empress died of cancer. She was buried, with the pomp and ceremony due to her rank, in the Church of the Holy Apostles, whose construction was begun by Justinian and herself many years earlier and which was not finally consecrated until 28 June 550, two years to a day after her death. Antonina saw that her mission was hopeless: the grief-stricken emperor was in no condition to make major decisions of policy. So she asked that her husband might be recalled. Hostilities had recently broken out again in Lazica, which was not covered by the peace treaty with Persia, and Justinian had in mind sending Belisarius once again to the eastern front. So in late autumn 548 the great marshal left Italy for the last time, his task uncompleted.

None of the historians of the period has described Justinian's reaction to the death of Theodora. He had no doubt had some months to prepare himself, and he was not a man to give away his feelings. It may be possible to infer something from an event which took place many years later. In 559 an army of Huns from beyond the Danube invaded Thrace and advanced, slaughtering and pillaging, to within thirty miles of Constantinople. Belisarius, by now elderly and overweight, was recalled from retirement to deal with the menace; and he hastily gathered together a scratch force of citizen militia. Age and idleness had not dulled his tactical brilliance, and he succeeded in convincing the Huns that his pitiful force was many times larger than it actually was. Outmanoeuvred and demoralized, they were defeated with the loss of four hundred dead. Meanwhile, Justinian, jealous of Belisarius' renewed glory, recalled him and took the field himself, for the first and last time. He was by now about seventy-seven. Needless to say, there was no battle. It was all done by diplomacy and money, and soon the Huns were being seen across the Danube by the emperor's nephew Justin, their pockets filled with the rich ransom paid by the emperor for the Roman prisoners they had taken. On 11 August Justinian made a triumphal entry into his capital after this curious victory. The official record of the ostentatious ceremony survives; it states that as the procession passed before the Church of the Holy Apostles it halted while the emperor went in to offer a prayer and light candles before Theodora's tomb.

7 The bitter fruits of victory

The situation in Italy called for action, but action was precisely what Justinian was incapable of in 548, after Theodora's death. Belisarius was recalled, but no new commander-in-chief was appointed. In early summer the Slavs invaded Illyricum from across the Danube. They took strong-point after strong-point as no attempt was made to relieve them, penetrated as far as Dyrrhachium (Durazzo) and withdrew unmolested with their booty and their long column of prisoners destined for the slave markets. All the while the Roman army in Illyricum, fifteen thousand strong, followed closely on their heels but never ventured to engage them, whether from lack of courage or from lack of clear orders. In Egypt the Nile flood was abnormally large, and the rich delta lands remained under water till long after the accustomed time for sowing. In the Bosphorus a sea monster – probably a killer whale – which for years had terrorized fishermen was washed ashore; it was found to be thirty cubits long and ten wide. A number of minor earthquakes in Constantinople and elsewhere contributed to the general malaise. Prophets of doom, magicians and soothsayers found a ready hearing. Soon the dissatisfaction of the people took a political turn. There were riots in the capital, led by the circus factions, which were repressed with no little bloodshed.

Now that Theodora was gone, the emperor turned for support to two of his oldest collaborators, his cousin Germanus and Belisarius. Belisarius was appointed Master of Soldiers in the east, but kept in the capital and put in command of the imperial bodyguard. Justinian treated him with the utmost regard, and was clearly anxious to have him at hand. A gilded statue of the great marshal was set up in one of the squares of Constantinople by the emperor's order. All this may have been comforting to both Justinian and Belisarius, but it did nothing to solve the pressing military problems of the empire.

Reminded of his own mortality by the death of Theodora, Justinian must have turned his thoughts to the question of the succession. He was far too sure of the value of his own work to leave its continuation to chance. Germanus was the obvious successor: a man of long military experience, well-liked by all classes, steady and reliable; but without the personal ambition that might make him wish to hasten his succession. Now that Theodora was gone, her implacable enmity no longer stood in his way. It is likely that Justinian had Germanus in mind as Belisarius' successor in Italy. But in the meantime a curious conspiracy came to light. The Armenian general Artabanus, in concert with another Armenian, Arsaces, sought a secret interview with Justin, the elder son of Germanus. Pointing out to the young man that Germanus and his whole family had been unjustly kept in the background, and playing upon the ill-feeling recently aroused over the division of the rich estate of Boraides, another cousin of the emperor, the Armenians proposed that Justinian be assassinated and Germanus put in his place.

Justin had the presence of mind to protest that neither he nor his father would have anything to do with such a project, and at once reported the proposal to Germanus. Germanus was in a quandary: to report the proposal to Justinian and to keep silence might be equally dangerous. He decided to take into his confidence Marcellus, the Count of the Excubitors, a palace officer of grim and sombre character but of unquestioned probity. Marcellus arranged an interview between Germanus and one of the conspirators, at which Leontius, a distinguished jurisconsult, was present concealed behind a curtain. The Armenian repeated the proposal to assassinate Justinian and Belisarius and added Marcellus to the list of proposed victims. Meanwhile Germanus had taken the precaution of informing two senior military colleagues of what was afoot. There followed a trial for high treason before the senate. Germanus and Justin were pronounced innocent thanks to the evidence of Marcellus, Leontius, and the two military officers. But a few days later, at a meeting of the emperor's council, Justinian attacked his cousin bitterly for not having informed him of the conspiracy at once. As for the conspirators, they were treated with exemplary clemency. Artabanus was merely removed from office and confined to his palace in the capital; within a year he was once again appointed to an important military command in Sicily.

Such was the official version of these events. What really happened we shall never know, since all the participants took the utmost care to cover up their tracks. For Justinian, however, this was a further blow; and his confidence in Germanus was gravely shaken.

Final victory in Italy

When the campaigning season reopened in the spring of 549, there was still no unified command in Italy, and no clear directive from Constantinople. The Gothic fleet ravaged the coastal cities of Dalmatia, challenging that sea power without which Justinian's restoration of a Mediterranean empire was an impossible dream. In early summer Totila once again led the Gothic army against Rome. The city was garrisoned by three thousand elite troops under a tried and resolute officer, Diogenes, who had long served under Belisarius; and the walls were once again in good repair. But the Goths had their agents even among the Roman soldiers. On 16 January 550 some disaffected Isaurians opened the Porta Ostiensis – near the immense church of S. Paolo fuori le Mura – and the Goths rushed in. Most of the garrison was put to the sword, and the survivors forced to take service under the Goths. Diogenes and a few of his officers succeeded in making their way under the cover of the winter night to Civitavecchia, the only fortress nearby to remain in Roman hands.

The last time Totila had held Rome, he had behaved as an invader, as had Alaric and Gaiseric before him. This time he conducted himself as a legitimate sovereign, so confident was he in his fortune. The fugitive inhabitants of the Eternal City were sought out in their refuges throughout Italy and persuaded to return. Such

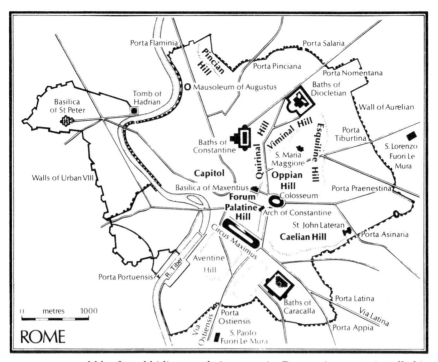

Porta Flaminia
Porta Salaria
Pincian Hill
Porta Pinciana
Porta Nomentana
Tomb of Hadrian
Mausoleum of Augustus
Baths of Diocletian
Basilica of St Peter
Wall of Aurelian
Baths of Constantine
Viminal Hill
Esquiline Hill
Porta Tiburtina
S. Lorenzo Fuori Le Mura
Quirinal Hill
S. Maria Maggiore
Walls of Urban VIII
Capitol
Oppian Hill
Basilica of Maxentius
Colosseum
Porta Praenestina
Forum
Palatine Hill
Arch of Constantine
Porta Asinaria
St John Lateran
Caelian Hill
Circus Maximus
R. Tiber
Aventine Hill
Porta Portuensis
Porta Latina
Baths of Caracalla
Via Latina
0 metres 1000
Via Ostiensis
Porta Ostiensis
Porta Appia
ROME
S. Paolo Fuori Le Mura

senators as could be found hiding on their estates in Campania were reinstalled in the city. For the first time Goths were settled in Rome. In the summer of 550 Totila, who had succeeded in rounding up the necessary charioteers and other skilled artistes, presided at chariot-races in the Circus Maximus, an unequivocal assertion of sovereignty. Justinian was sensitive enough to be wounded by such a blow to his prestige. When Totila sent an embassy to Constantinople proposing peace terms which would have put him in the position which Theodoric had held, the emperor refused to receive the envoys: there was to be no compromise. Totila's answer to this rebuff was an invasion of Sicily in 550. In spite of the successes which his fleet had scored, the Gothic king was too much of a realist to try to hold the island. But when he withdrew from Sicily at the end of 550, not only had he enriched his war-chest with a vast quantity of booty, he had struck a blow at Roman prestige which echoed from end to end of the Mediterranean. And he had hurt Justinian personally. For in the enactment which regulated the affairs of Sicily after its capture by Belisarius, it was made clear that the whole island and its revenues were to form part of the emperor's patrimony, and its administration to depend directly upon the emperor, without the intervention of a Praetorian Prefect.

It was rather the news of the invasion of Sicily than that of the capture of Rome which finally forced Justinian's hand. In the summer of 550 he appointed Germanus commander-in-chief in Italy, and promised him more troops and money than Belisarius had ever had. At the same time he gave him in marriage as his second wife the Gothic princess Matasuntha, widow of King Vitiges and grand-daughter of Theodoric. The implications of this marriage and this military command were not lost on contemporaries. Matasuntha's descent from the ancient royal line of the Amals would win her widespread support among the Goths, particularly the nobility. Germanus himself was *persona grata* to the Roman landowning aristocracy, both of east and of west. The western Roman upper classes, though by now wholly alienated from Totila, were far from enthusiastic to be subject to Constantinople. They had their traditions; and they could not expect to act as an effective pressure-group in the remote court by the Bosphorus. Though there is nowhere a direct statement of Justinian's intentions, it is hard to resist the conclusion that he hoped, if all went well, to restore the western Roman empire, with Germanus as junior co-emperor in the west and successor designate to himself. The restored western empire would be one in which Roman and Goth were once again reconciled. All other considerations apart, Italy would not be defensible against Franks, Alamans and Lombards without the Gothic army. Contemporaries saw in the still unborn child of Germanus and Matasuntha a pledge of the everlasting amity of Goth and Roman.

Germanus had great resources put at his disposal by Justinian. And his own personal fortune enabled him to supplement the imperial army with mercenaries from beyond the Danube paid for out of his own pocket. He was well liked by the army, and popular throughout the empire. The news of his appointment, his marriage and his military preparations produced disquiet and indecision among the Goths, as indeed it was intended to do. The isolated Roman garrisons, and the main Roman force at Ravenna, felt that the tide of fortune was at last turning. The new forces were massed in Illyria, and were to enter Italy by land from the north-east. A fresh Slavonic invasion, which penetrated as far as Naissus (Nish) delayed the advance to Italy. Such, however, was Germanus' reputation, and the memory of the defeat which he had inflicted on their kinsmen the Antae a quarter of a century earlier, that the Slavs hastily retreated before him into Dalmatia without offering battle. Then the unforeseen happened: Germanus fell ill and died at his headquarters in Sardica (Sofia) at the beginning of autumn. The son born to him and Matasuntha, who was to symbolize the union of Goth and Roman, was born posthumously. There was to be no western emperor, and no successor designate for Justinian.

Political solutions would have to wait. But the military problem was pressing, and Justinian remained unshaken in his resolve to put an end to the Gothic kingdom by destroying its armed forces. The man who in the spring of 551 was appointed commander-in-chief in the west, and who was given unprecedented support in troops and money, was the Praepositus of the Sacred Bedchamber, the eunuch Narses. The new commander was already in his early seventies. But his mind was as sharp, his judgment as unclouded and his action as resolute as they had ever been. His military experience was certainly limited. He had been for a time joint commander in Italy with Belisarius. But he was a close friend of John, the nephew of Vitalian and senior officer remaining in the west, upon whom he could rely for advice on technical matters. He had studied the arts of war. And above all he had enjoyed the daily confidence of Justinian and Theodora for twenty years. The authority which he carried was unmatched save by the emperor himself and Belisarius. And being a eunuch he was not a candidate for the imperial purple. A strange choice, then, and one which must have caused soul-searching among the generals; but a wise one. Justinian realized that Roman authority would never be firmly established in Italy by tactical victories, however brilliant, now that Totila was able to operate with massive support from the peasantry and the poorer classes of the cities. Nothing would suffice but the physical annihilation of the Gothic army, in other words of the whole male population of military age, in so far as they were not willing to serve under Roman command. The empire had the resources to do this. What was needed was to concentrate them at the right time and place. The problem was one of logistics rather than of tactics; and in such matters Narses' long experience was unparalleled. That he proved in fact to be a good field commander was incidental, and merely made things easier.

Narses left Constantinople in spring 551. The winter months had no doubt been spent in discussing the scale and strategy of the campaign. Narses, who had on earlier occasions shown that he was not afraid to speak his mind to the emperor, insisted on fulfilment of all his conditions in regard to men, ships, equipment and money. He spent the summer making a tour of inspection of military establishments in Thrace and Illyria and did not reach his headquarters at Salona (Solin, near Split) until autumn. Totila, realizing that he was now to meet the full force of the Roman empire, rose to the occasion with typical grandeur of design. He took Civitavecchia, sent an army to besiege Ancona and a fleet of forty ships to blockade the port from the sea and despatched the main body of the Gothic fleet, now some three hundred vessels, to ravage Corfu and the neighbouring mainland and to interfere with Roman supply-ships sailing to the invasion bases in Dalmatia. However a dash across the Adriatic by John, nephew of Vitalian, in summer 551 led to the defeat of the Ostrogoth fleet off Ancona and the withdrawal of the besieging army. The more far-seeing Gothic leaders, among whom Totila must be numbered, saw in this defeat the beginning of the end. But their resolution did not flag.

In autumn 551 a Gothic fleet succeeded in ousting the unsuspecting Roman garrisons from Corsica and Sardinia, which came under the command of John the Troglite in Africa. At the same time a Gothic army began the siege of Croton in Calabria, the last remaining Roman naval base in those regions. It is always hard to see what the losers in a war were trying to do. And there is not much information on the details of military operations in Italy at this period, since the most reliable informant, Procopius, left the theatre of war with his master Belisarius. But it does appear that Totila was trying to establish Gothic naval superiority in western waters, now that his position in the Adriatic had been drastically weakened. The fact that he left Gothic garrisons in several key ports of Sicily when the main Gothic force withdrew fits this hypothesis. The Mediterranean falls into two clearly defined halves, and there have been many periods in its history when sea power has been divided into two zones. Whether Totila's western orientation implied a search for alliances in the west is impossible to say. They would not have been far to seek. The Visigothic kingdom in Spain was worried by the strengthening of the Roman garrisons on the south shore of the Straits of Gibraltar. And dissidence and rebellion within the Visigothic royal house provided ample opportunity for outside intervention. But whatever may have been Totila's long-term plans – and all that is known of the man strengthens the conviction that he did have long-term plans – they were never brought to fruition.

In April 552 Narses left Salona at the head of an army of at least thirty thousand men. The interior of Istria and Venetia were occupied by a Frankish army which was trying to profit by the confused state of affairs in Italy. And Totila's general Teia had breached the dykes of the Po and its tributaries, making the plain of north Italy impassable to an army from Verona to the sea. Narses surmounted these difficulties by marching along the coast and building pontoon bridges over the mouths of the river. On 6 June he entered Ravenna, bringing with him money to meet all the arrears of pay of the Roman forces in Italy. After only nine days' delay he set off again southwards. The Gothic garrison of Rimini tried in vain to halt his march. Turning westwards, the Roman army crossed the Appennines by an easy pass and pressed on down the Via Flaminia through Tuscany. Totila, who had by this time been joined by Teia and his corps, marched from Rome up the same road to meet them. In the last days of June the two armies met at Busta Gallorum, where in 295 BC the Romans had won a great victory over the Gauls. This was the first and the last great infantry battle of the war. Narses, unlike Belisarius, did not share the disdain for unmounted troops which was so general in late antiquity. Indeed he caused many of his cavalry units to fight on foot, while his superbly trained archers provided covering fire. The Goths had archers too; but in accuracy and rate of fire they were no match for the Romans, and Totila finally ordered them to throw away their bows and fight at close quarters with their spears. The Goths were outnumbered and outfought. Six thousand of them fell on the field of battle, and many more were killed in the pursuit which ensued. Totila himself was fatally wounded and died a few hours later in the village of Caprara.

The outcome of the war was decided. The power and wealth of the empire had at last been concentrated in Italy, and all hope of a settlement favourable to the Goths was lost. Just because compromise was now ruled out, they fought on with the courage of despair. The Gothic leaders who had survived the battle gathered at Pavia, where they elected Teia as king. Meanwhile Narses continued his march southwards, taking the Gothic strong-points of Perugia and Narni, and storming Rome. There were still considerable Gothic forces at large in southern Italy. When the Roman senators who had taken refuge in Campania tried to return to Rome, a

Gothic detachment fell upon them and massacred them. When Narses began his advance into Italy, Totila had obliged the leading men of the cities of Italy to send their sons to the Gothic headquarters as hostages. Teia now had these young men put to death. Totila had similarly deposited the reserves of bullion and treasure of the Ostrogoth kingdom in Cumae, which was heavily garrisoned. It was against Cumae, on the coast west of Naples, that Narses next directed his attack, beginning regular siege operations against the well-defended city. Teia resolved to try to relieve the garrison of Cumae, which was under the command of his brother Aligern. By forced marches through the high Appennines he succeeded in eluding the Roman forces who were trying to block his route to the south; and by early autumn had occupied a strong position on the southern slopes of Mount Vesuvius, not far from the ruins of Pompeii. From this position he had access to the sea, where the Gothic fleet was still operating from its bases in Calabria and Sardinia. He probably hoped to relieve Cumae by sea. But he reckoned without Narses, who at once marched the main body of his army to Vesuvius and encamped opposite the Goths, separated from them only by the ravine of a mountain torrent, the Dracon. For two months the two armies faced one another, while Narses waited for his plans to take effect. The Goths were being supplied by sea, and their defensive position was a strong one. However Narses had ordered the Roman fleet to sail round from the Adriatic. When at last it appeared off Campania, the Gothic admiral, mindful of the crushing defeat he had suffered the previous year, surrendered to the Romans. With their supplies now cut off, and under continuous bombardment from the siege engines which Narses had mounted on high wooden towers on the Roman side of the ravine, the Goths could hold out no longer. They retreated a few miles southwards to the Mons Lactarius, a position protected by steep crags and virtually impregnable; but they no longer had any food. The Romans closed in on them. Surrounded on all sides, the Goths waited for a few days and then on 30 October made a sudden assault on the besieging Romans, in a desperate attempt to break out. The battle consisted of closequarter fighting by infantry, with Teia in the front rank among his soldiers. Before long he was killed; and the Romans displayed his head upon a spear, in the hope of inducing the Goths to surrender. Their hope was vain. All day long the grim butchery continued, until darkness forced both sides to fall back. The next morning the fighting began again. Towards evening the surviving Goths agreed to negotiate with Narses, and a truce was declared. According to one account, they were permitted to take their movable property and settle anywhere outside of Roman territory. According to another they were allowed to return to their homes in peace. It mattered little, for they were no longer dangerous. The bulk of the fighting men and almost all the leaders were dead, and as a nation the Ostrogoths had ceased to exist.

What remained were mopping-up operations of little interest. Slowly the Gothic garrisons here and there in central Italy and in Liguria were starved or beaten into surrender. Compsa, the last Gothic garrison south of the Po, held out till spring 555. Verona and Brescia remained in Gothic hands even longer. It was not until 20 July 561 that Narses took Verona, the last Gothic stronghold, and sent the keys of the city to Justinian as a token that the whole of Italy, from the Straits of Messina to the loftiest peaks of the Alps, had at last been restored to the Imperium Romanum.

While the slow conquest and pacification of Italy had been going on, Justinian had turned his attention to the westernmost of the barbarian kingdoms established on the former territory of the empire, that of the Visigoths in Spain. The Visigoths, like the Vandals and the Ostrogoths, were Arians. The relations between the ruling minority of Goths, who alone could bear arms, and the Roman majority were on the whole friendly. But there were sources of friction, which could be exploited by the government in Constantinople.

The lightning success of Belisarius in Africa had greatly alarmed the Visigoths. Their king Theodis took great pains not to provide the Romans with a *casus belli*, and rejected all appeals for help from the Vandals. As an additional precaution he seems to have occupied the Vandal fortress of Septem (Ceuta) across the Straits of Gibraltar from Spain. It was no doubt to evict this Visigothic garrison that in 534 Belisarius had sent a detachment from Carthage to Septem. He built a great fortress on the peninsula, which remained a distant outpost of Constantinople until it was surrendered to the Arabs by its commander in 711. In the meantime the Roman force remained there, supported by a fleet. The Visigoths were by now under no illusions about the emperor's ultimate intention.

For thirteen years there was an uneasy peace at the western end of the Mediterranean. By 547 things were going badly for the Romans. Most of Italy was in the control of Totila, and a large-scale Berber revolt was raging in Africa. King Theodis, now an old man, decided that it was safe to evict the Roman garrison from Septem and thereby seize control of the vital crossing from Africa to Europe. His troops crossed the straits and set siege to Septem. The Roman commander in Africa, John the Troglite, had clear instructions that Septem must at all costs be held. Difficult though his situation was, he detached a considerable force and sent it off by sea to relieve the besieged fortress. They took the Visigothic army by surprise and destroyed it. The explanation of this untoward defeat given by Visigothic sources is that the Romans attacked on a Sunday, when the pious Visigoths were all attending religious services. Ruling Visigothic circles were dismayed, and fell into disarray. Within a year King Theodis was assassinated, and a little later his successor Theodegisel met the same fate.

Justinian always preferred to support one side in a civil war rather than to undertake a war of aggression. Roman agents passed to and fro between Spain and their bases in Septem and in the Balearics preparing the ground. It was not long before the emperor was given just the chance he was waiting for. In 551 a member of the Visigothic royal family, Athanagild, rebelled against King Agila, the successor of Theodegisel, and appealed to Justinian for help. At about the same time the Roman inhabitants of Cordova rose in revolt against Agila, and defeated the army which he sent to repress them. Justinian was not slow to react. In spite of the heavy military commitments in Italy, he sent a small force to Spain in the spring of 552 to support Athanagild and to protect the citizens of Cordova. Its commander, a western Roman named Liberius, was a man of at least eighty-five, who had been Praetorian Prefect of Italy under Theodoric sixty years earlier, had for twenty-five years been governor of Southern Gaul when it was a province of the Ostrogothic kingdom and had lately been in command against Totila in Sicily. Not the dashing young leader of a forlorn hope, but an expert in western affairs. In particular his long years in Gaul on the very frontier of Visigothic Spain would have given him valuable contacts in that country.

Justinian was counting on a political rather than a military victory. And indeed the Visigothic army, torn between Agila and Athanagild, seems to have offered little resistance. The imperial troops swiftly occupied the territory between the sea and the line of the Segura and the Guadalquivir, as well as seizing the bridgehead of Cordova to the north of the river. Agila tried to encircle the armies of Liberius and Athanagild by making a counter-attack against Seville. But it was easily repulsed. In spring 555 Agila was murdered by his own troops, who rallied to the cause of Athanagild. For a time it looked as though Justinian had won Spain almost without a battle. But Athanagild had no intention of becoming a puppet of the emperor; and in any case he could only retain the loyalty of his own people by taking an independent stand. So he thanked the Roman commander and requested him to withdraw his troops as they were no longer needed. In fact the Roman troops, who were not numerous and who depended on a long and uncertain line of communication, had to cede a good deal of the territory which they had conquered. But the empire retained a foothold in Spain until long after Justinian's death. The exact frontiers of the province are not certain. It included the towns of Assidona (Medina Sidonia), Seguntia (Gisgonza), Malaga, Basti (Baza), Cartagena and Cordova, and may have comprised some points in the Algarve in southern Portugal. At any rate Justinian's dominions now extended to the Atlantic. The new province was attached for civil purposes to the Praetorian Prefecture of Africa, its garrison was put under the command of a separate Master of Soldiers in Spain, reporting directly to the emperor. The Guadalquivir frontier was to be regarded as merely a temporary truce-line. In the meantime, the first task was the destruction of the remaining centres of Ostrogothic power in north Italy, a task which Narses pursued with unswerving concentration to the end.

The narrative has been carried on to 561 in order to give a continuous account of the reconquest of Italy, the cornerstone of Justinian's programme of restoration. It is time now to return to the 540s and to look at other aspects of the problems of the empire.

In 546, when Totila was hammering on the gates of Rome and the fruits of ten years of war seemed all but lost, the Church of S. Vitale in Ravenna was completed. Justinian determined to make of the new church a symbol of his claim to be the only legitimate sovereign in Italy, the man to whose hands God had entrusted the Christian empire. Artists were sent from Constantinople to make mosaic portraits of Justinian and Theodora in the apse of the new church; portraits which by their splendour would outdo all that Theodoric had done to adorn his capital, and by their symbolism would declare to all that Justinian and his consort were the elect of the Lord. The portraits are still there, as impressive and moving as on the day they were unveiled. They give us some idea of the metropolitan art of the age of Justinian, of which so few examples have survived through centuries of wars, earthquakes and pillage – such mosaics were particularly attractive to those in search of booty, since they contained minute cubes of gilded glass, which looked like gold.

On one side of the apse Justinian is represented bringing his offering to the church; on the other side Theodora. On Justinian's left stands Archbishop Maximian. Among the other dignitaries represented, the man on Justinian's right, with a long moustache, may well be Belisarius. The others cannot be identified, but they are certainly portraits of individuals and not conventional figures. Behind the emperor and his dignitaries are seen four members of the palace guard, their spears sloped on their right shoulders, the one visible shield bearing the Chi-Rho monogram of Christ. The emperor is wearing a purple chlamys, attached on his right shoulder by a huge jewelled brooch. On his head is a jewelled diadem, from which hang two large pearls on each side. On his feet are the jewelled purple shoes which were one of the insignia of monarchy. He carries a large golden paten. And his head is surrounded by a nimbus. The dignitaries who accompany him wear white garments, the effect of which is to emphasize still more the distinction between the emperor and his entourage.

In the facing mosaic Theodora, who is represented as taller than any of the other figures, wears a long purple robe over a white dress with a deep brocade fringe. On the fringe are embroidered the Three Kings bringing their offerings to the infant Christ, a theme which parallels that of the mosaic itself. The empress wears an elaborate diadem, from which depend four strings of pearls. She has turquoise earrings, a rectangular pendant of gold and malachite, and a necklace of bluish stones. Her shoes are jewelled. Her head is surrounded by a nimbus. She carries a jewelled gold chalice. On her right are two beardless male figures, presumably eunuchs belonging to her bedchamber. One wears a white cloak and one a yellow cloak, both over white tunics. On her left appear seven female figures, doubtless ladies of her suite. All are richly dressed in long brocaded and jewelled garments and wear stoles of various colours. On the extreme left of the mosaic stands an elaborate marble font surmounted by a dove with outspread wings. An embroidered curtain in front of – or behind (there is no true perspective) – the font is held aside by the right arm of one of the eunuchs.

The figures are all unnaturally elongated, and curiously two-dimensional. Their bodies are depicted frontally, although they are intended to be moving across the plane of the mosaic. They have no connection with their background. That of the

Justinian mosaic is a plain gold surface surmounted by a design of green lozenges with plant motifs in one corner. That of the Theodora mosaic is more varied: behind the empress herself is a gold apse surmounted by a vault in shades of green, resting on two columns with Doric capitals; the font is backed by a rectangular niche; and the ladies-in-waiting by a gold surface surmounted by a red, white and blue hanging.

The almost unbelievable richness of the colour, the hieratic, other-worldly figures and the religious significance of the iconography were meant to impress the beholder with the power, in this world and the next, of the principal figures. They are a superb example of the image of himself which Justinian wished to project in Italy at this dark hour when so many of his plans seemed to be ruined. The emperor had abated none of his claims to ecumenical sovereignty.

It may be asked whether the portraits are in any sense likenesses of Justinian and Theodora. Lifelike resemblance was not demanded of imperial portraits in antiquity – any more than it is demanded of royal portraits on coins or postage stamps today. Theodora, who was about fifty at the time, and perhaps already in her terminal illness, is no doubt made to look younger than she actually was. Justinian's face is paler than the literary descriptions of him would lead us to expect. The artist has not used any of the red colour which appears on the cheeks of Archbishop Maximian and certain of the other figures. Yet there can be no doubt when the composition as a whole is viewed, with its strongly individual faces, that these are likenesses – albeit somewhat idealized – of Justinian and Theodora, and not mere conventional representations of rulers. One has only to look at the long procession of martyrs over the colonnade of the nave of the near-contemporary church of S. Apollinare Nuovo at Ravenna, who are entirely conventional and unindividualized, to be aware of the difference. Here then, in the apse of S. Vitale, we have the closest surviving likeness of Justinian and Theodora.

The nearby church of S. Apollinare Nuovo was constructed by Theodoric as an Arian place of worship. Towards the end of the reign of Justinian it was reconsecrated as a Catholic church by Archbishop Agnellus (553-66). Agnellus had two mosaics placed on the façade, representing Justinian and himself. The portrait of Justinian survives, somewhat damaged. It shows a much broader, heavier face, not at all like that in S. Vitale. But it has recently been convincingly argued that this was originally a portrait of Theodoric, and that Agnellus merely changed some of the features and the inscription. If so one wonders what the surviving Goths of Ravenna thought when they saw the portrait of their great king clumsily relabelled in the interests of Byzantine political propaganda.

8 Emperor and Pope

In spite of his occasional protestations that the spheres of emperor and patriarch were separate, Justinian was not the man to make a clear-cut distinction in practice between church and state. He was responsible for the correct religious views of all his subjects. The history of the church since the age of Constantine showed that uniformity of doctrine was not to be obtained by administrative methods, backed in the last resort by the sanction of force – or at any rate not by these alone. And Justinian, autocrat though he was by temperament, preferred persuasion to force.

The major religious problem throughout his reign was that of the nature of Christ. Did he combine in himself divine and human natures in an indissoluble whole, as the ecumenical Council of Chalcedon had decided in 451, or did his divine nature so predominate over his human nature as to make him God rather than man, as the Monophysites believed. The problem had sharp political overtones. For reasons which perhaps lie deep in the cultural past of the Mediterranean world, the south-eastern provinces of the empire, Egypt, Syria and Palestine, had strong Monophysite sympathies. In Egypt the whole countryside, outside the Greek city of Alexandria, was by the sixth century solidly Monophysite. The Monophysite church, whose liturgy and religious literature was in Coptic – the native tongue of the mass of the population – provided the framework for the nationalist and separatist sentiments of a vast and industrious population only superficially hellenized. In Syria and Palestine the position was less clear. But a vigorous Monophysite literature in Syriac bore witness to a cultural alienation which could readily turn to political separatism. The ultimate solution was to convince the Monophysites of the error of their ways, and to restore throughout the east a uniform Chalcedonian orthodoxy. In the meantime nothing must be done to alienate still further the inhabitants of these eastern provinces. So Justinian was forced by the logic of the situation to combine constant pressure and occasional selective persecution with concessions to the Monophysites, provided they could be made without sacrifice of principle. In this delicate task he was helped by Theodora's sincere, if somewhat emotional, attachment to the Monophysite cause. The imperial pair could speak with two voices: the rigidity of Justinian's official policy could be tempered by the backstairs intrigues of his wife.

Direct interference in Egypt was on the whole avoided. Provided the Egyptians paid their taxes and supplied the cheap corn needed to feed the capital, they could be left to wallow in their heresy.

Syria was a different matter. It was a strategically sensitive region, lying as it did along the Persian frontier. It merged imperceptibly into Asia Minor, the heartland of the eastern empire. And the Syrians were forceful, enterprising men, who played an important role in the life of the empire. So it was above all in regard to

Syria that Justinian sought to maintain a delicate balance, sometimes aided, occasionally thwarted, by his passionate and unscrupulous empress.

All this would have been difficult enough. But there was also the problem of the west. Monophysite views had never taken root in the Latin world, where the mass of the Roman population was solidly Chalcedonian. Its Gothic masters adhered to Arianism, a heresy of a different kind, originating in the fourth century and by now only of marginal importance in the Roman world. If Justinian wished to reconquer and hold the lost western provinces, he must be seen to be the champion of Chalcedonian orthodoxy. Above all he must retain the support of the Roman Church, which in the absence of an emperor had attained a power and independence unknown in the Greek east. If he appeared by his concessions to Monophysite views to be deviating from the views of Rome, his mission of restoration would at once lose credibility in the west – not only in Italy, the immediate theatre of operations, but in Africa, in Visigothic Spain, where Justinian was anxious to establish a foothold, and in Merovingian Gaul where he hoped to find allies against the heretical Goths. Thus the problem which faced Justinian was not merely that of avoiding an open breach between the Monophysite east and the Chalcedonian ruling circles of Constantinople, but of keeping the east in communion with the Pope in Rome. It was a task which called for all of Justinian's skill, flexibility, and powers of diplomacy. Above all it required patience, and as men grow older their patience often becomes exhausted.

In the first fifteen years of Justinian's reign and the first twenty-five of his effective power his policy of persecution combined with concession had reduced Monophysitism outside Egypt to apparent powerlessness. The ruling classes in the cities were firmly Chalcedonian. Monophysite bishops, hounded by emperor and patriarch, were not replaced when they died, resigned or were exiled. Justinian might reasonably expect that in his lifetime Monophysitism outside Egypt might become a vestigial survival, a mere historical curiosity, and that thus any possible source of tension between himself and the Pope would be removed. In the meantime Theodora's Monophysite sympathies provided a useful safety-valve. And her monastery in the Great Palace, which Justinian often visited, kept in honourable retirement in the capital many Monophysite leaders who might otherwise have been active in Syria.

In 543, however, Theodosius, the exiled Monophysite Patriarch of Alexandria, consecrated as bishop of Edessa a fanatical Syriac-speaking monk from Mesopotamia, Jacob Baradaeus. Jacob had no hope of ever setting foot in Edessa, a key city of northern Syria, firmly held by a Chalcedonian bishop; but from the Monophysites' point of view the claim was worth making. Theodora had a hand in his consecration, for the Monophysite king of one of the Arab buffer-states, Harith the Ghassanid, whose support had to be maintained at all costs, had beseeched her to intervene so that a Monophysite bishop might be ordained for his people. So the imperial authorities turned a blind eye to Theodosius' ordination of

Jacob Baradaeus. They soon had cause to regret their laxness. Jacob combined a ferocious asceticism, which won him the admiration and devotion of the mass of the oppressed Syrian peasantry, with a talent for underground organization which made him the ideal leader of an embryo resistance movement. Moving with lightning speed, and sure of concealment by his humble followers, he travelled from city to city and from province to province, rousing the dying faith of the Monophysite masses, re-establishing their ecclesiastical hierarchy and demonstrating the powerlessness of the imperial authorities to grapple with the force of an idea, backed up by organization. Jacob's activity, which lasted until his death, extended not only throughout Syria, but both into Egypt and throughout the whole of Asia Minor. He even ventured into Constantinople itself, where he ordained twelve bishops. In all he ordained about thirty bishops and some thousands of priests and deacons. Everywhere the Chalcedonian hierarchy felt its position challenged, and everywhere the confidence of the Monophysites was restored. In Alexandria the orthodox patriarch Zoilus had to flee the city in 546 as a result of disorders which the army suppressed with difficulty, and his successors found themselves involved in a series of unsavoury financial scandals. All this strengthened the position of the Monophysites.

Some time between 548 and 565 Justinian founded the monastery on Mount Sinai later dedicated to St. Catherine, in the valley below the mountain where Moses received the tablets of the law, on the traditional site of the Burning Bush. The region had been a centre for hermits and ascetics since the fourth century, and it was primarily to provide protection for these against Beduin raids that the monastery was established. It was surrounded by a formidable defensive wall, and a detachment of soldiers from Thrace was stationed nearby. At the same time it was probably intended to be a focus of Chalcedonian orthodoxy in a region dominated by Monophysite sympathies, and a visible symbol and reminder of the faith of the emperor. The monastery is still there, and still houses a community of Greek Orthodox monks. Of its numerous buildings only the wall and the church date from the original foundation. During repair work some years ago an inscription was revealed on one of the roof-beams of the church commemorating the late empress Theodora, and thus showing that the church was built after her death in 548. The monastery became in the course of centuries a treasure-house of manuscripts and works of art. The Codex Sinaiticus, one of the oldest manuscripts of the Bible, was discovered there by Konstantin Tischendorff in 1844; it is now in the British Library in London. Among the early icons in the monastery the recently discovered superb St. Peter may well have been painted in the lifetime of Justinian.

The revival of Monophysitism, at the very moment when things were going badly for the imperial armies in Italy, put Justinian in a dilemma: he needed to establish his claim in the west to be God's chosen vessel; but in western eyes he appeared to be temporizing with an abominable heresy.

A great deal of his time in 543 was spent in pondering the problem of building a bridge to the dissident Monophysites without losing credibility in the west. His principal religious adviser at the time, Theodore Ascidas, Metropolitan of Caesarea, an ambitious and intriguing cleric, suggested that the way out was to issue a formal condemnation of Nestorianism, which was anathema to Chalcedonians and Monophysites alike. Nestorius had in the previous century expounded the view that Christ was essentially a man, chosen as such by God to be the vehicle for a superimposed divine nature. His doctrines had considerable support among Christian communities in Persia and further east, but little in the Roman empire. After much discussion with Theodore Ascidas, the emperor issued, at the end of 543 or beginning of 544, an edict condemning the works and the person of Theodore of Mopsuestia and certain works of Theodoret of Cyrus and Ibas of Edessa. These early fifth-century theologians had put forward views which could be interpreted, in the light of what happened later, as Nestorian. Here, Justinian felt, was common ground for all Christians from Alexandria to Rome. There is nothing that unites men so much as a common enemy.

The Monophysites received the imperial decree with marked coolness. What they wanted was condemnation not of Nestorianism but of the doctrines approved at Chalcedon. In the Greek east a judicious combination of pressure and patronage secured the assent of most leading clerics, including Menas the Patriarch of Constantinople. In the west, on the other hand, where men knew little of Nestorianism and cared less, the edict provoked a storm. The emperor was on his own initiative going beyond the positions agreed upon at Chalcedon, and making concessions to a hateful Egyptian doctrine. Stephen, the *apocrisiarius* or legate in Constantinople of Pope Vigilius, excommunicated Patriarch Menas, an urgent warning to Justinian of what the Pope's reaction was likely to be.

In view of the state of affairs in Italy where Totila had snatched victory from the jaws of defeat, and in Africa, where Solomon had only begun the pacification of the country, the emperor needed all the support he could get from Pope Vigilius and the western church in general. This was no moment for bringing the full weight of imperial authority to bear on the Pope. So throughout the rest of 544 and the earlier part of 545 he treated Vigilius with the utmost respect, and seemed prepared to overlook his failure to condemn the Three Chapters, as the offending works and subsequently their authors came to be called. Indeed it was rather in Constantinople that Justinian had to face difficulties. An attempt to impose the Roman date for Easter instead of the Alexandrian led to a boycott of the butchers' shops for a week before the beginning of Lent, an ominous warning that the favour of Rome might turn out costly for Justinian.

By the autumn of 545, Totila was preparing to give siege to Rome. It was no part of Justinian's plans to present the Gothic leader with so choice a hostage as the Pope. And at the same time the emperor saw an opportunity to bring the obstinate prelate more directly under his own control. So on 22 November 545 an officer of the imperial guard accompanied by a detachment of excubitors from Constantinople arrived in Rome, seized Vigilius in a church where he had just celebrated the liturgy, and put him on board a boat which immediately set sail down the Tiber for Porto. Unconfirmed tradition has it that it was Theodora who persuaded Justinian to take this radical step. The Pope was not at all displeased at being arrested. He had no desire to become a pawn in Totila's hands. And he was confident that he could sustain his position in the matter of the Three Chapters.

For a time he was held in what amounted to honourable captivity in Sicily. On 25 January 547 he arrived in Constantinople, where Justinian came down to the harbour to welcome him. The scene as Pope and emperor met was doubtless moving. But no sooner were the celebrations of welcome over than Justinian began putting pressure on his distinguished guest to subscribe to his condemnation of the Three Chapters. Personally, Vigilius had little interest in the alleged Nestorianism of three eastern theologians, whose works he had probably never read. But he was in a quandary. If he condemned the Three Chapters, he risked being disowned by the western clergy on whose support his strength depended. If he refused, he would fall foul of Justinian in his own capital – and, what might well be more dangerous, he would win the enmity of Theodora, whose protégé he had been. By nature a vacillator, Vigilius soon yielded to Justinian's pressure. On 29 June 547 he was formally reconciled with his Constantinopolitan colleague Menas; and on the same day he handed to Justinian and Theodora a signed declaration of his condemnation of the Three Chapters. This document was to be kept secret until Vigilius had time to organize a formal enquiry into the views of the three allegedly Nestorian theologians. In this way the Pope's credit in the west was saved for the time being. But the outcome of the enquiry was evidently determined in advance. Seventy bishops, mostly westerners, who had not subscribed to Justinian's decree, were convoked to a synod. All went well until the third session when Facundus, bishop of Hermiane in Africa, a learned and subtle theologian, produced proof that the Council of Chalcedon itself had approved the very letter of Ibas of Edessa which Justinian now condemned as heretical. Vigilius, who was anxious to get public support for the attitude to which he had secretly committed himself, hastily brought the proceedings to a close and announced that the vote would be taken in writing some time later. Meanwhile the imperial agents set to work to bribe or coerce those of the bishops whose support could not be counted upon. They were successful. Facundus may have been the only bishop to vote in favour of the Three Chapters. On Saturday 11 April 548 Pope Vigilius issued his *Judicatum*, addressed to Patriarch Menas. This document roundly condemned the Three Chapters and added, to cover the Pope against the attack developed by Facundus, that he remained wholly and unshakably attached to the doctrines promulgated by the Council of Chalcedon.

If Justinian thought that he had at last obtained the ecclesiastical unity which he had so long striven for, he was soon disillusioned. Those western bishops who were outside the immediate reach of Justinian were unwilling to accept Vigilius' *Judicatum*. The death a month or two later of Theodora, who had been even more zealous than her husband in bringing constraint to bear on obstinate clergy and a great deal less scrupulous, made them less hesitant to take a public stand on the matter. In Italy many sees were vacant because of the long years of war, and opposition to Vigilius there was feeble. But the clergy of Dalmatia rejected the *Judicatum*; those of Dacia sent a letter to Justinian defending the Three Chapters, and deposed their own primate for accepting it; those of Gaul – a region subject to the Pope in matters of religion but entirely outside the boundaries of the empire – wrote to Vigilius demanding an explanation; the general synod of African bishops broke completely from communion with the Pope until he agreed to withdraw his *Judicatum*. Throughout 549 western hostility to the *Judicatum* hardened, and in Constantinople itself underground opposition groups began to form and to disseminate their propaganda. Justinian at last realized that his manoeuvres had had no effect upon the Monophysites, but had succeeded in splitting the Chalcedonian majority into two mutually hostile camps, divided largely along ethnic and geographical lines. Reluctantly he gave up for the time being the idea of summoning an ecumenical council to condemn the Three Chapters in accordance with the papal *Judicatum*. In fact the original of the *Judicatum* was handed back to Vigilius in August 550. But at the same time the unfortunate Pope was made to swear a solemn oath, confirmed in writing, that he would do all in his power to get the Three Chapters condemned. This oath was to remain secret.

Had Justinian decided in 550 that the whole matter of the Three Chapters had been a dreadful mistake, he might well have obtained some kind of actual religious unity on the basis of an agreement not to raise certain disputed questions. But he was losing something of his earlier flexibility without remitting anything of his tenacity of purpose. He was demoralized and isolated by the death of Theodora. And above all he was growing more and more convinced that he was a better theologian than the leaders of the church and that it was his duty to put their house in order. Now approaching seventy, he devoted more and more of his time to theological studies, under the guidance of Theodore Ascidas. The principal fruit of these was a long treatise on dogmatics which ended with a condemnation of the Three Chapters. Confident that no one could any longer fail to be convinced by the lucidity of his reasoning, and exasperated by the failure of the vacillating Vigilius – who was now entirely under the influence of the Roman deacon Pelagius – to carry out the terms of his recent oath, the emperor determined to put before the church a *fait accompli*. In July 551, at the suggestion of Theodore Ascidas, he published his dogmatic treatise in the form of an imperial edict having the force of law. Any subsequent ecumenical council could only formally confirm it.

This turned out to be a major blunder, uniting those whom Justinian was eager to separate and dividing those he wished united. And at a time when it was of supreme importance to retain the loyalty of the Roman population of Italy, this ill-timed intervention of the imperial theologian played straight into the hands of Totila and of those western Romans who still dreamed of an independent western empire in close alliance with the Goths.

Vigilius, under pressure from the western clerics in Constantinople, called on

Theodore Ascidas to induce Justinian to withdraw the new edict, which he stigmatized as contrary to the faith of Chalcedon. It was also, incidentally, a breach of the agreement of August 550 between emperor and pope. Neither Theodore nor Justinian took any account of Vigilius' remonstrances, and the unhappy Pope, to keep the support of his western colleagues, had to break off relations with the bulk of the Greek hierarchy. Justinian was not a man to be trifled with in such matters. Vigilius, who up to now had been living in considerable state in the Palace of Placidia, the official residence of his *apocrisiarius* in Constantinople, decided to move to a place of greater safety. He chose as his refuge the basilica of St Peter of Hormisdas. It was there that he drew up, on 14 August, a document formally excommunicating the Patriarch Menas and his clergy and signed by himself and a dozen other western bishops. Hesitating to provoke Justinian too far, the Pope refrained for the moment from publishing this sentence. But the emperor took his gesture not merely as an act of political opposition but as a personal affront. Vigilius had spurned his own lucid exposition of the problem. In a fit of temper he decided to resort to force. A detachment of palace guards, under the command of the Praetor of the Plebs, Comitas Dupondiaristes, who was responsible for law and order in the city, was dispatched to the church to arrest the Pope and the dissident African bishops. There was a scuffle, in the course of which several bishops were injured. Then the inept police officer lost his head and ordered his men to drag Vigilius from the altar to which he was clinging. The Pope, whose legs and beard the gendarmes had seized hold of, clung all the harder to the altar, which toppled over, nearly crushing him. By this time a crowd had gathered, whose angry cries of indignation mingled with the lamentations of the bishops and the orders and counter-orders of the harassed Praetor. Soon his men began to lose their nerve, and some of them refused to pursue their distasteful task any further. The Praetor decided to withdraw his forces in haste; and the Pope and his clergy, battered but undefeated, remained in possession of the church.

The next day a group of exalted dignitaries – headed by Belisarius himself, Cethegus the leader of the senate of Rome, Peter the Patrician, Master of Offices, and Justinian's nephew Justin – made its way from the palace to the church of St Peter of Hormisdas, where it took a solemn oath in the emperor's name that no harm would be done to Vigilius if he returned to his official residence. This the Pope at once did. But soon he realized that he was virtually under house arrest. Justinian's tactical withdrawal did not mean that he had given up any of his designs.

Within a few months Vigilius decided that he was being compromised in the eyes of the western clergy whose loyalty he so much needed. On the night of 23/24 December 551, he gave the imperial guards the slip in the darkness and fled across the Bosphorus to the Church of St Euphemia in Chalcedon, where a century earlier the Council of Chalcedon had held its sessions. The Pope's choice of a refuge was significant. He clearly wished to brand those who condemned the Three Chapters as enemies of the Catholic faith of Chalcedon. Once again Belisarius and other high officers of state were sent to assure Vigilius of the emperor's good will.

And a day or two later Justinian sent a referendary to Chalcedon with a personal message for the Pope. But Vigilius had learned his lesson, and refused to budge. The news spread, and crowds began crossing the water to visit the rebellious prelate. At the beginning of February 552 he published a pastoral letter, giving an account of his sufferings and embodying a confession of faith which ostentatiously did not condemn the Three Chapters. A few days after this the imperial guards broke into the church and arrested the western bishops there. But they did not venture to lay hands on Vigilius: the repercussions in Italy and Africa would have been too costly for Justinian to contemplate. Vigilius' reaction was immediate and effective. In spite of the arrest of most of his entourage, he succeeded in having posted up in most of the churches of Constantinople the text of his sentence of excommunication of the Patriarch Menas, passed six months earlier.

The blow to Justinian's pride was hard. But he had not been thirty-five years in power without learning when and how to withdraw. Negotiations between emperor and pope went on during the spring. Finally in June the Patriarch Menas, Theodore Ascidas and the other excommunicated bishops were sent to St Euphemia to make honourable amends to the Pope. An agreement was reached to annul all statements made concerning the Three Chapters since the agreement to suspend discussion – and this of course included the emperor's edict. On 26 June Vigilius returned to his palace in Constantinople and was publicly reconciled with Justinian. But if he thought he would be left to enjoy his victory, he soon learned his mistake.

In August the Patriarch Menas died, and was succeeded by Eutychius. Justinian saw the moment as opportune to revive his scheme for an ecumenical council and issued invitations to eastern bishops to attend. In January 553 the assembled eastern bishops invited Vigilius to preside at the new council to be held to settle once and for all the question of the Three Chapters. The Pope was pleased by the honour, but decided to play for time. For everything would depend on whether he could carry the majority of the western bishops with him or whether Justinian could pack the western delegation with men favourable to his own point of view. So he first asked permission to call a local synod in Italy or Sicily to formulate a common western attitude. Justinian had no choice but to forbid this. It would not only have given Vigilius power to control the voting of the western delegates at the council, but would also have enabled him to delay its meeting for as long as he liked. In return, however, the emperor asked Vigilius to nominate those western bishops who were to be invited. This put the cunning Pope in something of a dilemma. If he nominated bishops who supported the Three Chapters he would violate the oath he had given to Justinian to work for their condemnation. If he nominated bishops ready to condemn the Three Chapters, he would lose all authority in the west. Vigilius delayed his reply as long as he could and in the end submitted only a short list of names, and that too late for them to be effectively invited. In fact the only westerners who attended were a group of African bishops who had been vetted before departure by the Praetorian Prefect of Africa.

After more wrangles over procedure, the ecumenical council – the fifth in the history of the church – finally opened in Hagia Sophia on 5 May 553. Justinian refrained from attending in person, and took great pains to foster the illusion that the council was free to reach its own independent decision. This impression was doubtless somewhat marred by the imperial letter read at the opening session, in which the emperor reminded the assembled prelates that they had all already condemned the Three Chapters. In any case the council was packed with bishops ready to follow Justinian's lead. Vigilius, for whom time was running out, tried to retain some freedom of action by staying away from the council. The debates, pompous and vacuous, went on without him. By 14 May he declared that he had at last made up his mind, and drew up his *Constitutum*, signed by himself and a handful of western clerics. It condemned as heretical many passages of Theodore of Mopsuestia, but refused any wholesale condemnation of the Three Chapters: an attempt, therefore, at compromise. But Vigilius, weak and indecisive as ever, delayed its publication for eleven days in the hope that the emperor would make some overture. Finally on 25 May he invited Belisarius, Cethegus and Justin the emperor's nephew to convey his *Constitutum* to Justinian. He must have known that the emperor would not be satisifed with it, but he had not reckoned with the changed political situation. Narses' victories had now firmly established Roman power in Italy. The Gothic army faced total defeat, and the Gothic kingdom was virtually annihilated. Justinian no longer depended on the goodwill of the Roman citizens of Italy: they were under the iron heel of his soldiery. So he decided to take his revenge on Vigilius for the humiliations he had endured. An imperial referendary was sent to the assembled council with a packet containing the originals of Vigilius' secret declaration anathematizing the Three Chapters and of his oath of 15 August 550 that he would do all in his power to further their condemnation. Its third item was an imperial decree declaring that Vigilius had by his conduct placed himself outside the church. Vigilus' humiliation was complete.

On 2 June the final session of the council pronounced fourteen anathemas, dealing with the Three Chapters and with certain other heresies. Vigilius for a time refused to endorse it. He had in effect been deposed by the council. But Justinian was in no hurry to replace him. He had taken the measure of Vigilius: a new pope might be harder to deal with. He had not long to wait. By December Vigilius capitulated, and in a letter to the Patriarch Eutychius he formally anathematized the Three Chapters. But this was not enough for Justinian. The wretched Pope was obliged in February 555 to publish a second *Constitutum*, circumstantially condemning the Three Chapters. He was now of no further use to Justinian, who allowed him to return to Rome. Vigilius did not live to see the city again, but succumbed to a kidney disease in Syracuse in June.

A new Pope now had to be found. Most leading western clerics were opposed to the condemnation of the Three Chapters. But the appointment of an eastern Pope would almost certainly have led to a schism in the church. With a boldness and sureness of touch which recalled his younger days, Justinian offered the papacy to the deacon Pelagius, the spokesman of the Roman nobility and hitherto one of the stoutest opponents of the emperor's religious policy. The implied condition was the condemnation of the Three Chapters. Pelagius took the bait, either because he had decided that opposition was useless now that Justinian was in absolute control of devastated Italy, or out of ambition. When Pelagius, a Roman of the Romans, reached Italy, he was met by universal hostility, and could only enter the city under the protection of Narses' troops. It was many months before three bishops could be found to consecrate him. In time he slowly won control of the church as far as the Po, for he was decisive and a hard-working and realist administrator. But he had to adopt a very equivocal attitude to justify himself. Thus the prestige and influence of the papacy in reconquered Italy remained low. In the long run, and despite a series of tactical defeats, Justinian had won, in that he had kept the Pope in communion with the eastern church and in subservience to the imperial government.

But it was a victory which cost more than it gained. The Monophysites of Egypt and Syria remained sullen and unreconciled, providing more and more the rallying point for opposition to the empire and all that it stood for. In fact Justinian, by trying too hard to secure unity of doctrine throughout the empire, had in the end divided the church irreparably. From being a group – or rather a collection of groups – within the church which was dissatisfied with the decisions of the Council of Chalcedon of 451, the Monophysites became in the course of Justinian's reign a counter-church, with its own hierarchy, its own ecclesiastical literature, largely in Syriac or Coptic, its own monasteries, and its own style of religious and social life. The breach has never been healed. In the west disillusion and cynicism were the prevailing moods. Italy was devastated as it had never been before. Its olive groves and vineyards had been cut down and burnt. Its roads lay neglected, its bridges demolished. Of its cities, many were in ruins, some actually abandoned by their citizens, all reduced to a fraction of their former population and despoiled of their treasures. War and plague had decimated the people, and the survivors sheltered like wild beasts in the ruins of their former prosperity.

Narses, with an energy which belied his age, set about reorganizing Italy. In the military sphere, fortifications were rapidly built to control the passes across the Alps, and a number of special frontier commands established. Land formerly belonging to Ostrogoths was redistributed, most of it to the Byzantine soldiers who replaced the former Gothic garrisons along the northern frontier. In the civil sphere a number of measures for the restoration of normality were comprised in a long imperial edict of 13 August 554, known as the Pragmatic Sanction. All acts of Amalasuntha, Athalaric and Theodahad are confirmed, as well as all measures undertaken by Justinian and Theodora. All acts of Totila are declared null and void. The normal processes of civil litigation are restored, and the jurisdiction of military commanders restricted to cases involving their own troops. The ancient status and privileges of the city of Rome are restored.

. A series of provisions deals with such matters as lost title-deeds, persons carried off to captivity, irregular weights and measures and so on. But the most striking feature of the Pragmatic Sanction is the way in which it restores and guarantees the privileges of the upper classes, the sole element in Italian society on whose support Justinian could now count. All property belonging to refugees was to be restored to them in full and at once, with no compensation to those who might have acquired it in good faith. All slaves freed by Totila were to be returned forthwith to their former masters; all tenants to their former overlords:

> We ordain that slaves or tenants, who have been retained by anyone, be returned to their masters together with the offspring they may have produced in the meantime.
> If during the accursed period of Gothic tyranny any man of servile condition be found to have married a free woman, or any female slave to have married a free man, we grant by these presents to the free person the right of divorce, while the slave is to be returned to the possession of his or her master, and no prejudice is to be caused to the master as a result of past events. If however they wish to maintain their present marriage, they are to suffer no prejudice to their personal freedom, but the children are to follow the status of their mother. (Justinian, *Pragmatic Sanction* 16, 15.)

The bishop and the notables of each province of Italy were to have the right to appoint from their own number a provincial governor, a striking concession to the local magnates. All senators were to have unrestricted right to come to court in Constantinople, and to go to Italy for as long as they liked in order to restore their estates to their former productivity. The whole enactment is couched in terms of restoration of the past, in all its minutest details. That the half-century of Gothic rule and the twenty years of war had profoundly changed the social and economic structure of Italy seems not to have occurred to Justinian. Or if it did occur to him he pushed it at once to the back of his mind. Innovations – and he made many – had to be disguised as restorations. In fact the terms of the Pragmatic Sanction were never carried out in full. Power remained in the hands of the army, and it was Narses and his fellow-generals who actually administered the regions in which they exercised military command. The old ruling class had been shattered, and no amount of legislation sufficed to reconstruct it. The fugitive *coloni* could not be found and returned to their masters. And as there was a great shortage of labour, owners of estates had to lease out portions to independent smallholders – often someone else's former tenants – on relatively favourable terms. The Roman senate, which had crumbled away in the war years, was maintained only by large-scale granting of the dignity of patrician to the notables of Italy and by a reduction by two-thirds of the sum to be paid by honorary consuls on their nomination. All in all, the glorious restored empire in the west was a very ramshackle affair.

As Narses was mopping up the last pockets of Gothic resistance in Italy, in Constantinople an unexpected disaster befell one of Justinian's greatest works. The dome of the Church of the Holy Wisdom, weakened by an earthquake, collapsed as it was being cleaned on 7 May 558. Justinian set the younger Isidore, son or nephew of one of the original architects, to rebuild the dome. He did so successfully, making its pitch higher than that of the original daringly flat dome. The restored church was formally opened on 24 December 562, in the presence of the eighty-year-old Justinian; and the ceremonies went on for several days in both the church and in the palace. Paul the Silentiary, the most distinguished of a school of poets in the classical manner which flourished in Justinian's later years, wrote at the emperor's behest a long and graphic description of the church in hexameters, which he read to Justinian in a series of sessions. It gives us the clearest idea of how men of the time saw the great church.

A few months earlier the emperor had to face an unpleasantness of a more personal character. A plot was discovered to assassinate him. The principal conspirators were Ablabius, a retired official of the mint, Marcellus, a bullion-dealer, and Sergius, nephew of a minor functionary – men of no particular standing. It was not the first such plot that had been forestalled, and Justinian might merely have congratulated his police officers and forgotten the matter. But there was the question of motive. One of the conspirators – the other two managed to kill themselves – declared under interrogation that three members of Belisarius' staff, Isaac, Vitas and Paul, were privy to the plot. When they were interrogated in turn by Procopius, the Prefect of the City, they implicated Belisarius himself. Was there anything in the charge? Justinian probably disbelieved it; but he could not be sure. And he was in any case indignant that Belisarius had not kept a more vigilant eye on the activities of his subordinates. Accordingly he summoned a consistory, at which all the chief dignitaries of the capital were present, and caused the depositions to be read, including those implicating Belisarius. The ageing marshal was shocked and wounded at this public slur upon his loyalty. He was even more displeased to find most of his entourage withdrawn and himself put under house arrest. When the Church of the Holy Wisdom was reinaugurated, the two greatest of the old emperor's collaborators were not with him: Theodora had been dead for fourteen years, and Belisarius was in disgrace. In the poetic address to Justinian which served as a prologue to the description of the Chruch of the Holy Wisdom, Paul the Silentiary says of Theodora:

These things, my Lord, enable the soul of the empress, blessed and happy, fair and wise, to speak freely to God on your behalf, she whom in life you had as your pious collaborator, and whom after death you made the pledge of your greatest oath to your subjects, an oath you have never broken, nor may you ever break. (Paul the Silentiary, *Description of Hagia Sophia* 58-65.)

Not a word is said of Belisarius. But the emperor is congratulated on his courage in facing a villainous conspiracy.

9   The final years

Already in the reign of Justin I Roman diplomacy had been active at the southern
end of the Red Sea, when the Christian – but Monophysite – kingdom of Axum in
Ethiopia had been encouraged by the Romans to attack and occupy the Yemen,
whose rulers, recent converts to Judaism, were Persian protégés. It was
considerations of trade rather than war which prompted this lively interest in so
remote a region.

Since the early empire, Roman trade with India, Indonesia and China had been
highly organized. The principal imports from the east were spices and perfumes,
largely from southern India, Ceylon and Indonesia, and silk yarn from China.
Spices, in particular pepper, were important articles of general consumption in a
society which killed most of its calves in autumn – through shortage of winter
feeding stuffs – and salted or pickled the carcases. Anything which improved – or
disguised – the flavour was in high demand. It is interesting that amongst the booty
seized by Alaric when he sacked Rome in 410 was five thousand pounds of pepper.
Ancient medicine also made much use of spices. Silk was much too dear to be in
general use in the ancient world; but as a mark of social distinction it played an
important role. Upperclass women wore silk dresses, naturally. And embroidered
or brocaded silk robes were by the time of Justinian the official garb of high officers
of state, given to them as a part of their salary. Silk garments were also distributed
to potentates outside the empire as a mark of imperial favour. The government had
therefore a special interest in maintaining the supply of silk yarn at reasonable
prices.

The trouble was that the Persian empire straddled the trade routes from the east.
Goods from China came either by sea via Ceylon to ports in the Persian Gulf, or
through central Asia by caravan to the Persian frontier. Those from India and
Indonesia came by sea to the Persian Gulf. Both categories of goods were then sold
by Persian merchants at frontier markets between the Persian and Roman empires.
Sometimes this trade was left in private hands, sometimes it was under state
control. But the Persian merchants, or the Persian government when it interested
itself in such matters, were always able to restrict supply and to charge a monopoly
price. There is a good deal of information on how the silk trade worked in the sixth
century. No private Roman citizen could buy silk direct from Persia. State
functionaries, the *commerciarii*, bought all raw silk offered by the Persians at a
number of scheduled frontier posts. This was both a device to keep the price down
by cutting out competitive buying, and a means of ensuring that the state got the
large quantities of silk it needed before private merchants got their hands on it. The
commerciarii then either sent the silk to one of the imperial factories, or sold it at
purchase price to silk merchants or direct to weavers. At the beginning of
Justinian's reign there were large stocks in the hands of the government, which

could be used to keep the internal price stable.

The ideal solution to the problems of eastern trade was to use routes which cut out the Persians altogether. This was the aim in establishing Roman control of the mouth of the Red Sea. Roman merchants from Egyptian ports could now sail direct to Ceylon and buy silk and other commodities there. Apparently the policy was a failure. The Persian traders were too strongly entrenched in the Ceylon market, and succeeded in buying up all the silk available and keeping the Romans out. The Romans may have been more successful in circumventing the Persian monopoly of spice and perfume. As a counter-measure, the Persians put up their prices. Justinian tried to block the price of silk on the free market within the empire, with the result that a black market soon flourished.

By 540, when the Second Persian War broke out and direct importation of silk stopped, the old-established silk industry of Beirut and Tyre was ruined, and the stocks left in the hands of the state were too low to meet the demand for robes of office and diplomatic presents. Peter Barsymes, the Syrian-born finance minister who replaced John of Cappadocia, drove out the private merchants and manufacturers by enforcing price control. For a time an attempt was made to supply the market from imperial factories. But soon Barsymes took over many of the private factories, with their skilled workmen, and ran them on state account. Thus a state monopoly, not merely of the import of silk but of its processing, was created.

After the peace of 545 raw silk from China began to appear at the frontier markets again. But the silk trade did not revert to its previous pattern. Many of the craftsmen from the private factories had emigrated to Persia – they were Syriac speakers, equally at home in Beirut and in Ctesiphon. And most of the owners, if they were not completely ruined, had invested their capital in some other enterprise. So the state monopoly continued to operate, with few exceptions. And periodical Persian pressure continued to keep prices up and stocks dangerously low. The problem was a continuous source of worry to the emperor and his finance minister.

In 552, however, a radically new solution was proposed. Some monks, probably Nestorians, approached Justinian, explaining that they had connections in Soghdiana (the region of modern Samarkand and Bukhara) and that from there they could obtain silkworm eggs and so render the empire independent of foreign silk supplies. Justinian welcomed the chance of undermining the Persian monopolists and the monks set off on their long journey, aided and supported by all the resources of the Roman empire. When they returned a year or two later they brought with them the precious eggs and enough technical knowledge to enable state silk spinneries to be set up on the Syrian coast.

The importation of silkworm eggs from Soghdiana did not at once end the empire's dependence on Persia for supplies. It was a very long time before local production could meet the demand of the market; and certain kinds of silk goods continued to be imported from China. But it reduced the Persians' bargaining power; and it opened up a new route, north of the Caspian Sea, from Chinese-controlled Soghdiana, to Roman-held ports on the Black Sea, which entirely circumvented Persian territory. The cost of transport on the northern route, however, made it uncompetitive. The wealth of the east flowed, as before, to ports on the Persian Gulf.

Religious orthodoxy and trade were continuing sources of anxiety on the eastern frontiers in the twilight of Justinian's reign; there were no major military operations. In 554 Al-Harith, Prince of the Christian Ghassanid Arab state, invaded the territory of the pro-Persian Lakhmid Arabs and killed their prince, Al-Mundhir. In the following year Gubazes the king of Lazica was murdered at the instigation of Roman officials, and there followed a series of revolts among the Laz tribes, who naturally looked for Persian support. For a time it looked as though the two empires might be dragged into war by their allies. But neither Justinian nor Chosroes was eager to face the expense and uncertainty of a clash along the long frontier from the Caucasus to Mesopotamia. The matter was handled through diplomatic channels. A truce was signed in 552, which also covered the client states of both parties. And in 556 the Persian ambassador Izad-Gushnasp and his Roman counterpart Peter the Patrician signed a fifty-year peace treaty at the frontier city of Daras. The Persians agreed to waive all claims on Lazica, in return for an annual payment of thirty thousand gold *solidi*. The rest of the frontier remained unaltered, as it had been for the last two hundred years. And the two turbulent Arab buffer-states were forbidden to attack the territory of either empire, but allowed to make war upon one another without in any way engaging their protectors. For the remaining years of Justinian's life all was calm on the eastern frontiers.

On the northern frontier, which followed the line of the Danube and the Drave, the situation was less reassuring. Far beyond the frontier great movements of peoples were beginning, building up more and more pressure upon the Roman defences. The traditional method of dealing with threats on the northern frontier was to divide the enemy. There had not been for centuries a major state facing the Roman legions across the Danube, only a confusion of tribes and ethnic groups, whose changing rivalries and alliances provided an ideal opportunity for Roman diplomacy. So Justinian contented himself with repulsing invading armies where he could, strengthening the fortifications of the cities, and distributing gold coins and silk garments among the barbarian rulers. The campaigns in Africa and Italy strained the empire's resources of men and money. But they were a part of the great restoration of the Christian Roman empire, a fitting concern for the successor of Constantine. Punitive expeditions among Slavs and Huns could be left till later.

In 548 there was a major invasion by the Slavs, who penetrated as far as the walls of Dyrrhachium, the main port of embarkation for Italy. Although there was a Roman army of fifteen thousand men in the western Balkan peninsula, it either could not or would not come to grips with the invaders, who withdrew in autumn, laden with booty and captives. This was disquieting. Even more alarming

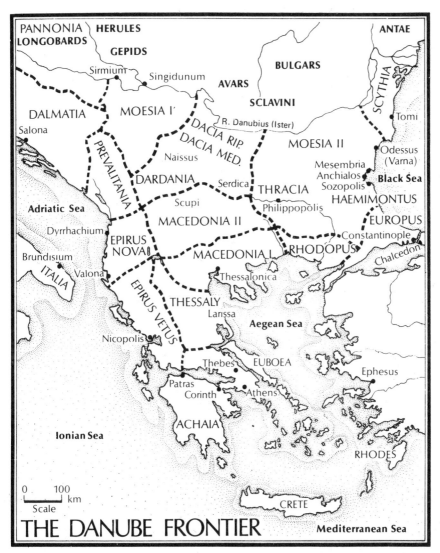

PANNONIA HERULES ANTAE
LONGOBARDS
GEPIDS
Sirmium Singidunum BULGARS
AVARS SCYTHIA
MOESIA I' SCLAVINI Tomi
DALMATIA R. Danubius (Ister)
Salona DACIA RIP. MOESIA II Odessus
Naissus DACIA MED. Mesembria (Varna)
Anchialos
PREVALITANA Sozopolis Black Sea
DARDANIA Serdica THRACIA HAEMIMONTUS
Scupi Philippopolis
Adriatic Sea MACEDONIA II EUROPUS
Dyrrhachium Constantinople
EPIRUS RHODOPUS Chalcedon
Brundisium NOVA MACEDONIA I
Valona
ITALIA EPIRUS Thessalonica
VETUS
THESSALY
Nicopolis Larissa
Aegean Sea
Thebes EUBOEA
Patras Ephesus
Corinth Athens
ACHAIA
Ionian Sea
RHODES
0 100
km CRETE
Scale
THE DANUBE FRONTIER Mediterranean Sea

was the progress which these northern barbarians were making in military art and
science. For the first time they attacked and took a number of walled towns, instead
of by-passing them. The point was not lost on Justinian, who sent his military
engineers to strengthen the defences of many cities and to build fortresses at key
strategic points. But no fighting men could be spared from the urgent task of
destroying Gothic resistance in Italy.

Worse was to come. In 550 a great force of Slavs, perhaps operating under the
control of the Hunnic Bulgars, swept through Thrace. One column reached the
long walls built by Anastasius, about thirty miles west of Constantinople. There

they defeated the Roman garrison and took prisoner its commanding officer, whom they flayed and then burned alive. Unable to penetrate the strongly fortified line, they turned west towards Rhodope, burning, pillaging and massacring as they went. Another Slav force crossed the Danube farther west and marched via Naissus (Nish) towards Thessalonica. But the presence of Germanus, on his way to take up the supreme command in Italy, was enough to make them turn back. Once again the invaders showed themselves able to take fortified places. And some groups even wintered on Roman territory. Their thoughts were evidently turning from pillage to settlement. Preoccupied though he was with events in Italy, the emperor was constrained to take military measures. A considerable force was mustered in the capital, and marched off in the spring of 551, under the command of a eunuch general named Scholasticus and Justin the elder son of Germanus. The barbarians were to be taught a lesson; but the Roman army did not get far. Near Adrianople it ran into a new invading army of Slavs and suffered a crushing defeat. In the same year another Hunnic people, the Kotrigurs, who had been hired as mercenaries in a war between two Germanic groups in central Europe, found time on their hands. They crossed the Danube near Belgrade, advanced as far as Philippopolis in Thrace, and sent out advance parties in the direction of Thessalonica and Constantinople. Chastened by the defeat of Scholasticus and Justin earlier in the year, and unwilling to withdraw any of his best fighting troops from Italy, Justinian turned to the well-tried methods of Roman diplomacy. Another Hunnic community, the Utigurs, established at this time in the steppe land between the Don and the Volga, was approached by imperial envoys, liberally supplied with money and arms and urged to attack the Kotrigurs in their home territory north of the Danube. They were eager to respond to the call, for little love was lost between the two kindred peoples. The Utigurs crossed the Don, swept through the Ukraine – they were nomad horsemen – and fell on the rear of the Kotrigurs. The scratch force of old men and boys which met them was annihilated, and the women, children and herds ravaged by the invaders. The news of this disaster brought the main force of the Kotrigurs back in haste across the Danube, leaving much of their booty behind them in Thrace.

Once again the traditional policy led to short-term success. The Kotrigurs and the Utigurs remained for years at each other's throats, and their continuing strife gave ample opportunity to the warlike proclivities of their Slav and Bulgar neighbours. For seven years relative calm reigned on the Danube frontier. Occasional raiding-parties crossed the river, but there was no major invasion. Meanwhile the Roman fleet cruised unmolested up and down the river till it froze in winter, and the fortifications along its southern bank were strengthened. The foundations of the great fortresses of Belgrade, Smederevo and Vidin, upon which Byzantines, Hungarians and Turks later built, were probably laid at this point. But Justinian, ageing and increasingly a prisoner of the great design which he had formed in the prime of youth, did nothing to tackle the root of the problem. The peoples pressing on the frontier were neither decisively repulsed nor incorporated into the empire. And the main weight of the imperial armies was deployed in Italy and in the east.

In 558, probably as a result of a change of rulers, the Kotrigurs and the Utigurs made peace. The policy of divide and rule had failed. The new Kotrigur leader Zabergan, anxious to establish his reputation amongst his followers, decided to invade Roman territory. Crossing the frozen Danube in March 559 he pressed on into Thrace. There his army, which included contingents of dependent Slavonic people, split into three columns. One marched through Macedonia into Greece. It got as far as Thermopylae, where the fortifications had recently been repaired. There the vigorous resistance of a small Roman force under the logothete Alexander stopped the raiders' advance. The second column tried to break into the Thracian Chersonese (the Gallipoli peninsula), which was protected by a wall across the narrow isthmus. The Roman commander there was a young man named Germanus, a native of Justiniana Prima and perhaps a distant kinsman of Justinian. At any rate the emperor had brought him to Constantinople, given him an excellent education and promoted him at an early age to high responsibility. Germanus repaid his benefactor well. The Kotrigurs were held at the wall and suffered heavy losses. When some of them tried to turn the defences of the peninsula by crossing the gulf on boats or rafts built of reeds in the delta of the Maritza, the young general was ready for them. A fleet of armed merchant ships and fishing boats destroyed the Kotrigur vessels. Six hundred men were drowned. This disaster was too much for the invaders, who hastily withdrew towards the Danube. The third column made for Constantinople. The long walls running across the peninsula, about thirty miles from the city, had recently been damaged by an earthquake and gave little protection. A scratch force of palace guards and citizen militia, with little military experience, was sent to meet the Kotrigurs and, predictably, defeated. There was panic in the city. Those who could transported their families and their movable goods across the Bosphorus to Asia. Refugees poured into the capital from the nearby countryside. To lodge and feed them presented a problem to the authorities; and their presence sapped still further the morale of the citizens. As the elderly emperor – Justinian was now seventy-seven – paced the corridors of the Great Palace by night, his thoughts were sombre. Persia had been forced to make peace. The kingdoms of the Vandals and the Ostrogoths had been destroyed and the provinces they had occupied restored to the empire. In far off Spain, Roman power had been asserted once again. Yet within a day's march of his capital barbarians whose very name was unknown to the annals of the past were burning and pillaging unmolested. Soon worse news arrived. The Kotrigurs had reached the river Athyras, only eighteen miles from the walls of Constantinople. The city itself was impregnable, and the Romans still had undisputed command of the sea. But the blow to Justinian's prestige was not to be borne. And might not the panic-stricken populace turn against an emperor who did not seem to enjoy the favour of God? In his moment of crisis Justinian turned to his oldest collaborator, Belisarius, who had lost nothing of his tactical brilliance. He set out with a tiny force, which he supplemented by arming peasant refugees. Splitting up his levies into numerous detachments and attacking where least expected, he succeeded in luring Zabergan into an ambush and killed four hundred of his men. The Kotrigur's nerve broke, and he fled back to his base camp near Arcadiopolis (Lüle-Burgaz). The situation was saved; but Justinian was displeased that it was not he himself who had saved it and recalled Belisarius to the capital at once. The Kotrigurs continued to ravage Thrace. In the meantime the emperor had been arranging the reinforcement of the Danube fleet. It was the news of this – with the implied possibility that he might not be able to get back home across the river – that forced Zabergan to conclude a treaty with the Romans, whereby they would be escorted back to their homeland and would receive a regular subsidy. An inglorious outcome, perhaps. Some felt that Belisarius should have been given the chance to defeat the Kotrigurs in a pitched battle. But what if he had lost?

However, the emperor was uneasy. Throughout the summer he had been with his court at Selymbria in Thrace, supervising personally the repair of the long walls, and anxious to show himself in the role of a man of action. For fifty years he had scarcely left his capital, only occasionally crossing to spend the summer in one of his palaces on the Asian shore of the Bosphorus. The disturbance of his routine must have been almost traumatic for a man of his age and fixity of habits. That he undertook it is a measure of the anxiety he felt. When the treaty with the Kotrigurs was finally signed, he took the even more unexpected step of returning to Constantinople as a triumphant victor. Entering the city by the Golden Gate, Justinian and his entourage proceeded through the streets, lined by cheering crowds to the Great Church to return thanks for the glorious victory which God had vouchsafed to his people. It was on this moving, albeit somewhat pathetic, occasion that Justinian dismounted by the Church of the Holy Apostles, which he and Theodora had built twenty-three years earlier, and lighted candles by her tomb.

The wisdom of Justinian's policy of limited military reaction and subsidies was soon to be tested, though the moment of truth did not come until some years after his death. The Huns of Attila, and their descendants the Bulgars, the Kotrigurs and the Utigurs, were pastoral peoples of the steppe and semi-desert lands of central Asia, who had been driven westwards in search of new pastures by a combination of factors. The progressive dessication of their ancient home, and in particular of the Tarim Basin, reduced the grazing land available. The varying development of the different steppe peoples brought new tribes and confederations to dominance over their neighbours, and reduced to subjection or drove into exile the previous masters. And above all, the policy of the two great empires to the south of the steppe lands, Sassanian Persia and China, favoured now this people, now that, in their constant search for security on their northern frontiers.

In the fifth century A D one of the pastoral peoples of the steppe had established its rule throughout Mongolia and Manchuria, north and east of the Great Wall. In so doing they had learnt that herds of men are more profitable than herds of sheep and cattle, and with true herdsman's instinct had picked up the techniques of domination and exploitation. The Chinese, who viewed with disquiet this powerful and extensive empire on their frontier, called them Chou-Chuan. The peoples of Europe knew them as Avars. Their own name for themselves may have been Uighur or the like – from which the Franks drew their word 'ogre', such was the terror that the Avars inspired in the hearts of peaceful peasants. About 555 the Turkic subjects of the Avars revolted against their overlords. The long arm of the Wei empire probably had something to do with this event, for the Chinese too preferred to rule by dividing. There was a massacre of the Avars; and the survivors, some twenty thousand in number, fled westwards along the strip of grazing land that stretches from the Pacific to the plains of Hungary. By 557 they had reached the plains north of the Caucasus. There they contacted, through the intermediacy of the king of the Christian Alans, the Roman commander-in-chief in Lazica, who was none other than the emperor's cousin, Justin son of Germanus. What they wanted was land to settle on, and recognition as allies of the empire, which in practice meant the payment of a subsidy by the imperial treasury. Justin, who had no doubt long been aware of the approach of the Avars, realized that this was not some everyday frontier incident, to be dealt with by the local commander. He sent off the Avar envoys to see Justinian in Constantinople. When they arrived at the capital in January 558 they created a furore by their bizarre and alarming appearance, and in particular by their long hair, arranged in a kind of pony-tail. Justinian too realized that the newcomers might change the balance of power on the northern frontier. To impress the envoys, he met them surrounded by his full consistory – even by the whole senate, according to some sources. Some of the Avars had doubtless years before waited upon the emperor of China in the courts and palaces of Lo-Yang; they would be connoisseurs of ceremony and protocol. The outcome of the long negotiations was that Justinian accepted the alliance of the Avars, but did not for the moment grant them land for settlement within the empire.

In the next year the great invasion of the Kotrigurs preoccupied both emperor and government. Justinian's decision not to fight them, however, was certainly influenced by the hopes which he placed in his new Avar allies. In fact from 558 onwards the Avars first attacked and defeated the Transcaucasian Huns, and then, moving swiftly westward to the western Ukraine and Bessarabia, fell upon the Antae. Justinian intended that they should play the part of imperial policeman. But the Avars were accustomed to rule vast territories themselves, and did not accept easily a subordinate role. By 561 they were established on the lower Danube. Their Khagan, Baian, demanded to be settled in Scythia (Dobrudja), south of the Danube delta. This region was much too close to the populous centre of the empire, and to the plains of Thrace from which it drew its best soldiers, to be entrusted to such uncertain allies. Justinian temporized. Baian lost his patience and decided that if he could not get what he wanted by negotiation, he would cross the Danube and take it. But the military commander in Thrace – once again Justin son of Germanus – learned of the plan through his spies and warned the emperor. The Avar envoys were detained in Constantinople until Justin had strengthened the defences and concentrated his river fleet in the threatened area. When the envoys were finally allowed to return to their master, Justin insisted on taking from them at the frontier the arms which they had bought in the capital. Baian was furious, but there was little he could do about it. He continued to receive subsidies as an ally, but was given no land within the empire. The next year he and his people, despairing of getting what they wanted from Justinian, set off at full gallop through Europe for the kingdom of the Franks, where they hoped to drive a harder bargain. This move was probably encouraged by the Roman government, for it took place just when Narses was engaged in evicting the Franks from northern Italy. However the Avars, defeated in battle in Thuringia, concluded a treaty with the Merovingian king Sigebert and returned to the region north of the lower Danube. Until Justinian's death they remained there, theoretical allies of the empire, while Justin son of Germanus watched them suspiciously from his fortifications on the Roman side of the river. Within a generation of his death they were to control a great empire stretching from France to the Black Sea and to hammer on the gates of Constantinople.

Historians have sometimes asserted that in his later years Justinian lost his grip on political affairs and devoted himself wholly to sterile speculations and discussions on theology. The analysis of events on the northern frontier in the second half of Justinian's reign suggests that this is an exaggeration. The policy may not have been the best possible open to the empire, but it was consistent and uniform, the product of a powerful mind fully alert to every detail. Justinian was old, perhaps inflexible; but certainly not senile. It remains true, nevertheless, that after the death of Theodora more and more of his attention was directed to religion, and that he approached it essentially as an administrative problem. The reasons for this interest are clear enough. His consort's death was a reminder of his own mortality and of the necessity of accounting to his Maker for the empire which had been entrusted to him. At the same time, many things were going wrong. The great enterprise of restoration, which began with such rapid successes, seemed to be running into greater and greater difficulties. New problems were arising on the Danube frontier. The effects of the great plague were serious and lasting. Justinian would not have been a man of his age if he had not looked for the cause of these setbacks in incorrect religious doctrine and observance, displeasing to the Almighty. And he would not have been the man he was had he not believed that he himself could clear up the mistakes and set the world once again on the right course. Just as he had restored lucidity and simplicity to the chaotic muddle of Roman law, so he would free the true doctrine of the church from the jungle of heresy and schism that had grown up around it.

The problem of the succession and the death of Justinian

As he grew older, the emperor became more and more personally involved in detailed theological controversies and in the minutiae of church organization. In 561 he saw fit to issue a law fixing the date of Christmas and Epiphany, which had been celebrated at different times in different regions. His last legislative enactment, Novel 137 of 26 March 565, is a long series of regulations on clerical discipline, a matter which some might feel to be beneath – or beyond – imperial notice. The church historian Evagrius, writing some years after Justinian's death, reports that towards the end of his life the emperor published a decree declaring that the body of Christ was incorruptible and his sufferings only apparent, and required all bishops to subscribe to the decree. This doctrine, known as Aphthartodocetism, was one held by a faction of extreme Monophysites. Historians have supposed either that Justinian underwent a sudden and dramatic conversion, or that he was confused and did not realise what he was doing. Neither supposition is convincing. The emperor was a competent theologian. He had again and again said exactly the opposite in the past, and he does not appear to have displayed any other signs of senile dementia. The decree, if there was one, does not survive. Evagrius, though generally well-informed, may have misunderstood some of the many criticisms made of Justinian in the last years of his life. In general his account of the reign of Justinian lacks coherence. The matter is a mystery, and will probably always remain one. In October 563, when he was eighty-one years of age, Justinian suddenly decided to undertake the long and arduous pilgrimage to the Church of St Michael at Germia in Galatia (Yerma near Ankara). It was probably the first time for half a century that he had been more than a few days' journey from Constantinople. Whether he was impelled by some dream or vision, or was following the advice of one of the monks and theologians with whom he increasingly surrounded himself, is not known. But it was a remarkable undertaking for a man of his age and sedentary habits, and bears witness to the deep anxiety which coloured his last years.

Not least among the causes of this anxiety was the problem of the succession. Theoretically the emperor was chosen by senate, army and people. In practice their choice could be so circumscribed as to fall inevitably upon one man. Anastasius, who came to power late in life, was content to leave posterity to solve its own problems. Justin had marked out his nephew to succeed him by advancing him rapidly in the hierarchy of rank, by leaving more and more of the decisions of policy in his hands and finally by having him appointed as co-emperor a few months before his own death. Neither of these courses was open to Justinian. On the one hand his sense of mission and the habits of fifty years of power made it impossible for him to leave the succession open. He was convinced that no one knew so well as himself how to run the empire and was determined that it should continue to be run in the same way. On the other hand to designate a successor was to diminish his own autocratic power; and this he could not accept, even in the ninth decade of his life. So things were allowed to drift. His cousin Germanus, married to Matasuntha the grand-daughter of Theodoric and entrusted with the supreme command in Italy, seemed in 549 to be marked out as Justinian's eventual successor, perhaps after a period as subordinate emperor in the west. But Germanus died in 550. He was the last of Justinian's male cousins, Justus and Boraides having died before him. For a time the question of the succession was quietly allowed to drop.

But as the emperor grew older, it could not be avoided. In 560 Justinian suffered from severe headaches, and the rumour spread through the capital that he was dead. There were disorders in the city, and two dignitaries, the *curatores* George and Aetherius, were accused of plotting to elevate to the throne Theodore, the son of Justinian's foreign minister Peter the Patrician. There was an investigation, but nothing was proved. Justinian, now restored to health, no doubt preferred to forget the matter rather than draw attention to his own mortality. The next two years were marked by frequent riots and street battles between the circus factions, the outward sign of the disquiet and discontent of the populace. It was fertile ground for a conspiracy against the emperor's life. In autumn 562 just such a conspiracy was discovered, that of Marcellus, Ablabius and Sergius, in which the name of Belisarius was involved.

It is not known what actually happened. It seems utterly unlikely that Belisarius, who had given Justinian forty years of loyal service and again and again shown his own lack of ambition for political power, was really involved in a plot to murder him. But he can hardly have failed to discuss the problem of what would happen if Justinian were to die; and he had never learnt the discretion of a courtier. At any rate nothing was proved against him, and six months later the emperor restored him to favour and to the enjoyment of all his dignities and privileges. He had probably never seriously suspected him.

This mysterious plot underlined the urgency of the problem of the succession. The choice was in effect limited to members of the emperor's family. Justinian had always had a strong sense of family solidarity; and by this time no outsider could have maintained his claim against the emperor's powerful kin. He had outlived all his kinsmen of his own generation. In the next generation there were five adult males, who had by now been for years in high office. But the real choice was between the two Justins, one the son of his sister Vigilantia, the other the son of his cousin Germanus, who could not easily be by-passed in favour of their younger kinsmen. The obvious course would have been to designate one of the pair as *nobilissimus* or *Caesar*, or even to make him co-emperor, as the old emperor Justin had done for Justinian himself forty years earlier.

Justin, son of Germanus, was born about 525. He had, like most of Justinian's male relations, followed a military career. And he had inherited some of the prestige and popularity of his father, as well as some of his military brilliance. In recent years he had held high commands in sensitive frontier areas: in Lazica, and in Thrace where he dealt briskly and efficiently with the Avars. But his military duties had kept him away from the capital, and he was perhaps out of touch with the emperor's thinking on matters of high policy. The other Justin, son of Justinian's sister Vigilantia, was a somewhat older man, born some time before 520. He was the only one of Justinian's kinsmen who was not a soldier. What he did in his earlier years is unknown. Procopius never mentions him. Indeed his first recorded public appearance was during the delicate negotiations with Pope Vigilius in 552. Presumably he had held various offices in the palace bureaucracy. At any rate he clearly enjoyed his uncle's confidence. He had married Sophia, a niece of Theodora, an alliance which guaranteed him powerful support in court circles even after the empress's death in 548. In 552 he held the office of *cura palatii*, with the rank of consular, later raised to that of patrician. His office, though not one of the highest, gave him control of the palace bureaucracy. It also involved permanent residence at court, where he had the ear of his uncle and ample opportunity to manoeuvre and advance his interests. He seems to have been an able and energetic man, upon whom the ageing emperor came more and more to rely. And he had an ambitious wife, who had kept a foot in the Monophysite camp even after embracing the faith of Chalcedon. In 559 he was in charge of conducting Zabergan and the Kotrigur army back through Thrace to their homeland beyond the Danube. In 562 and 563 he played a prominent part in suppressing the riots of the circus factions. All in all, not an unworthy candidate for the succession.

The two Justins seem to have been on good personal terms. Indeed some sources state that in the old emperor's last years they made a compact each to support the other if he was chosen to succeed. The world waited for an announcement, but none was given. Meanwhile Justin son of Germanus, at the head of his army, continued to watch the threatening Avars across the Danube; and Justin the son of Vigilantia to attend to the hundred and one details of daily government business.

Justinian seemed indestructible. Age had slowed him, and he was no longer so readily accessible and affable to all who wished to see him. The time that he did not spend in the endless study of state papers and reports was devoted to abstruse theological discussion. But he continued to attend meticulously to every detail of the government of his empire. In March 565 came the news of the death of Belisarius, his oldest collaborator and the one man whom he could trust to put into effect whatever arrangements he might make for his succession.

The summer of 565 wore on, and night after night the lights burning in the Great Palace by the Sea of Marmora bore witness to the old emperor's unsleeping vigilance for the welfare of his people. They were still burning on the night of 14 November, when, without any signs of illness, Justinian suddenly died. The only officer of state present at his deathbed was Callinicus, the Praepositus of the Sacred Bedchamber. It was he who was the only witness to the emperor's last words, in which he designated as his successor Justin the son of his sister Vigilantia. Did Justinian really bring himself in the end to make a choice, or did Callinicus make it for him? Only Callinicus knew.

No sooner was Justinian dead than Callinicus, accompanied by such senators as he could find, hastened to Justin's palace near Seraglio Point. Roused from their sleep in the middle of the night, Justin and Sophia were hailed as emperor and empress. After a brief show of reluctance, they accepted their destiny. As the first cocks were crowing they entered the Great Palace, to the acclamations of the regiments of the guard. The new emperor's first act was to double the guards on the gates, as a precaution against popular unrest. His second was to lay out the body of his uncle on a gilded bier and to cover it with a winding-sheet on which his spouse, with admirable forethought, had had embroidered representations of the principal episodes in Justinian's life. Later in the morning Justin and Sophia appeared in the Kathisma of the Hippodrome, while the assembled citizens greeted them with the traditional cry of '*Tu vincas, Iustine*'. On the next day, clad in a purple robe and half-smothered in the gold and jewels which were the spoils of Africa and Italy, Justin made his way in solemn procession to Hagia Sophia, where he was elevated upon a shield by four stout soldiers. The aged patriarch John placed a diadem upon his head, and he took his place for the first time on the imperial throne within the chancel of the great church, while clergy and people intoned their blessings. There followed a second and more spectacular appearance in the Hippodrome, at which the new emperor distributed largesse and paid off in gold coin the debts of his predecessor. On the same afternoon Justinian's funeral took place. The body, lying upon a gilded and glittering catafalque, was borne from the Great Palace, followed by Justin and Sophia, the senate and the high officers of state, Patriarch, bishops and clergy, soldiers and palace guards, all bearing candles. The citizens of Constantinople, some weeping, some feigning tears, lined the streets through which the resplendent cortège passed. In the Church of the Holy Apostles, built by himself and the empress twenty-three years earlier, the old emperor was laid to rest in a sarcophagus of porphyry beside Theodora – the peasant boy and the bear-keeper's daughter.

Of their tombs and of the church no trace remains today. But some idea of the building can be gained from the Basilica of St Mark in Venice, which is modelled upon it.

Among the hundreds of thousands who lined the streets on that November day there were perhaps few who had much affection for Justinian. He had been a man with a mission, a hard – though never a gratuitously cruel – ruler. But there were few who could remember a time when he had not ruled over and represented the Roman empire. The crowds were uneasy; perhaps they knew it was the end of an age.

10 *Epilogue*

'Justinian had meant his reign to inaugurate a new era,' writes Professor George Ostrogorsky, 'but it really marked the close of a great age.' If one had to put one's verdict on Justinian as a statesman in a single sentence, one could hardly do it better. His restoration of the ancient grandeur of the Roman empire was a failure, it did not last, and it could never be repeated. Most of Spain and the whole of Gaul were left in foreign hands, though Roman sea power made the Mediterranean once more a Roman lake. Italy, devastated by a generation of warfare, its cities in ruins and its population decimated, was overwhelmed two years after Justinian's death by the Lombards, a Germanic people then settled in the plain of Hungary. Only the extreme south, as well as a few ports and cities in central Italy, an enclave round Ravenna and the islands of the Venetian lagoon remained in Roman hands. Yet Justinian's policy ensured a Byzantine presence in Italy which lasted, in political terms, until 1071, in cultural terms much longer, and which made its unique contribution to the early Italian Renaissance. It was to a south-Italian Greek that Petrarch turned when he wanted to read Homer in the original. The Byzantine element in Italy survives even today in two tiny enclaves of Greek speakers, one in Calabria, the other in Apulia. Cordova was lost to the Visigoths in 584, and by the 620s they had evicted the Romans from their last remaining strongholds in Spain. In Africa the growing pressure of Berber tribesmen confined Roman authority more and more to the cities and their neighbourhood. Yet Roman Africa flourished long after Justinian's reconquest. In 697, however, the Arabs, who had already conquered Egypt, Palestine and Syria, invaded Latin north Africa and quickly took Carthage. Fourteen years later they captured Septem, the last remaining Roman outpost on the African continent. Thus the reconquered west, which had cost the empire so much in money and in blood, proved unable to defend itself against serious attack. And outside Africa it was never much more than a hollow sham. It might well have been better for the peoples of the west if stable kingdoms, in alliance with the empire, had developed, in which the Roman and German elements could gradually fuse together, as they did in Frankish Gaul. But that the matter had to be settled by the sword was not Justinian's choice. He sought political solutions in Africa and above all in Italy, which might have resulted in just such a system of semi-independent states under ultimate – but remote – Roman sovereignty. The situation was not yet ripe.

In the east Justinian sought peace and maintenance of the status quo. Whether he should have foreseen that sixty years after his death Persia would be powerful enough to launch a real war of conquest is an open question. What is certain is that both he and the Great King of Persia, by arming, encouraging and training their respective Arab vassal principalities, did much to raise the level of military skill of the Arabs as a whole – a skill which in the next century they used to defeat Roman armies, wrest Egypt, Palestine and Syria from the empire, and threaten the heartland of Asia Minor, as well as to destroy completely the Sassanid Persian empire.

Justinian certainly underestimated the rapid growth of pressure on the northern frontier. Within a generation of his death Avars and Slavs had occupied much of the northern Balkans, within two generations the Avars were besieging Constantinople itself, and by the end of the next century his namesake Justinian II regarded a breakthrough from Constantinople to Thessalonica as a great victory. It was not that Justinian did not react to the build-up of peoples in the north. We have seen that he was constantly engaged in the traditional practice of buying the support of one foreign nation against another. And the surviving monuments bear witness to the ubiquity and solidity of the new fortifications which he built. The charge is rather that he got the scale of the threat wrong; that he used traditional methods out of inertia when he ought to have concentrated the strength of the empire either on repulsing the new invaders or on absorbing them; that he failed to notice a turning-point in history. There is much in the charge. But how many statesmen have shown the kind of foresight which his critics demand of Justinian? One searches in vain the copious literature of the age for even a glimmering of the idea that the greatest threat to the empire came from the north. Justinian, like all his contemporaries, was the prisoner of traditional conceptions. He dealt with the northern barbarians by traditional methods, which concentrated on avoiding needless bloodshed. And with a few exceptions he dealt with them well. The Avars, who were to transform the situation in the generations after his death, did not appear on the scene until Justinian was seventy-five.

In internal matters, Justinian fought to maintain the unity of the Roman empire against a variety of centrifugal tendencies – not least that represented by the great territorial magnates, who detested him. He realized to the full the importance of ideological unity in maintaining the coherence of the vast community. The close fusion of church and state so long characteristic of the eastern Roman empire was in a large measure his work. Western scholars, to whom it seemed natural that the one universal church should be independent of the many often short-lived states which grew up, have sometimes called this close fusion of church and state 'Caesaropapism'. To do so is to use a pejorative term instead of attempting to understand the reality. It certainly corresponded to the needs of the time, and gave the empire the strength to resist the long and unrelenting Arab pressure in succeeding centuries. Certainly Justinian sometimes overreached himself in his attempts to force ecclesiastical unity on his subjects. The story of his relations with Pope Vigilius is a sorry one from both sides. But when one reflects on the savagery with which religious disputes were conducted at later periods and in other lands, one is struck by the relatively reasonable and civilized procedures employed by Justinian. In this respect he contrasts favourably with Philip II of Spain, with whom Gibbon compared him in a famous passage (*Decline and Fall of the Roman Empire*, ed. J. B. Bury, vol. 4, 432).

Some – but by no means all – Marxist historians have accused Justinian of presiding over a restoration of slave-owning society, and of so trying to turn back the clock of history. The charge cannot be substantiated. There is no evidence that slavery was more extensive, or more intensive, in his reign than before. What is true is that it is often mentioned in his legal enactments. But the context is generally that of clearing up old obscurities or setting aside obsolete provisions. In reconquered Italy he ordered the re-enslavement of those freed by Totila. But it is difficult to see what else he could have done, since his declared purpose was to restore the status quo at the death of Amalasuntha and since he needed the support of the middle and upper classes of Italian society.

His great corpus of Roman law brought the law into accordance with the needs of the age, cutting out antiquarian survivals and distinctions without a difference. To start from scratch and devise a code of law which reflected the realities and the concepts of the early Byzantine world would have been inconceivable at the time. Justinian – and Tribonian – redesigned and refurbished the venerable edifice of Roman law. The excellence of their workmanship is borne out by the way in which later generations took it as the starting-point from which to develop their own legal systems. No work of legislation except the Ten Commandments has had such lasting effect.

Justinian's Great Church still survives, admired alike by tourists and by architects. It stands as a reminder of the high excellence of all the arts in the age over which he presided, an excellence far surpassing anything achieved since the second century and serving as an unattainable model for succeeding generations. It was an age of lively experiment in literature, one in which side by side with the most rigorous classicism arose new literary forms such as the elaborate hymns of Romanus together with the use of the vulgar tongue in literature. And it was an age of hard intellectual argument. Theological disputation was often conducted by piling up quotations from the Fathers, it is true. But when John Philoponus argues against Proclus that the universe was created in time, and not always there, a sharp and tough intellect is wrestling with a genuine philosophical problem. And the last of the neo-Platonists, men like Simplicius and Damascius, were not merely erudite; they were rigorous and courageous searchers for truth. All this, of course, cannot be put to the credit of Justinian. But he was a generous, intelligent and understanding patron; and he set a standard of excellence which found ready acceptance among his contemporaries.

What of Theodora in all this? She remains an enigmatic and rather alarming figure, a woman enjoying immense power in an age which had no institutional structure for such exercise of power. Later tradition tended to close its eyes to her. It is only recently that she has begun to be appreciated – and often oversimplified and misunderstood. Yet if a civilization can be judged by the way it treats its women, that of the age of Justinian and Theodora deserves to be rated high.

In spite of all the failures, his empire was powerful – far more so than the Roman empire had been since Theodosius or would ever be again. And its fame and prestige spread far beyond its borders. It is symptomatic that a local worthy in north Wales in the sixth century, living in a society which had not seen a Roman soldier for two centuries, and where men had almost forgotten how to speak Latin, dated his tombstone by the name of the man who was in that year consul in Constantinople under Justinian. How did he obtain such information?

To some of his contemporaries, however, particularly those attached to old and wealthy senatorial families, Justinian was the devil incarnate. Rumour had it that as he paced the galleries of the palace by night his head would sometimes vanish from his shoulders and reappear again later. And his mother, so some said, claimed to have had intercourse with a demon before conceiving her son. This uncompromisingly negative judgement of Justinian is most clearly expressed in Procopius' *Secret History*, a document which cannot have been widely circulated during the emperor's lifetime; its almost paranoic tone scarcely justifies the confidence which some scholars have placed in it. It probably reflects the author's quasi-Manichaean point of view.

Justinian was remembered in the Byzantine world as the builder of Hagia Sophia and as a legislator, rather than as the ruler who restored Roman power in the western Mediterranean. For centuries after his death the empire had all it could do to retain control of Asia Minor and the eastern Mediterranean. But the idea of a reconquest of the lost provinces never faded completely from men's minds. Western states were given *de facto* rather than *de jure* recognition. And as the Arab threat disappeared, and the territories in Europe overrun by the Slavs were brought again under Byzantine control, emperors began to try to reassert Byzantine power in the west, and particularly in southern Italy. The second half of the tenth century saw a steady advance of Byzantine control in the heel and toe of Italy. There were no great battles. But every advantage was taken of the quarrels between the Lombard principalities and of the power-vacuum left by the Arabs as they withdrew from their bridgeheads on the Italian coast. In the wake of the army and sometimes even preceding it came Byzantine monks and Byzantine settlers, reinforcing the surviving Greek elements among the population. The emperor Basil II (976-1025), under whom Byzantine power reached its zenith in the Middle Ages, certainly saw himself as a second Justinian, though no two men could have been more different in character. So too in the twelfth century Manuel I (1143-85) for a time re-established Byzantine power in regions of south Italy, while the rhetoricians and panegyrists recalled the great days of Justinian and Belisarius. But the balance of power in Europe had radically changed. Manuel's victories were only obtained by skilfully exploiting the differences between the Holy Roman Empire and the papacy, between Venice and Genoa, between the Normans of south Italy and their neighbours. And within twenty years of Manuel's death, crusaders from the west had captured Constantinople itself. There was no place for dreams of reconquest. And Justinian had never sufficiently captured the popular imagination to become a folk hero, as did the Iconoclast emperors Constantine V and Theophilus. He never passed into legend. The west too remembered Justinian.

Dante met his shade, who traced for him the history of the Roman empire from Aeneas to Charlemagne (*Paradiso*, Canto 6).

His great marshal Belisarius did live on in the imagination of the common people. Out of a confused recollection of his successive short-lived disgraces there grew a story that he was blinded by Justinian and reduced to begging in the streets of Constantinople until, in a great emergency, Justinian had need of him again. This story is referred to as generally familiar by John Tzetzes in the middle of the twelfth century. And there survives a poem in early vernacular Greek – in its present form probably first written down in the thirteenth or fourteenth century, but depending on earlier oral versions – which recounts, with copious moral reflections, the same story. This legend found its way into western literature. It was the basis upon which Marmontel constructed his novel *Bélisaire* (1767), which was a veiled attack on the autocracy of Louis xv. The novel was many times reprinted, and among the numerous translations is one into Greek (Venice, 1783).

Theodora might well have become the subject of many a legend had the *Secret History* of Procopius been known to wide circles of readers. But it was hardly read by the Byzantines – copies were doubtless always rare – and was unknown in the west until a manuscript was discovered by N. Alemanni at the beginning of the seventeenth century. However, she was remembered. In the eleventh century tourists were shown a small house under a portico, where she was alleged to have made her secret assignations with Justinian. In Syriac legend she was revered as the protector of the Monophysites. Her sordid antecedents were conveniently forgotten, and she became the daughter of a pious Monophysite senator. There may have been a tradition about Theodora in the medieval west. At any rate in the eleventh century Aimoin de Fleury recounts how the young Justinian and the young Belisarius met two ladies of easy virtue called Antonina and Antonia. Justinian fell in love with Antonia, who exacted from him a promise that if he became emperor he would marry her. When in the end and to his great surprise he did become emperor, he insisted on keeping his promise, to the horror of the senators (*Historia Francorum* 2.5). The story is decked out with many folk motifs. It nevertheless suggests a tradition about Justinian and his empress independent of that furnished by the Latin translations of Byzantine chronicles then available in the west.

Baronius, the great ecclesiastical historian of the Counter-Reformation (his *Annales Ecclesiastici* appeared between 1588 and 1607), can find no words strong enough for Theodora. In his thunderous Latin periods he calls her a second Eve, a new Delilah, another Herodias dripping with the blood of the saints. After the rediscovery of the *Secret History*, she was attacked by lay and ecclesiastical writers alike, and endless efforts were made to find lovers for her by reading between the lines of Procopius. The eighteenth century took a poor view of the eastern Roman empire in general. And Gibbon at first dismisses Theodora with the tart observation that her strange elevation cannot be applauded as a triumph of female virtue. But later he recognizes her strength of character and her sincerity.

In the nineteenth century interest in Justinian and Theodora began to revive. Novels in many languages, and usually of poor quality, attempted an imaginative recreation of their story. Victorien Sardou wrote a play entitled *Théodora*, which opened on 26 December 1884 in the Théâtre de la Porte Saint-Martin in Paris, with music by Massenet and with Sarah Bernhardt in the title role. The Nika revolt, the disgrace of Belisarius and the death of Theodora were telescoped into a few days; and she was given a lover, one Andreas, the leader of the Green faction. Her intrigue was discovered, and she was strangled on the orders of Justinian. Lack of historical veracity did not prevent Sardou's play enjoying a long run and several revivals. It was translated into German and adapted as a novel several times over. It was no doubt the success of Sardou's play which led Benjamin Constant, a Belgian painter working in Paris and specializing in harem scenes for the tired businessmen of the Third Republic, to exhibit at the Salon of 1887 paintings of Justinian and Theodora, which attracted lively attention. Tastes change, however, and the portrait of Theodora was sold in London in 1909 for £378, and the next year for £52 10s. Attempts to trace it have proved vain. It may well be lying forgotten in the cellars of some English provincial art-gallery. A more serious result of the interest aroused by Sardou's play was the publication in 1904 by the young French historian Charles Diehl of a work entitled *Théodora, impératrice de Byzance*. Diehl's book was both a solid work of scholarship and an elegant and sympathetic, if somewhat romantic, account of an extraordinary woman.

Of a very different character from Sardou's play was Robert Graves' novel *The Count Belisarius*, first published in 1938. Mr Graves adheres closely to what the sources tell us, and fills out their many gaps by a sensitive reconstruction based on close study and real understanding of the age. *The Count Belisarius* is one of the most remarkable historical novels of the twentieth century, and has been many times reprinted.

The Byzantine court was photogenic if nothing else, and one might have expected Hollywood to make an epic on Justinian and Theodora. But the only film traceable is a low-cost Italian production of 1953, *Teodora, Imperatrice di Bisanzio*, which seems to have been little shown outside its country of origin. The title role was played by Gianna-Maria Canale. The imperial pair quarrelled when Arcas, an ex-lover of Theodora, turned up. But they were eventually reconciled and, standing side by side, faded out into a picture of the mosaics of S. Vitale.

Table of Dates

THE WEST	CONSTANTINOPLE AND THE EASTERN EMPIRE	THE EASTERN FRONT
	c. 482 Birth of Justinian.	
	c. 495 Justinian brought to Constantinople to be educated.	
518 End of schism between Pope and eastern Church.	518 Death of Anastasius. Justin I becomes Emperor. Promotion of Justinian. Persecution of Monophysites begins.	
519 Consulship of Eutharic, son-in-law and heir of King Theodoric.		
	520 Consulship of Vitalian. Vitalian assassinated by Justin I and Justinian.	
	521 Consulship of Justinian.	
522 Death of Eutharic. Consulship of Boethius and Symmachus.		
523 Hilderic becomes king of Vandals and begins pro-imperial, anti-Ostrogothic policy.	*c.* 523 Germanus defeats Antae.	523 Massacre of Christians in Yemen by Dhu-Nuwas. With imperial support King Elesboas of Ethiopia invades Yemen.
524 Theodoric executes Boethius and Symmachus.		524 King Kavadh of Persia drives Romans out of Iberia.
	525 Justinian appointed Caesar by Justin I. Marriage of Justinian and Theodora.	525 Ethiopian conquest of Yemen.
526 30 August: death of Theodoric. Amalasuntha becomes regent for her son Athalaric.	526 Serious earthquake at Antioch.	526 War with Persia. Belisarius in command.
	527 Justinian made co-emperor. Death of Justin I. Succession of Justinian.	527 Belisarius continues operations against Persia.
	528 Codification of law begun.	

THE WEST	CONSTANTINOPLE AND THE EASTERN EMPIRE	THE EASTERN FRONT
	529 7 April: First version of *Code* issued. Closure of Academy in Athens. Revolt of Samaritans.	
530 King Hilderic of the Vandals deposed by Gelimer, who revives anti-Imperial policy.	530 John of Cappadocia appointed Praetorian Prefect. Mundus defeats Slav raids in Balkans.	530 Belisarius defeats Persians at Dara.
		531 Belisarius defeated by Persians at Callinicum. Death of King Kavadh and accession of Chosroes I.
	532 January: Nika riots. Massacre of rioters by Belisarius and Mundus.	532 Everlasting Peace signed with King Chosroes.
533 June: Belisarius sails to Sicily, lands in North Africa. September: Belisarius defeats Gelimer at Tenth Milestone and occupies Carthage. December: Vandal army destroyed at Tricamarum.	533 December: Publication of *Digest*.	
534 Surrender of Gelimer to Belisarius. Solomon left in command in Africa. Amalasuntha negotiates secretly with Justinian. October: death of Athalaric. Amalasuntha marries King Theodahad.	534 Belisarius celebrates triumph for conquest of Africa. Publication of second version of *Code*.	
535 Amalasuntha imprisoned by Theodahad and murdered. Mundus invades Dalmatia. Belisarius captures Syracuse and begins occupation of Sicily.		
536 Mutiny in Africa. Theodahad negotiates with Justinian. Ostrogoths recover Dalmatia and kill Mundus. Belisarius invades Italy, takes Naples. Theodahad deposed and succeeded by Vitiges. December: Belisarius occupies Rome.		

THE WEST	CONSTANTINOPLE AND THE EASTERN EMPIRE	THE EASTERN FRONT
537 Germanus suppresses mutiny in Africa. Vitiges besieges Belisarius in Rome.	537 26 December: dedication of Hagia Sophia.	
538 Vitiges abandons siege of Rome. Narses arrives in Italy. Liguria and Milan occupied.		
539 Ostrogoths recover Milan and massacre its population. Recall of Narses. Vitiges negotiates for peace.		539 Vitiges' envoys appeal to King Chosroes for help.
540 Belisarius accepts surrender of Ostrogoths and enters Ravenna.	540 Slav raiders threaten Constantinople and ravage Greece.	540 Chosroes invades Syria and captures Antioch.
541 Autumn: Totila elected king of Goths and reopens war against imperial forces.	541 John of Cappadocia dismissed as a result of intrigue by Theodora.	541 Chosroes invades Lazica. Belisarius takes over command in east.
542 Totila captures many strong-points in Italy.	542 Peter Barsymes organizes state monopoly of silk trade. Summer: outbreak of bubonic plague in Egypt, which rapidly spreads throughout the empire.	
543 Totila takes Naples.	543 Plague continues to rage. Jacob Baradaeus consecrated Monophysite bishop of Edessa. Peter Barsymes appointed Praetorian Prefect.	
544 Belisarius returns to take command in Italy.		
545 December: Totila begins siege of Rome.		545 Truce with Persia.
546 New mutiny in Africa. Assassination of Areobindus. John the Troglite appointed commander in Africa.	546 Justinian issues edict condemning Three Chapters.	
547 Totila abandons Rome, and Belisarius reenters the city. Completion of Church of S. Vitale in Ravenna.	547 Pope Vigilius arrives in Constantinople.	

	THE WEST	CONSTANTINOPLE AND THE EASTERN EMPIRE	THE EASTERN FRONT
548	Belisarius recalled from Italy. John the Troglite defeats Moors in Africa.	28 June: death of Theodora. Slav raids penetrate as far as Dyrrhachium.	
549	Totila begins new siege of Rome. Completion of Church of S. Apollinare in Classe, near Ravenna.		
550	January: Totila captures Rome, and invades Sicily. Imperial forces enter Visigothic Spain.	Germanus appointed to command in Italy and married to Matasuntha, granddaughter of Theodoric. He repulses Slavonic raiders in Balkans but dies in autumn. Narses appointed commander in Italy and begins preparations.	
551	Totila besieges Ancona. Imperial naval victory at Sena Gallica. Totila makes peace overtures, which Justinian rejects.	Open breach between Justinian and Pope Vigilius. Kotrigurs invade Balkans. Justinian incites Utigurs against them.	Bessas recaptures Petra in Lazica from Persians. New truce with Persia.
552	Narses arrives in Italy and defeats Goths at Busta Gallorum. Death of Totila. Narses recaptures Rome and destroys Gothic force at Mons Lactarius.		
553	Franks and Alemans invade Italy.	May: fifth ecumenical council condemns Three Chapters, in spite of opposition by Pope Vigilius. December: Vigilius under pressure condemns Three Chapters.	
554	Narses defeats Franks and Alemans and begins pacification of Italy. Visigoths check imperial expansion in Spain.	_c._ 554 Silkworm eggs smuggled into empire from Soghdiana, and Byzantine silk production begun. Publication of _Pragmatic Sanction_.	
555	Pope Vigilius dies in Sicily on way back to Rome. Capture of Compsa, last Gothic strong-point south of Po.		King of Lazica murdered by Roman authorities. Pro-Persian revolt in Lazica.

THE WEST	CONSTANTINOPLE AND THE EASTERN EMPIRE	THE EASTERN FRONT
556 Consecration of Pope Pelagius.		
		557 New truce with Persia.
	558 Dome of Hagia Sophia collapses. Recurrence of bubonic plague. Invasion of Balkans by Kotrigurs. Avar envoys in Constantinople.	558 Avars under Baian establish contact with Justin son of Germanus in Caucasus.
	559 Belisarius, recalled from retirement, defeats Kotrigurs.	
561 Narses takes Verona, last Gothic stronghold.		
	562 Conspiracy to assassinate Justinian. 24 December: re-dedication of Hagia Sophia.	562 Fifty Years Peace with Persia.
	563 Justinian undertakes pilgrimage to Germia in Galatia.	
	565 January: Justinian promulgates doctrine of Aphthartodocetism in new attempt to reach compromise with Monophysites (?). March: death of Belisarius. 14 November: death of Justinian and accession of Justin II.	

Notes on Sources

The period of Justinian's life and reign was covered by a series of narrative histories written by contemporaries, in the sophisticated historiographic tradition inherited from Herodotus, Thucydides and Polybius. Unfortunately not all of these works survive in their entirety. English translations are mentioned where these exist.

1 *Procopius* An account of Justinian's wars was composed by Procopius of Caesarea in Palestine, a lawyer by training and for many years military secretary and to some extent confidant of Belisarius. The first two books deal with operations against Persia from the beginning of the century down to the 550s. The next two deal with the campaign against the Vandals in Africa, its antecedents and consequences. The last four deal with the long war against the Goths in Italy and the events which led up to it. Procopius was an eyewitness of much of what he recounts and collected information on other matters carefully and critically. His history is extremely detailed and is the main source for the first two-thirds of Justinian's reign. He is less well-informed on events in Constantinople than on what happened in the field, but what he says must always be taken seriously. On the whole he is favourable to Justinian in his history of the wars, but he often criticizes his measures from the point of view of the commander in the field.

As he was writing his history of the wars, or more probably after its completion, he composed – for private circulation rather than for publication – his *Secret History*, a blistering attack upon Justinian and Theodora purporting to be the 'inside story' lying behind the narrative of his published work. It contains much which is known to be true from other sources, a great deal which cannot be verified and some statements which are known to be untrue. The tone is scurrilous and the work is animated by passionate hatred. It is probably the product of a period of deep disillusionment with the emperor and his policy some

time in the 550s. It may also reflect a quasi-Manichaean view of the world, which could easily be reconciled with conventional Christianity. Used with care, it is a valuable supplement to the history of the wars. But its chronology is very sketchy; and narrative and interpretation are so closely interwoven that they sometimes cannot be distinguished.

Shortly after writing the *Secret History*, Procopius was invited by Justinian to write an account of his buildings and public works. This work, *On the Buildings*, is panegyric in tone, but contains much information on buildings no longer surviving, such as the Church of the Holy Apostles in Constantinople and the numerous churches and monasteries which Justinian had built in Palestine.

Editions

Procopii Caesariensis opera omnia, ed. J. Haury, 3 vols., Leipzig, 1905-6 and reprint (Greek text).

Procopius, trans. H.B.Dewing and G.Downey, 8 vols., Loeb Classical Library, London, 1914-40.

Procopius, trans. Averil M.Cameron, Washington Square Press, New York, 1967 (select passages).

Procopius, *The Secret History*, trans. G.A. Williamson, Penguin Books, London, 1966. The best recent study of Procopius is Averil M. Cameron, *Procopius and the Sixth Century*, London-Berkeley-Los Angeles, 1985.

2 *Agathias* A continuation of Procopius' history, covering the years 552-68, was written by Agathias of Myrina in Asia Minor, a lawyer and poet. His sources of information and his historical judgment are alike inferior to those of Procopius. But his account of events is detailed, and he had a wide-ranging curiosity.

Editions

Agathiae Myrinaei historiarum libri quinque, ed. R.Keydell, Berlin, 1968 (Greek text); English translation by J.D.Frendo, *Agathias; The Histories*, Berlin-New York, 1975.

See also Averil M.Cameron, *Agathias*, Oxford, 1970.

3 *Menander Protector* A continuation of Agathias' history was written by a member of the palace guard under the emperor Maurice (582-602). It took the story of events from 558 down to 582. Menander's history survives only in excerpts made for a historical encyclopedia in the tenth century. He was a careful, critical historian, with good sources of information and a grasp of the political realities of the time.
Editions
R. C. Blockley, *The History of Menander the Guardsman,* Liverpool, 1985. Text and English translation of the surviving fragments.

4 *Peter the Patrician* A Byzantine diplomat under Justinian, who rose to the dignity of Master of Offices, composed one or more works on the history of his own times. Of these there survive only excerpts dealing with diplomatic negotiations and with court ceremonies. They preserve much detailed information.
Editions
Historici Graeci minores, ed. L.Dindorf, I, Leipzig, 1870 (Greek text). There is no English translation.

In addition two ecclesiastical histories cover the reign of Justinian. These are primarily concerned with the affairs of the church. But they incidentally supply information on the civil history of the time.
1 *Evagrius* Evagrius of Epiphaneia (Hama) in Syria, who practised at the bar at Antioch, wrote at the end of the sixth century an ecclesiastical history in six books, dealing with the years 431 to 594. He gives attention to secular matters as well, and in particular mentions the early Slavonic invasions of the Balkan peninsula. For the age of Justinian he used a variety of earlier historians, including many whose work is now lost.
Editions
The Ecclesiastical History of Evagrius with the Scholia, ed. J.Bidez and L.Parmentier, London, 1898 (Greek text).
English translation: *Evagrius, A History of the Church from AD 431 to AD 594*, E.Walford, Bohn's Ecclesiastical Library, London, 1851.

2 *John of Ephesus* John wrote the history of the Church from its foundation until 585 from a Monophysite point of view. The surviving portion of his work, which was written in Syriac, covers the years 521 to 585. It contains valuable information on social life and attitudes, particularly in the provinces of the empire. His other work, *The Lives of the Eastern Saints*, contains much interesting detail on the spread of Monophysitism and its persecution.
Editions
Iohannis Ephesini Historiae Ecclesiasticae pars tertia, ed. E.W.Brooks, Louvain, 1935 (Syriac text).
English translation: *The Third Part of the Ecclesiastical History of John, Bishop of Ephesus*, R. Payne Smith, Oxford, 1860
E.W.Brooks, *Lives of the Eastern Saints*, Paris, 1925 (English translation).

At a lower level of historical analysis come the early Byzantine world chronicles. In principle these recount the history of the world from the Creation to the writer's own time. In practice they deal in detail largely with recent events in the Roman empire. Their concept of historical causation is a narrowly theological one, and they show little grasp of political realities or of human character. Nevertheless they often provide valuable information not preserved in other sources, and since they recount events year by year they are often useful in establishing their chronology.

1 *Malalas* John Malalas, an advocate of Antioch, composed about the end of Justinian's reign a chronicle extending from the Creation to 563. Side by side with much that is trivial, it preserves a great deal of information on the age of Justinian, particularly regarding events in Syria.
Editions
Ioannis Malalae Chronographia, ed. L.Dindorf, Bonn, 1831 (Greek text).
The Chronicle of John Malalas, trans. M.Spinka and G.Downey, VIII-XVIII, Chicago, 1940 (from an Old Slavonic version which is in

places fuller than the surviving Greek text). An English translation of the whole Chronicle with a historical commentary is in preparation by a group of scholars in Australia.

2 *John of Antioch* John, of whom nothing else is known, wrote a chronicle from the Creation to 610, probably some time in the seventh century. The full text is lost, but from the surviving excerpts it appears to have been a work of higher quality than the run of these chronicles.

Editions
Fragmenta Historicorum Graecorum, ed. K.Muller, IV, Paris, 1851 (Greek text). There is no English translation.

3 *Paschal Chronicle* This compilation by an unknown author of the early seventh century covers the period from the Creation to 629. It contains some information on the age of Justinian not available in other sources.

Editions
Chronicon Paschale, ed. L. Dindorf, Bonn, 1832 (Greek text). There is no English translation.

4 *John of Nikiou* John, an Egyptian ecclesiastic of the seventh century, wrote a chronicle covering the period from the Creation to the Arab conquest of Egypt. It is valuable in particular for Egyptian affairs. The Greek text is lost. What survives is an Ethiopic version of excerpts from a lost Arabic translation.

Editions
Notices et extraits des manuscrits de la Bibliothèque Nationale, ed. H.Zotenberg, 24, Pt. 1, 125-605, Paris, 1883 (Ethiopic text).
The Chronicle of John, Bishop of Nikiou, trans. R.H.Charles, London, 1916. (Not always reliable).

5 *Theophanes Confessor* Theophanes, a Byzantine monk of the early ninth century, compiled a chronicle covering the years 284 to 814. For the age of Justinian it includes much material from primary sources now lost.

Editions
Theophanis Chronographia, ed. C. De Boor, Leipzig, 1883 (Greek text). There is no English translation of the section dealiing with the sixth century.

6 *Marcellinus Comes* Marcellinus, a court official of Justinian from Latin-speaking Illyria, composed a continuation of St Jerome's Latin adaptation of the chronicle of Eusebius. It covers the years 379 to 548, and deals almost entirely with affairs in the eastern empire. An unpretentious work, it preserves much valuable information.

Editions
Chronica minora 2 (Monumenta Germaniae historica, auctores antiquissimi 8), ed. Th. Mommsen, Berlin, 1894 (Latin text). There is no English translation.

7 *Victor Tunnunensis* Victor, an African bishop, was exiled from his see by Justinian for opposition to imperial policy in the matter of the Three Chapters, and ultimately confined to a monastery in Constantinople. His Latin chronicle, covering the years 444 to 563, is useful in particular for African affairs.

Editions
Chronica Minora 2 (Monumenta Germaniae historica, auctores antiquissimi 8), ed. Th. Mommsen. Berlin, 1894 (Latin text). There is no English translation.

Several other contemporary works of quasi-historical character are valuable as sources for the reign of Justinian.

1 *John the Lydian* John, a civil servant of antiquarian tastes in Constantinople, wrote a treatise on the history of the Roman magistrates which contains valuable information on the institutional history of the period, and in particular on the activities of Justinian's minister of finance, John of Cappadocia.

Editions
A.C.Bandy, *Ioannes Lydus, On Powers, or The Magistracies of the Roman State*, Philadelphia, 1982. (Greek text and English translation).

2 *Cosmas Indicopleustes* The author, a retired sea-captain of Alexandria, composed towards the end of Justinian's reign a long treatise (*The Christian Topography*) directed against the Aristotelian natural philosophers of Alexandria, and designed to prove that the world was shaped like the tabernacle of Moses. He incidentally supplies much picturesque information on the eastern trade of the empire and on Byzantine economic and military policy towards the Ethiopian and Arab states at the mouth of the Red Sea.

Editions

E.O.Winstedt, *The Christian Topography of Cosmas Indicopleustes*, Cambridge, 1909 (Greek text).

Wanda Wolska-Conus, Vol I, Paris, 1968 (text and French translation).

The Christian Topography of Cosmas an Egyptian monk, trans. J.W.McCrindle, London, 1897.

3 *Corippus* Flavius Cresconius Corippus was a school-master in Carthage when he published, about 550, his panegyric on John the Troglite, the Roman commander in Africa. Some fifteen years later he wrote a poem in honour of Justinian's nephew, the emperor Justin II. The former poem recounts in some detail, though with all the conventional trappings of epic poetry, the story of the pacification of Africa. The latter is valuable for its account of the death of Justinian and the succession of Justin II and for its clear expression of many aspects of the political ideology of the period.

Editions

Monumenta Germaniae historica, auctores antiquissimi 3.2, ed. J.Partsch, Berlin, 1879 (Latin text).

Flavii Cresconii Corippi Iohannidos libri viii, ed. J.Diggle and W.F.R.Goodyear, Cambridge, 1970 (Latin text).

Averil M.Cameron, *Flavius Cresconius Corippus, In Laudem Iustini, Augusti minoris*, London, 1976. (Text and English translation).

4 *Paul the Silentiary* Paul was a gentleman-usher (*silentiarius*) at court in the latter part of the reign of Justinian. As well as a collection of occasional poetry included in his anthology by his friend Agathias, he wrote a long description in hexameter verse of the Church of the Holy Wisdom at Constantinople, which was recited in the presence of Justinian at the second dedication of the church in 562. There also survives from his hand a similar description of the Ambon or 'pulpit in the church. These poems are as lucid as their ornate, traditional style permits and give us an idea of the Great Church as it was originally conceived and as it struck the eyes and minds of contemporaries.

Editions

P.Friedländer, *Johannes von Gaza und Paulus Silentiarius*, Leipzig-Berlin, 1912; Hildesheim-New York, 1969 (Greek text).

W.R.Lethaby and H.Swainson, *Sancta Sophia*, London-New York, 1894 (English translation).

A source of a somewhat different kind is provided by Justinian's legal corpus, comprising the *Digest*, the *Code*, the *Novellae*, and the *Institutes*, together with prefatory matter, authorizing edicts, etc. The *Code* contains a number of dated legal enactments of Justinian. The *Novellae* comprise his legal enactments after the publication of the *Code*, and are a most valuable source, not only for the legislation itself, but for official ideology and propaganda.

Editions

Th.Mommsen, R.Krueger, R.Schoell and G.Kroll, *Corpus Iuris Civilis* 3 vols, Berlin, 1867-1954 (Latin and Greek texts). See also J.Wenger, *Die Quellen des römischen Rechts*, Vienna, 1953. There is no English translation of the whole corpus.

Justinian's theological works are published in J.P.Migne, *Patrologia Graeca*, vol. 86, Paris, 1865, 945-1151. One of his hymns is still in liturgical use in the Orthodox Church.

Further Reading

1 GENERAL HISTORIES OF THE PERIOD

A.H.M.JONES, *The Later Roman Empire 284-602; a Social, Economic and Administrative survey*, 3 vols and portfolio of maps, Oxford 1964. A narrative survey of the fourth to sixth centuries is followed by detailed studies of the institutions, social classes, trade, the church etc. Very important, but hardly a beginner's book.

A.H.M.JONES, *The Decline of the Ancient World*, London 1966. A short account based on the author's *Later Roman Empire*.

J.B.BURY, *A History of the Later Roman Empire from the death of Theodosius to the death of Justinian*, second edition, 2 vols, London 1923. A large-scale narrative history. Less concerned with social and economic matters than Jones. The second volume is devoted to the reign of Justinian.

J.W.BARKER, *Justinian and the Later Roman Empire*, Madison, Wis. 1960. A useful introduction (with bibliography).

E.STEIN, *Histoire du Bas-Empire*, vol II. Paris 1949. The most detailed study of the period. Indispensable for the serious student, but inclined not to see the wood for trees.

2 JUSTINIAN AND HIS REIGN

W.G.HOLMES, *The Age of Justinian and Theodora. A History of the Sixth Century*, second edition, London 1912. Detailed but unexciting.

P.N.URE, *Justinian and his Age*, Penguin Books 1951. A stimulating introduction to some of the problems.

A.VASILIEV, *Justin the First. An Introduction to the Epoch of Justinian the Great*, Cambridge, Mass. 1950. The fullest study of the reign of Justinian's uncle and predecessor.

CH.DIEHL, *Justinien et la civilisation byzantine au VIe siècle*, 2 vols, Paris 1901. A brilliant and highly readable study of the age, but on certain points out of date.

B.RUBIN, *Das Zeitalter Justinians*, vol 1 [all published], Berlin 1960. The first volume of what was to be the major modern study of Justinian. Immensely learned, but long-winded and sometimes irrelevant. Heavy going even for those whose German is good.

G.W.DOWNEY, *Constantinople in the Age of Justinian*, Univ. of Oklahoma Press, 1960. A popular but scholarly account of life in Justinian's capital.

3 THE WEST

J.M.WALLACE-HADRILL, *The Barbarian West: Early Middle Ages, A.D. 400-1000*, London 1952.

C.DAWSON, *The Making of Europe*, London 1939.

H.ST.L.B.MOSS, *The Birth of the Middle Ages, 395-814*, London 1937.

4 CHURCH HISTORY

A.FLICHE and V.MARTIN (ed.), *Histoire de l' Église*, vol 4, *De la mort de Théodose à l'élection de Grégoire le Grand*, Paris 1937. The most detailed and reliable study of the period. The complete series is being translated into English, but the translation of vol 4 has not yet appeared.

J.PARGOIRE, *L'église byzantine de 527 à 847*, Paris 1905. The first chapters give a balanced account of Justinian's religious policy.

P.R.COLEMAN-NORTON, *Roman State and Christian Church. A Collection of legal documents to A.D. 535*, London 1966, 3 vols. Vol 3 contains translations of all Justinian's religious legislation up to 535, with full discussions.

W.H.C.FREND, *The Rise of the Monophysite Movement*, Cambridge, 1972. Justinian's attitude to the Monophysites is discussed on pp. 255-295.

5 ART AND ARCHITECTURE

A.GRABAR, *From Theodosius to Islam*, London 1966. Superbly illustrated.

D.TALBOT RICE, *The Beginnings of Christian Art*, London 1957. A more general survey of a longer period.

W.F.VOLBACH and M. HIRMER, *Early Christian Art*, London 1958. Well illustrated.

R.KRAUTHEIMER, *Early Christian and Byzantine Architecture*, Harmondsworth 1965. Brilliant.

O.S.VON SIMSON, *Sacred Fortress. Byzantine Art and Statecraft in Ravenna*, Chicago 1948. A popular account of monuments of the period in Ravenna.

F.W.DEICHMANN, *Frühchristliche Bauten und Mosaiken in Ravenna*, Baden-Baden 1958.

D.TALBOT RICE, *The Art of the Byzantine Era*, London 1963.

J.BECKWITH, *Early Christian and Byzantine Art*, Harmondsworth 1970. Reliable and splendidly illustrated.

E.KITZINGER, *Byzantine Art in the Making*, Cambridge, Mass. 1977. Chapter 5, pp 81–98 offers a good introduction to the art of the age of Justinian.

6 LITERATURE

The fundamental reference works on Byzantine literature are H.G.Beck, *Kirche und theologische Literatur im byzantinischen Reich*, Munich, 1959, and H.Hunger, *Die hochsprachlich profane Literatur der Byzantiner,* Munich, 2 vols., 1978.

F.H.MARSHALL, Byzantine Literature, in N.H.Baynes and H.St.L.B.Moss, *Byzantium, An Introduction to East Roman Civilisation*, Oxford 1948. A short sketch.

F.A.WRIGHT, *A History of Later Greek Literature, 323 B.C. to 565 A.D.*, London 1932.

F.IMPELLIZZERI, *Storia della letteratura bizantina*, I, *Da Costantino agli Iconoclasti*, Bari 1965. The most detailed account of the literature of the period, with copious bibliographies.

7 THE CORPUS JURIS

H.JOLOWICZ, *Historical Introduction to the Study of Roman Law*, second edition, London 1952, pp. 488-516.

W.KUNKEL, *An Introduction to Roman Legal and Constitutional History*. Oxford 1966, pp. 152-64. Two brief but reliable accounts of Justinian's legislation.

P.COLLINET, *Études historiques sur le droit de Justinien*, 3 vols. Paris 1912–25. Much here is only for the specialist. But vol I contains a good and detailed general survey.

L.WENGER, *Die Quellen des römischen Rechts*, Vienna 1953. pp. 562–679. An indispensible reference work.

On Tribonian cf. A.M.HONORÉ, *Tribonian*, London, 1978. A learned and sometimes controversial work.

8 CONSTANTINOPLE

D.TALBOT RICE, *Constantinople: Byzantium-Istanbul*, London 1965.

M.MACLAGAN, *The City of Constantinople*, London 1968.

D.JACOBS, *Constantinople: City on the Golden Horn*, New York 1969.
Three well-illustrated histories of Constantinople from its foundation by Constantine until the present day.

G.DAGRON, *Naissance d'une capitale: Constantinople et son institutions de 330 à 45*, Paris, 1974. Masterly study of the foundation and early history of the city.

R.MAYER, *Byzantion Konstantinopolis Istanbul: Eine genetische Stadtgeographie*, Vienna–Leipzig, 1943. Interesting study by an urban geographer.

Sources of Illustrations

1. Louvre, Paris. Photo Hirmer
2. Museo Nazionale, Florence. Photo Hirmer
3. Bibliothèque Nationale, Paris
4. Castello Sforzesco, Milan. Photo Hirmer
5. Castello Sforzesco, Milan. Photo Bulloz
6. Palazzo dei Conservatori, Rome. Photo André Held
7. Bayerische Staatsbibliothek, Munich
8. Biblioteca Medicea Laurenziana, Florence
9. British Museum, London. Photo Peter Clayton
10. British Museum, London
11, 12. Original formerly in the Bibliothèque Nationale, Paris. Photo of electrotype copy Peter Clayton
13. British Museum, London
14. Museo delle Terme, Rome. Photo Deutsches Archaeologisches Institut, Rome
15. Staatliche Museen, Berlin
16. Musée du Bardo, Tunis
17. Director of Antiquities, Amman
18. Museum of Antiquities, Antioch
19. Musée du Bardo, Tunis
20. Photo Josephine Powell
21. Photo Josephine Powell
22. Photo Bildarchiv Foto Marburg
23. Photo Scala, Florence
24. Photo Alinari
25. Courtesy of Professor I. Ševčenko, Harvard University
26. Photo Josephine Powell
27. Photo Hirmer
28. Museo Storico Artistico della Basilica Vaticana, Rome
29. Nationalbibliothek, Vienna

Index